MILITARIZING MEN

MILITARIZING MEN

*Gender, Conscription, and War
in Post-Soviet Russia*

Maya Eichler

STANFORD UNIVERSITY PRESS
Stanford, California

Stanford University Press
Stanford, California

©2012 by the Board of Trustees of the Leland Stanford Junior University.
All rights reserved.

No part of this book may be reproduced or transmitted in any form or by any means, electronic or mechanical, including photocopying and recording, or in any information storage or retrieval system without the prior written permission of Stanford University Press.

Printed in the United States of America on acid-free, archival-quality paper

Library of Congress Cataloging-in-Publication Data
Eichler, Maya, author
  Militarizing men : Gender, conscription, and war in post-Soviet Russia / Maya Eichler.
    pages cm.
  Includes bibliographical references and index.
  ISBN 978-0-8047-7619-6 (cloth : alk. paper) —
  ISBN 978-0-8047-7620-2 (pbk. : alk. paper)
  1. Draft—Russia (Federation). 2. Masculinity—Russia (Federation).
  3. Gender identity—Russia (Federation). 4. Militarism—Russia (Federation).
  5. Chechnia (Russia)—History—Civil War, 1994—-Social aspects. I. Title
UB345.R9E53 2012
947.086—dc22   2011008956

Typeset at Stanford University Press in 10/14 Minion

I dedicate the book to the men and women in Russia and around the world who challenge the power of militaries and resist the gendered logic of militarization—sometimes at the risk of their own lives.

And to Priya Poesie, with hope for a less militarized future.

Contents

	Acknowledgments	ix
	Introduction: The Personal and Public Politics of Militarizing Men	1
1	Gender and Militarization in the Soviet Union	15
2	Militarized Masculinity and State Leadership in the Russian-Chechen Wars	35
3	The Societal Crisis of Militarized Masculinity: Conscription, Economic Transformation, and the Russian-Chechen Wars	59
4	The Soldiers' Mothers Movement: Contesting and Reproducing Militarized Gender Roles	85
5	Veterans of the Chechen Wars: Questionable Warriors or a Model of Masculinity?	108
	Conclusion: Masculinity, Soldiering, and War in Post-Soviet Russia	136
	Notes	145
	Referencees	195
	Index	219

Acknowledgments

I FIRST BECAME INTERESTED in the topic of gender and militarization in Russia in the mid-1990s. I had friends who were active in the Russian peace movement, mostly Quakers from Russia and abroad with whom I attended various workshops and retreats. Many of the Russian men I met in this context had turned to the Quakers for help in either evading conscription or fighting for their right to conscientious objector status. Through one of my friends I visited the offices of soldiers' mothers who were active in St. Petersburg. I was deeply impressed with these women's work and their gumption to take on the military. My interest in draft evasion and the soldiers' mothers movement re-emerged years later when I was introduced to feminist International Relations scholarship on the role of gender in processes of militarization. In particular, the work of Cynthia Enloe and Sandra Whitworth inspired this project. Reading their work, I found myself preoccupied with the question of what made the challenges to the military and state by soldiers' mothers so powerful. As I realized later, these women were challenging not only notions of patriotic motherhood but also something even more fundamental—namely, the common-sense idea that serving in the military is a citizenship duty of men and is important to their socialization as men.

I am enormously grateful to the following people who read earlier drafts of this book and generously shared their comments and suggestions: Claudia Brunner, Aurélie Campana, Deborah Cowen, Alison Crosby, Cynthia Enloe, Wenona Giles, Patrick James, Nadejda Marinova, Jennifer G. Mathers, Ananya Mukherjee-Reed, Sergei Plekhanov, Laura Sjoberg, Lisa McIntosh Sundstrom,

Sandra Whitworth, Elena Zdravomyslova, and Tatiana Zhurzhenko. I am particularly indebted to Valerie Sperling and one anonymous reviewer for their attentive reading and constructive comments. The book also benefited greatly from conversations with J. Ann Tickner and Soumita Basu. I am thankful for comments and criticism I received when presenting parts of the book at conferences, workshops, and seminars of the International Security Program of the Belfer Center for Science and International Affairs (Harvard Kennedy School), Canadian Political Science Association, Center for International Studies (University of Southern California), International Studies Association, Peace and Justice Studies Association, Twenty Years Feminist International Relations (University of Southern California), and Women in International Security Canada. I thank my editor at Stanford University Press, Stacy Wagner, for taking on this project and seeing it through. My thanks also go to editorial assistant Jessica Walsh, production editor John Feneron, and freelance copyeditor Martin Hanft. Any omissions or mistakes, of course, are my responsibility.

I acknowledge the financial support I received in support of conducting this research and completing the book from the Social Sciences and Humanities Research Council of Canada, the Ontario Government, the Canadian Consortium on Human Security, the York Centre for International and Security Studies, York University (Faculty of Graduate Studies), the University of Southern California (Center for International Studies), and the Harvard Kennedy School (Belfer Center for Science and International Affairs and Women and Public Policy Program).

My deepest gratitude goes to the men and women who generously agreed to share their stories and thoughts with me during my fieldwork in Samara. The Gender Studies Center at Samara State University sponsored my visa application and gave me use of their office space during my fieldwork. I thank the members of the Gender Studies Center, in particular Liudmila Popkova, Elena Zhidkova, and Natal'ia Sokolova. Serguei Oushakine took the time to discuss my research and put me in touch with Professor Popkova, and Gustava Z. helped me to prepare for my fieldwork trip. For her remarkable companionship during my stay in Samara I will always be grateful to Lena S. Thank you to Lena A. for her help with transcribing the interviews.

I am grateful to my friends and family for their emotional support and interest in my research undertakings. Finally, my greatest appreciation goes to Govind, whose love, help, and encouragement have sustained me and this project.

MILITARIZING MEN

Introduction

The Personal and Public Politics of Militarizing Men

> Precisely because the military can insinuate itself so deeply into family dynamics, industrial structures, the human psyche, the electoral system, class and racial interactions, historical memories, and popular cultures, when women question the gendered fiber of any armed forces, they find themselves engaged in analyzing the very definition of personhood and of the nation.
>
> Cynthia Enloe[1]

I MET VADIM at the office of a committee of soldiers' mothers in Samara, a city of one million located on the banks of the Volga. Now almost thirty years old, he had served as a conscript in the first Chechen war (1994–1996). Vadim had found it hard to reintegrate upon his return from Chechnya, but with the help of a local committee of soldiers' mothers attended school and later found employment as a financial specialist. The chair of the committee, who arranged our meeting, told me that Vadim had received an Order of Courage (*Orden Muzhestva*) for his actions during the war. But the war was not something Vadim was able to talk about. After more than ten years, he still suffered from the effects of his participation in the first Chechen war. We instead chatted about his experience of military life more generally. In spite of the memories of combat that still weighed on him, Vadim felt that military service had been an important life lesson, that it had helped him mature and become a man. He thought his transition from boyhood to manhood was confirmed by society, which treated him as an adult upon his return.[2]

Even for the many young men who do not see combat, military service in

Russia often is a damaging experience because of violent hazing practices and inadequate food and medical care. In early 2006, the case of the conscript Andrei Sychev shocked Russians and once again confirmed the dangers of military service. Sychev was brutally hazed by his fellow soldiers and, not receiving timely medical care, his legs and genitals had to be amputated. Every year hundreds of thousands of young men in Russia must confront the following dilemma: should I risk life and limb by heeding the draft call, or avoid the brutality and pain of Russian army life but take the chance of being seen as less of a man?

A young man's decision is shaped by the views of family members and society. Many Russian parents fear for their sons' health and life during military service and will do everything they can to keep them out of the army. However, it is the mothers rather than fathers who have publicly expressed this fear and organized in soldiers' mothers groups to improve service conditions and demand an end to conscription. For Russian men (whether sons or fathers) to publicly speak out against conscription is socially less acceptable and likely to be seen as unmanly. What it means to be a real man or a good mother lies at the heart of the state's conscription policy and societal resistance to it.

The Soviet state pursued a policy of mandatory military service for its male citizens. Military service was a key pillar of Soviet military power, but its significance went well beyond the defense of the country. As a duty of Soviet citizenship, military service was designed to mold young men into patriotic and loyal citizens. The military was also defined as *the* institution of male socialization, and military service was seen as a male rite of passage. During the 1980s, however, the Soviet state began to encounter increasing difficulties with draft evasion and an overall loss of prestige for the military. These changes were due in part to the Soviet war in Afghanistan and Mikhail Gorbachev's policy of *glasnost'*. The activism of soldiers' mothers brought public attention to the abuses and dire conditions conscripts faced during their service. Thus, in the final years of the Soviet Union, the prominent place of the armed forces in society and the militarized gender roles prescribed by the state were called into question.

Mandatory military service was one of the major fault lines of conflict between state and society that emerged with the demise of Soviet power and the transition to the postcommunist order. The new Russian state nonetheless upheld military service as a constitutional duty of young men, while promising the transition to an all-volunteer force sometime in the future. The first war in

Chechnya, which relied primarily on conscripts, further undermined the appeal of military service and exposed the deep problems plaguing the Russian armed forces. In addition to the widespread practice of hazing, the possibility of being sent to fight in Chechnya became another reason for the fear among young men and their families regarding military service. The waging of the second war (1999–2009), in contrast, more heavily involved contract soldiers and militarized state agencies other than the military (such as the Federal Security Service). President Vladimir Putin (2000–2008) aimed to restore society's faith in the military and its personnel, and stressed that military service was a duty of male citizens. The Putin regime itself was made up of significant numbers of militarized men originating from the security services. At the same time, draft evasion continued to be a problem and societal support for ending conscription remained strong. Interestingly, the very practices assumed necessary to achieve and assert manhood—such as hazing and combat—helped to undermine the appeal of military service in Russia. Hopes that Russia would move to an all-volunteer force in the foreseeable future were once again dashed in early 2010. The Ministry of Defense announced that it will continue to rely on conscripts to fill the ranks of Russia's armed forces, and will in fact expand the ratio of conscripts to volunteers.[3]

The issue of citizens' recruitment for military service and war is particularly salient today as many countries face challenges in filling their militaries' ranks. How states organize their military and recruit citizens for military service and war is fundamentally gendered: it relies on a particular understanding of men's role in society that links masculinity with the military. (Re)producing this link is important in order for militaries to attract male soldiers, bolster morale, and engage in combat. State policies such as male conscription and the waging of war are centrally informed by masculinity. The importance of masculinity, however, goes beyond the military sphere to the very core of state legitimation. To the extent that states depend on militarized justifications of their rule and reinforce a militarized form of patriotism, challenges to men's participation in the military and in war result in challenges to the very legitimacy of the state.

This book investigates the relationship between men's identities and the Russian state's conscription policy and waging of war in Chechnya. How did the state and military leadership on the one hand, and societal actors and individuals on the other, reproduce or contest the link between masculinity and the military in post-Soviet Russia? How have the postcommunist transformation and the Russian-Chechen wars affected the idea that a real man is one who has served in the military, if not fought in combat? And what does the politics of militarized masculinity tell us about state-society relations in post-Soviet Russia and about militarism as a source of legitimacy for the post-Soviet state?

The book shows that men's militarization has been challenged *and* reinforced in the context of postcommunist transformation and the Chechen wars. In post-Soviet Russia, the state has faced serious difficulties in its militarization of men. This is most evident in the large number of draft evaders and deserters, antidraft and antiwar activism by soldiers' mothers, and the lack of popular support for the Chechen wars (with the exception of the initial phase of the second war). The transition to capitalism also encouraged the emergence of new ideas of masculinity that anchor men's identities in the market economy and conflict with patriotic, militarized masculinity. In addition to these disruptions of militarism, Russia has experienced a partial resurgence of militarized gender identities. This trend can be observed in the official revival of militarist ideology under President Putin, but also in the activities of regional soldiers' mothers groups and veterans' organizations. The process of remilitarization from above and below aims to strengthen militarized patriotism and narrow the gap between state and society. Even though it does not resolve the conflict over conscription, it increases the potential of militarism as a source of legitimacy for the post-Soviet state.

Theoretical Lens: Feminist International Relations and Militarized Masculinity

There are many competing definitions of militarism and militarization. I do not use "militarism" to imply the dominance of the military over the state or society, but rather define militarism as an ideology that promotes a central role for the military and its personnel in state and society. This role is shaped by particular sociohistoric and political-economic contexts. Militarism might inform state policies such as increases to military budgets, special social policy toward military professionals, or universal conscription. War necessarily relies on militarism, as it privileges a military solution over other, nonviolent solutions. The terms "militarism" and "militarization" are sometimes used interchangeably. I differentiate between militarism as an ideology (or a set of ideas), and militarization as a process. I define militarization as any process that helps establish and reinforce a central role for the military in state and society, and demilitarization as a process through which the military's position is questioned and undermined. Thus militarization (and the adjective "militarized") will be used to underscore the socially and politically constructed nature of the military's importance. Politicians, society, and individuals become militarized when their beliefs and actions support a central role for the military. Militarization is thus achieved when militarism is not questioned but accepted as normal and necessary.[4]

This study builds on scholarship in feminist International Relations (IR), which developed out of a desire to make women's lives and experiences visible and to uncover the gendered assumptions of the discipline. Joan Scott argues that "gender is a primary way of signifying relationships of power."[5] Thus gender is about more than women and men and their relations. It structures social life more generally as it assigns power to those institutions, practices, and activities associated with masculinity. What has traditionally counted as political (and thus relevant) gained its predominance by association with men and masculinity. The political leader, citizen, or warrior has long been imagined as a man and as displaying masculine characteristics. This was understood as natural, and masculinity therefore, just as femininity, remained unexplored in mainstream IR.[6] In recent years, feminist IR scholars have begun to explore in more detail the role of masculinity in global politics.[7] Turning our analytical gaze toward masculinity does not mean a simple return to the original subject of IR. It is intended to problematize what mainstream IR has taken for granted for so long: men's identities, notions of masculinity, and gendered relations of power. To study men then is necessarily to study them in relation to women, and vice versa. A gendered analysis reveals how women and men are affected differently by international politics, the ways in which they are expected and encouraged to fulfill certain gendered roles, *and* how notions of masculinity inform key concepts of IR.

Feminists use the term "gender" to underscore that women's and men's identities are constructed in relation to one another rather than biologically given. What it means to be a woman or a man depends on historical, cultural, social, and economic contexts. Gender structures social life to such an extent that we can talk of any given society as representing a particular *gender order:* a set of dominant gender relations and notions of masculinity and femininity.[8] The gender order manifests itself in gendered power relations, a gendered division of labor, and dominant sexual practices. Feminist and gender scholarship has documented the central role that modern states—capitalist, state-socialist, or transitional—play in reproducing and shaping their respective society's gender order, including its material, institutional, and ideological aspects.[9] However, the state itself relies on the gender order for its own functioning and ideological legitimation, as is evident in the politics of militarization. The basic claims states make—to sovereignty, protection and security, the monopoly over the legitimate means of violence—are intrinsically tied up with particular gender relations and notions of masculinity and femininity. These claims have historically entailed dividing society into those who bear arms and defend state and nation (men) and those who are relegated to the private sphere and defined as in need of protection (women as well as children). A notion of militarized masculinity centrally underpins state sovereignty and the state's coercive power. States and militaries have worked hard to sustain the association of masculinity with the military and of femininity with the need for protection.[10] Without the militarization of men and their subordination to the state, the state would not be able to deliver on its claim of providing security. A particular gender order is thus implicit in militarization and state legitimation.

The focus of this book lies at the intersection of militarization/war and the gender order: the role of militarized notions of masculinity in state- and nation-building. In conceptualizing masculinity I follow R. W. Connell's important insights: first, masculinity needs to be understood in relation to femininity, as it is located within gender relations. That is, to make sense of masculinity and men, one must examine femininity and women, and vice versa.[11] Second, masculinities (and femininities) are produced at various sites: that of the individual, the institution (for example, the state, the workplace, the United Nations), and that of ideology/culture/discourse (such as advertisements, art, "common sense"). Third, masculinity is linked to power: men gain power in society not because of their biological identity as men but thanks to their "cultural association" with masculinity. What counts as masculine (or feminine) in a particular time and place depends not on men (and women) per se, but on what is considered to be power-enhancing (or power-degrading).[12] Fourth, we need to distinguish multiple masculinities. Connell argues that hegemonic masculinity gets defined in relation to various subordinate and marginalized masculinities (and femininities). Thus, gay men represent subordinate masculinity in an era that defines the heterosexual as the norm, and working-class ethnicized or racialized men embody marginalized masculinity in a society centered around middle- and upper-class white men. Finally, masculinities (and femininities) undergo change and are therefore best understood as historically (in addition to culturally) specific.[13]

Highlighting the intersections between the gender order and militarization, we can see state legitimacy as being partly organized around notions of hegemonic masculinity (for example, the soldier, men of the dominant ethnic/racial group, or institutionalized hegemonic masculinity embodied by the state or the military). This hegemonic masculinity is defined in opposition to notions of subordinate masculinity (such as the enemy, the deserter, or the homosexual). In addition, states (and the social forces they are allied with) rely on, and at times actively empower, various constructions of femininity, including female domesticity, patriotic motherhood, or women workers. A state's ability to wage war, and to gain legitimacy from the waging of war, depends on men's and women's adherence to particular militarized gender roles, in addition to a variety of other factors such as economic resources, weapons technology, or public opinion.

Militarism has profoundly gendered effects. It privileges the military, a masculine institution, and men as militarized protectors, and thus contributes to unequal gender relations. Masculinity is associated with a variety of characteristics, including strength, violence, aggression, risk-taking, and dominance. The pervasiveness of militarism is evident in the fact that most people intuitively accept the idea of men as more aggressive, violent, and willing to fight in war than women. Indeed, historically men have acted as the warriors in most societies. However, feminist IR scholars urge us not so readily to accept the presumably natural link between men and militarism. Feminists use the term "militarized masculinity" to challenge us to think about how masculinities and men *become* militarized, about the ways in which masculinity and the military *become* linked, rather than to assume and accept that men are essentially militaristic.[14] Men's militarism cannot be taken for granted, as it relies on socialization, state policy, and—increasingly—economic incentives.

Militaries and states have long propagated the notion that manhood is achieved through military experience, or put simply, that the military helps make men out of boys. Obligatory military service has been one of the most important tools in shaping men's militarized identities.[15] In militarized societies, state and military leaders define woman's patriotism in terms of her willingness to sacrifice her son, and man's military service as intrinsic to his citizenship and identity. Militarization is gendered in that women's and men's identities can become informed by militarism. A mother's militarization is evident in the pride and social recognition she gains from her son's military service. A man's identity becomes militarized if he believes military service to be necessary for his transition to manhood or his status as citizen.

I define militarized masculinity as the idea that military service (and combat) are central to men's identity, whether this is understood as a citizenship duty or a necessity of male socialization. Militarized masculinity is embedded in gendered state policies such as compulsory military service for men as well as the public expressions and actions of the state and military elite. At the societal level, changing political-economic conditions as well as societal receptivity for notions of militarized masculinity affect the link between masculinity and the military. Individual men and women reinforce or challenge militarized masculinity through their acceptance of military service as a duty of male citizenship and/or as key to masculine identity, which is reflected in men's willingness to serve and women's support for men undergoing service.

The study of the military, militarism, and militarization is crucial for feminist scholars, for analytical and political reasons. The military is one of the main sources of unequal gendered power relations in society. In conscription societies, men's mandatory military service defines citizenship in gendered terms and effectively elevates men's citizenship status over that of women. As gender signifies relations of power more broadly, militarized masculinity is a factor in political power relations. Association with hegemonic notions of masculinity often brings social and political advantages. Thus, an examination of how notions of militarized masculinity achieve or lose hegemony is important for understanding gendered social and political power. At the same time, the insight that men are militarized rather than being born militaristic opens up space for the reconsideration of gender roles and the militarized politics they help sustain.

Empirical Focus: Postcommunist Transformation and the Russian-Chechen Wars

The Russian postcommunist transformation forms the backdrop of this study. Liberal scholars and policy-makers initially assumed a linear transition from communist political and economic systems to democracy and capitalism. Others, such as path-dependency scholars, pointed to the negative effects socialist legacies would have on the progress of change.[16] Michael Burawoy and Katherine Verdery find it misleading to "conceive of the transition as either rooted in the past or tied to an imagined future. Transition is a process suspended between the two."[17] Their approach allows for a better appreciation of the complex interplay of continuities and changes that make up postcommunist transformations.

Postcommunist transformations touch all aspects of life. They are best viewed as a multiplicity of connected economic, political, ideological, social, and cultural processes that lead to fundamental changes in the economic and political system, the social and ideological order, and in cultural norms and practices. This transformation is by its very nature contested and dynamic, its outcome uncertain. The outcome depends on political and societal struggles over the path of reform and the nature of the new regime. Postcommunist transformation involves the redistribution of economic and political power as well as the restructuring of societal relations along class, gender, age, region, or nationality. Neither state nor societal actors fully determine the outcome of change. The state is a central agent, but even within the state, ministries, agencies, and levels of government often disagree on the course of reform. Similarly in society, various social actors work to influence or contest the government's policies.

In the early 1990s, the legitimacy of the new Russian state rested on the government promise of improved social and economic conditions. Russians associated democratization with outcomes such as "social order, economic stability, guaranteed welfare and a greater measure of distributive justice."[18] However, the economic policy of "shock therapy," adopted by Boris Yeltsin's reform government, created a social order characterized by increased economic disparities and the concentration of power in the hands of the "new" ruling class. This undermined the popularity of the government's neoliberal reforms and its definition of Russia as part of the West. Resistance to Yeltsin's program emphasized alternative conceptions of the Russian nation. The government shifted its own position in response, taking on a more nationalist, anti-Western stance. President Putin carried forth this more assertive stance vis-à-vis the West and in addition moved to strengthen the state and renew Russian patriotism. Economically, Russia continued its integration into the world capitalist system, while the ideological sphere saw a revival of state patriotism and militarism reminiscent of the Soviet era. In the context of the economic and ideological crisis of the postcommunist order, militarism together with nationalism and patriotism became central to political leaders' attempts to gain, or strengthen their grip on, power.[19]

Militarism and militarization are best understood within the dialectic of continuity and change that has accompanied Russia's postcommunist transformation. Changes in the military sphere and in military-society relations cannot be isolated from other aspects of transformation but have to be understood in the context of multiple, intersecting transformations: of the economy, society, the political system, and culture and values. This study views militarism and militarization as part of the reorganization of social relations and political power that has taken place during the postcommunist period. Such an approach does not take the militarism of—and between—states for granted, but instead investigates why militarism emerges and how it fits into broader social and political changes.

Military violence between Chechen separatist and Russia federal forces overshadowed Russia's postcommunist transformation.[20] The state waged two wars (1994–1996, 1999–2009) against the separatist republic of Chechnya, which declared independence in November of 1991. Competing explanations of this conflict have been put forward, which look to the history of Russian imperialism, the legacy of contradictory Soviet nationality policies, Russia's current economic and geostrategic interests in the Caucasus region, or a combination of these factors. Some authors emphasize that Chechen resistance to Russian imperialism dates back to the nineteenth century. They situate the most recent conflicts within a prolonged history of Russian-Chechen animosities and interpret them as part of the Chechens' historic struggle for national liberation.[21] Others argue that Russian-Chechen relations were aggravated by a Soviet nationality policy that was based on a "built-in contradiction between the principle of ethnoterritorial federalism and the actual repression of national aspirations."[22] On the one hand, Chechens faced forced deportations and assimilationist policies. In 1944 approximately 500,000 Chechens and Ingushes were deported to Central Asia on Joseph Stalin's order for alleged collaboration with Nazi Germany. On the other hand, the principle of ethnoterritorial federalism encouraged the idea of a Chechen people.[23] Furthermore, Soviet modernization policies during the 1960s to 1980s helped develop the republic's economy and educational system, but ethnic inequalities remained.[24] Those authors who look to contemporary rather than historic explanations stress the importance of economic and geostrategic factors for the Russian state. They note the key transportation routes (Rostov-Baku highway and railway) and oil pipeline that run through Chechnya, the local oil refining industry, as well as proximity to the Caspian Sea with its considerable oil reserves.[25]

While all these approaches offer important pieces to the puzzle, I favor an approach that situates the wars within the process of Russia's postcommunist transformation.[26] The wars can be partly understood as a response to threats to the unity of the Russian state. However, the wars must also be understood in connection with the legitimation of political power in the context of the economic and ideological crisis of the postcommunist social order. The political leadership in Russia has relied on militarism to bolster its rule, because of the lack of other easily available sources of legitimation.[27] Yet, this process has been contradictory. The new Russian state was able to draw on the Soviet legacy of a dominant military culture, but had to contend with weakened notions of militarized masculinity and "patriotic duty" at the societal level. The Chechen wars are typical of contemporary warfare in global politics. Fought against "separatists," "bandits," and "terrorists," the wars have not ended in clear victory or peace. In an age of the perpetual war on terror Russia faces the problem so many other countries do: how to mobilize its population in support of war.

Fieldwork

This study draws on fieldwork I conducted in Samara, which is the administrative center of Samara *Oblast'* in the Volga Federal District and located approximately 1,100 kilometers southeast of Moscow. During the Soviet period, Samara—then named Kuibishev—had been a "closed city" because of its concentration of military industry. I chose Samara for the following reason. One of the central components of my fieldwork was to carry out interviews with women who were active in the soldiers' mothers movement. Here my concern was to avoid the focus on Russia's "center" often found in the Western literature and reflected in the already substantial research that exists on the independent soldiers' mothers groups in Moscow and St. Petersburg. I had the hunch that this focus on Russia's two main cities might lead to a skewed view on gender and militarization. Nongovernmental organizations in Moscow and St. Petersburg are more likely to be in contact with Western organizations and be influenced by Western ideas. Instead, my aim was to examine how nongovernmental groups in Russia's regions address concerns about the military, and thus to contribute to a more complex understanding of the soldiers' mothers movement.[28] In hindsight Samara also presented a good place to conduct fieldwork on military matters, as troops from Samara region participated in both Chechen wars. This fact led to the development of numerous local and regional groups that work with Chechen war veterans.[29]

During my fieldwork in Samara from May to August 2006, I conducted twenty-four interviews primarily with soldiers' mothers, draft evaders, and veterans of the Chechen and other recent wars.[30] The interviews were semistructured and the questions focused on the interviewees' perspectives on military service and the effects of the wars on their lives, as well as on the activities of soldiers' mothers' and veterans' organizations. The interviews were informed by my feminist curiosity about men's and women's notions of militarized masculinity. However, the majority of questions did not explicitly ask about gender (such as "In your view, what attracts or deters men from military service?" or "How did the Chechen wars affect your life?"), but nonetheless revealed gendered attitudes and stories. I read the interviews through a feminist lens to identify what notions of masculinity and femininity the interviewees employed.

The fact that subjects such as the military and the Chechen wars are considered politically sensitive in contemporary Russia posed some difficulties for my research. My status as a foreign researcher compounded this problem. Among those who were skeptical or did not agree to an interview, the most common concerns seemed to be around the association of Westerners with human rights or espionage. I also encountered the view that people from abroad should not be interested in these kinds of topics and should instead concern themselves with their own society's problems. However, it must be noted that Russian scholars also encounter difficulties when conducting research on the military and Chechnya. As Tanya Lokshina pointed out in May 2007 in reference to her interviews with police veterans of the Chechen wars: "Unfortunately, Chechnya has become almost a taboo subject in Russia of late and a lot of police officers who served in Chechnya refuse to speak about their respective experiences in the conflict zone, even with anonymity warranted."[31] I encountered similar difficulties, yet my experiences were not universally difficult.[32] In one case, my status as foreign scholar was of advantage, as the leader of one of the Samara soldiers' mothers groups apparently refused to talk to local journalists but was willing to give me an interview.

Plan of the Book

The book explores the facets of militarized masculinity in post-Soviet Russia through five thematic chapters. Chapter 1, "Gender and Militarization in the Soviet Union," outlines the significance militarized masculinity had for Soviet state and society (including its gender order) and argues that the official notion of militarized masculinity began to be challenged in the late Soviet period as a result of the war in Afghanistan, Gorbachev's policy of *glasnost'*, and the activism of soldiers' mothers. Chapter 2 on "Militarized Masculinity and State Leadership in the Russian-Chechen Wars" examines how articulations and representations of militarized masculinity undermined the legitimacy of the first war, but helped mobilize support for the second. The analysis shows that there is no straightforward connection between the waging of war and manliness. Instead, leaders' attempts to use war as a means of appearing manly are shaped by a complicated interplay of militarized masculinities. In Chapter 3, "The Societal Crisis of Militarized Masculinity: Conscription, Economic Transformation, and the Russian-Chechen Wars," I analyze the policy of male conscription and the growing challenges to militarized masculinity as a result of violence and poor service conditions within the military, the emergence of new class-based notions of masculinity, and the Chechen wars. Chapter 4, "The Soldiers' Mothers Movement: Contesting and Reproducing Militarized Gender Roles," examines the soldiers' mothers movement in Russia by contrasting groups in Moscow and St. Petersburg with those in Samara. Soldiers' mothers groups in Moscow and St. Petersburg have challenged militarized masculinity by publicly opposing the wars and lobbying for the abolition of conscription. By contrast, soldiers' mothers in Samara shied away from publicly opposing the wars, and while they defend draftees' and conscripts' rights, they have tended to reinforce militarized gender roles. Chapter 5 on "Veterans of the Chechen Wars: Questionable Warriors or a Model of Masculinity?" explores how representations of Chechen war veterans have diverged from the image of the heroic warrior. It argues that the Chechen wars revealed numerous contradictions of militarized masculinity, both in the representations of unwilling and excessive warriors and in the difficulties veterans faced upon their return to civilian life.

Three threads are drawn through this book. The first concerns a gender analysis of militarization that is simultaneously situated at the state and societal levels, and also takes seriously the experiences and actions of citizens. I emphasize the importance of gender to state policies such as conscription and war, but I am equally concerned with how society and individuals reproduce or contest these policies. An analysis of militarized masculinity at the societal level makes evident the challenges to militarized state- and nation-building in post-Soviet Russia. Such an approach also reveals that the politics of militarized masculinity are as much personal and local as they are public, national, and global.[33]

Second, in this book I examine how gender can help produce ideological coherence but at the same time often points us to tensions and contradictions within social and political processes. Gender helps stabilize social relations and creates ideological support for state policies. For example, the idea that men are warriors and women are in need of male protection offers a justification for male conscription and the waging of war by men. But gender also helps us see disruptions to ideology and the potential for the transformation of social relations and political power. As states rely on militarized masculinity for their own functioning and legitimacy, the contestations of militarized masculinity offer insight into the challenges to gendered social and political power.

Finally, I explore contradictory and parallel processes of de- and remilitarization instead of assuming a linear process of militarization. Such an approach is especially suited to the study of postcommunist transformation and conceptualizes militarization and militarism in the context of the economic and ideological crisis of the postcommunist order. The following chapters explain how changing state-society relations manifest themselves in the contested politics of militarized masculinity, and how notions of militarized masculinity are reinforced as the state attempts to stabilize the new order and citizens struggle to find their place within it.

1 Gender and Militarization in the Soviet Union

ON MAY 8, 1967, Leonid Brezhnev presided over the unveiling of the Tomb of the Unknown Soldier on Moscow's Red Square. The memorial was dedicated to those who had died in the Great Patriotic War (1941–1945), as World War Two is commonly referred to in Russian. The ceremony celebrated the feats of the Red Army, and reaffirmed its status as a pillar of Soviet state and society. It was also an occasion to highlight the heroism of the soldiers who had fought in the war and call for society's deepest respect for them.[1] N. G. Egorichev, first secretary of the Moscow Committee of the Communist Party, portrayed veterans of the Great Patriotic War as role models for the younger generation. He stated in his speech that these heroes had shown "wholehearted courage and patriotism, fidelity to military duty, steadfast devotion to the Communist Party, to the Socialist Fatherland."[2] The Soviet leadership of the time constructed a heroic image of the Soviet soldier that was rooted in the experience of mass mobilization and sacrifice during the Great Patriotic War. The war and its heroes helped reinforce military service as a "sacred duty" of citizenship and an act of patriotism informed by the communist struggle and loyalty to the party. It was men who were imagined as the true heroes and model citizens in the official narrative of the Great Patriotic War, even though a great number of women had served in the Soviet military and many more had replaced men in the workforce during World War Two. Stalinist war propaganda had emphasized women's motherhood over their military heroism, and the postwar period saw women's swift demobilization. After the war, women's role as patriotic mothers who had willingly sacrificed their sons for the defense of the nation overshadowed their wartime contribution as combatants.

This chapter examines the relationship between gender and the military in the Soviet Union from two angles. First, it places gender roles in the context of war and militarism, which centrally shaped the development of Soviet state and society. Militarization was a process that shaped not only the economy or educational system but also Soviet gender relations and notions of masculinity and femininity. Universal male conscription was a key organizational feature in the militarization and mobilization of Soviet society and established a firm link between masculinity and the military. Second, I approach women's and men's roles in the military sphere through an analysis of the Soviet state's gender policies. The Soviet Union officially espoused a policy of women's emancipation but never extended it to the military sphere. A policy of obligatory male conscription together with the political and social importance assigned to the military reinforced gender inequality in the Soviet Union.

Demographic developments during the 1960s called into question the policy of women's equality and exposed anxieties over the balance of nationalities within the Soviet Union. Even more significant changes occurred during the late Soviet period, when the Soviet war in Afghanistan and Gorbachev's policies led to a reduced status for the military and difficulties for the state's conscription policy. Greater freedom of expression and organizing among soldiers' mothers contributed to public discussion of problems in the military such as systemic hazing and deaths among servicemen. Desertion and draft evasion became more common, indicating challenges to militarized masculinity. The final years of the Soviet Union were accompanied by the partial demilitarization of notions of femininity and masculinity.

The Significance of the Military for Soviet State and Society: Sketching the Outlines of "Militarized Socialism"

The changes that took place during the late Soviet period questioned the centrality of the military logic that had shaped Soviet state and society. This military logic, it should be noted, to a certain extent preceded the Soviet Union. Scholars underline the long Russian tradition of "defense-mindedness," which includes militarism as state ideology, comparatively high institutional autonomy of the military, and the state's ability to extract huge sacrifices from the population.[3]

The traditional fusion of civil and military spheres of the Imperial Russian state was wiped out in 1917 but soon came to be re-established to new political and ideological ends, though "in a modified form and on a different social basis."[4]

The Soviet state took shape in the context of a hostile international environment and multiple war experiences: defeat in World War One, the divisive and bloody Civil War, and the victorious but devastating Great Patriotic War. Manfred Sapper traces the origins of Soviet militarism to the state-making period after the October Revolution. He emphasizes the increase in societal violence that resulted from deserting and demobilized soldiers returning from World War One and the impact of the Civil War (1918–1921) that followed the Bolshevik seizure of power. The merging of military and civilian spheres rather than military dominance over politics distinguished this form of militarism. The early period of Soviet state formation saw the militarization of political, economic, and social life, as well as widespread violence and repression.[5] The Civil War was not followed by a process of demilitarization. Instead, most aspects of daily life, such as work or education, remained militarized. Sapper argues that the Civil War provided the legitimating ideology for Bolshevik rule.[6] The centrality of militarism and militarization to Soviet state and society established during Vladimir Lenin's rule was reinforced by Stalin's policies and society's experiences of World War Two.

The Stalinist period was characterized by the drive to catch up economically through rapid industrialization. This development strategy entailed "a massive extraction of resources from the population and their investment in heavy industry," which favored the growth of the defense industry.[7] In a 1931 speech Stalin linked Soviet development policy to socialist patriotism: "Do you want our Socialist fatherland to be beaten and to lose its independence? If you do not want this, you must put an end to its backwardness in the shortest possible time and develop a genuine Bolshevik tempo in building up the socialist economic system."[8] Stalin's appeal to patriotism, rather than Marxism-Leninism, became central to his mobilization of the population for war.[9] Soviet patriotism, as it became defined in the 1930s, meant loyalty to the Communist Party leadership. The one-party Soviet state equated loyalty to the state with loyalty to the party.[10]

The Great Patriotic War, which began with the German invasion of June 22, 1941, led to a further mobilization of people and resources by the state. It is well documented that broad sections of Soviet society—male and female—threw themselves into the war effort and that Soviet citizens suffered enormous deprivations and casualties (26.6 million dead). Roger D. Markwick and many others have described the war as a "watershed" in the history of the SU, which transformed the country into a "nation-state."[11] The Soviet leadership continued the characteristics of the war-mobilized society such as "the war economy, central planning, military strength of the state, and patriotism of society" in the postwar period.[12] These features of war mobilization had been decisive in defeating Nazi Germany and thus were accepted by society as central elements of Soviet life. Lev Gudkov argues that "readiness for mobilization [became] one of the legitimising principles of power."[13] The Great Patriotic War replaced the Bolshevik Revolution as the main event legitimating the Soviet regime, which solidified a prior shift from the emphasis on international class-struggle to Soviet patriotism that had taken place during the 1930s.[14] At the same time, victory against Germany elevated the status of the Red Army, establishing it as a "respected and trusted institution" of Soviet society for most citizens.[15]

Stalin created a narrative of the Great Patriotic War that portrayed himself and the party as the main heroes, and downplayed the role of Soviet citizens in defeating Nazi Germany. In 1947, the Soviet leader downgraded the Victory Day holiday (May 9) to a work day and eliminated most of the benefits for veterans of World War Two. With Nikita Khrushchev's reassessment of the Stalinist legacy, the narrative began to change, and by the 1960s there was a full-fledged "cult of the Great Patriotic War."[16] In 1965, Leonid Brezhnev re-established Victory Day as a holiday, which became an important annual ritual in the military-patriotic mobilization of society. This was part of a deepening of societal militarization during Brezhnev's rule (1964–1982) that included the expansion of military-education programs. In the context of declining economic growth rates and worries about the weakening loyalty and changing values of Soviet citizens, militarization became an increasingly important tool of domestic political legitimation. The 1960s also saw the expansion of welfare benefits for veterans, who now held the most privileged status in the Soviet welfare state. In exchange, the state and party leadership expected veterans' loyalty and participation in the mobilization of society.[17]

The entrenchment of militarism as an "integral component" of Soviet party-state ideology and of militarization as a fundamental societal process[18] gave rise to what some scholars have termed "militarized socialism." The deformation of socialist ideals into "militarized socialism" can be traced to the period of early Soviet history and World War Two but was reinforced as the Soviet leadership struggled with economic stagnation and weakening political support during the 1960s.¹⁹ The emergence of the Cold War and superpower rivalry between the United States and the USSR further strengthened the importance of the military for the Soviet regime. The military was seen as a key instrument in achieving superpower status and balance with the U.S. The arms race was particularly important in reinforcing the emphasis on defense production and the subordination of the economy to military needs. One outcome of this was to skew the Soviet economy toward a focus on heavy industry. While Premier Khrushchev (1958–1964) attempted to reduce ground forces, citing the increased importance of nuclear weapons and the possibility of peaceful coexistence between the Soviet Union and the West, the policy was reversed under Brezhnev. During his rule the Soviet Union experienced a further military buildup.²⁰ The geopolitical context of the Cold War strengthened the centrality of the military logic in Soviet state and society.

Gendering Military Service in the Soviet Union

A standing army and conscription were established in Russia during the reign of Peter the Great (1682–1725). Conscription was based on a quota system that obliged village communities to supply a certain number of peasants to serve as soldiers. During much of the eighteenth century military service was for life, but the length of service was reduced over time. On the urging of military reformers such as War Minister Dmitrii Miliutin, Alexander II introduced universal (male) military obligation in 1874. However, conscription was still not universally applied. There were exemptions based on ethnic background, profession, and "health or family hardships," and service length was shorter for educated men.²¹

In the early years of the Soviet state, the leadership's attempt to create an army of a new type shaped its policy on military service. Lenin envisioned an army that would serve the interests of the people (understood as the working class and peasants) and be staffed on a voluntary basis. The Workers-Peasants Red Army, founded in early 1918, was originally made up of volunteers but soon had to rely on conscripted soldiers. During the Civil War, the Bolshevik leadership was concerned with the political loyalty of soldiers and restricted its policy of conscription to workers and poor peasants. Draft evasions and desertions were frequent.²² In 1925, a new law on military service was introduced that "obligated all citizens to participate in the defense of the USSR, but limited activities involving weapons to workers."²³ Obligatory service applied only to men. The 1939 law on universal military service "removed social class criteria in service assignment, but reaffirmed the obligation of all male citizens to serve."²⁴

The policy on military service changed during the Great Patriotic War when both men and women were recruited en masse. The Soviet army numbered 5.5 million at the beginning of the war and quickly more than doubled in size through a mass mobilization of the population. The Antifascist Committee of Soviet Women was founded in 1941 to mobilize women for the war against Nazi Germany.[25] Childless women began to be drafted in 1942 after the heavy losses suffered during the early phase of the war. The shortage of manpower—as seen in other comparative contexts—was the main reason for the state's conscription of women.[26] However, many women voluntarily signed up for military service during World War Two and pushed for their right to participate in combat. Anna Krylova argues that the discourse of gender equality and the growing acceptance of women as fighters that preceded World War Two was an important factor in opening up combat roles for women.[27] As many as 800,000 women served in the Red Army during World War Two, at its high point making up 8 percent of the overall force. Women served primarily in medical capacities, antiaircraft units, as pilots, snipers, and in the partisan forces.[28] Official war propaganda called for the mobilization of women into the military and economic war effort, but also heavily relied on maternal images, in particular as part of the appeal to patriotism.[29] Thus, during the war the political leadership used contradictory notions of femininity—women fighters and patriotic mothers—to mobilize women for different aspects of the war effort. The official rhetoric of heroism came to include both women and men although disproportionately more men were decorated and celebrated as "Heroes of the Soviet Union." This was likely related to the fact that the distinction was primarily awarded to combatants, which limited the number of women who could be considered for the honor.[30]

After the war there was a return to a more "traditional" gender order in the military. In her study of female aviators, Reina Pennington examines the reasons behind women's almost complete demobilization and subsequent exclusion from military academies after the war. She argues that prevailing gender ideology regarding women's roles and the state's pronatalist policies stressed women's primary responsibility as mothers. The Soviet state viewed women's participation in the military as a temporary measure in the exceptional context of war, and not as part of a broader transformation of gender roles. Public remembrance of the war highlighted women's role as mothers rather than combatants. War-weariness among female soldiers may have also "limited the development of a feminist consciousness in the postwar Soviet Union," and weakened any resistance by female soldiers to their demobilization.[31] In addition, the official women's movement closely associated women and especially mothers with peace, which reinforced essentialist ideas about women's peacefulness and men's militarism. The Antifascist Committee of Soviet Women, renamed the Soviet Women's Committee in 1956, was the only organization speaking on behalf of Soviet women. As part of the Soviet Union's international Cold War propaganda, the committee stressed the achievements of Soviet women and their role as peace-builders.[32] In the domestic sphere, however, the state expected women to support husbands, sons, and brothers undergoing military service.

The 1967 law on military service restated the commitment to universal male conscription. In addition, Article 63 of the 1977 Constitution affirmed that "military service in the ranks of the Armed Forces of the USSR is the sacred obligation of Soviet citizens."[33] Soldiering and citizenship were intertwined and connoted as male, as this clause applied only to men.[34] The law on military service included the possibility of a female draft during wartime and permitted women to serve as volunteers.[35] In reality, female volunteers were limited to particular military professions (radio and telegraph specialists, switchboard operators, nurses, clerks, secretaries) and recruited during times of demographic need (World War Two, early 1960s, 1980s).[36] Women's participation in the military sphere was constructed as exceptional despite an official state policy of women's equality.

Soviet policy-makers considered men's obligatory military service as fundamental to reproducing the country's military might, but it was also aimed at fulfilling a number of important domestic functions. For example, conscripts were used in the civilian labor force in the agricultural and construction sectors (in continuation of czarist practices).[37] The most important domestic function of military service, however, was that of educator and socializer. Military service was considered a key tool in the proper ideological socialization of Soviet men. During their service, conscripts received political education as much as military training.[38] Obligatory male military service was embedded within a broader curriculum of military education that took place outside the military proper. This system included basic military training for draft-age and pre-draft-age men (since the reduction of military service by one year in 1967), a program of civil defense as part of the school curriculum (since the early 1970s), and a program of military-patriotic education for the general population.[39]

The Soviet Gender Order[40]

While there is an impressive literature on various aspects of "militarized socialism," its gender aspects are rarely touched upon except for Soviet women's combat participation during World War Two. Neither have feminist and other scholars paid sufficient attention to the significance of male obligatory military service for the Soviet gender order.[41] The military, however, offers an interesting site for analysis of Soviet constructions of masculinity and femininity. There existed a stark contradiction between the official Soviet image of emancipated womanhood and women's near-exclusion from the military. The Western feminist literature on the Soviet gender order focuses primarily on the economic and legal changes to women's status and the Soviet state's renewed emphasis on women's reproductive functions starting in the 1930s. It has shown that despite significant advances for women, Soviet policy did not fundamentally transform gender roles or overcome gender inequalities.[42] In the military sphere we also find an adherence to "traditional" gender roles both in Soviet women's marginal inclusion in the military and the gendered division of labor for those serving in the military. Moreover, Karen Petrone argues that the discourse of the male World War Two hero-soldier "undermined the revolutionary rhetoric of gender equality" that had characterized the 1920s.[43] The state's valorization of the military and of militarized masculinity was one of the ways in which male power was entrenched in Soviet society, in spite of the state's claims of having resolved the "woman question."[44]

Women as Workers and Bearers of the Nation

The Soviet state elite saw women as crucial to economic production as well as the reproduction of society, and expected women to fulfill the dual role of workers and mothers. Biological reproduction and motherhood were perceived as matters of state interest as the health of future generations of workers and their ideological commitment to communism depended on women's correct mothering.[45] Policy-makers thus considered women, in their role as biological and cultural reproducers, as important allies in the building of communism.[46] State policies assisted women as mothers through the provision of childcare services and maternity benefits. Women were treated as a special category of worker requiring protection from heavy and dangerous labor (although there were many exceptions). The number of women as a share of the total paid workforce increased from 25 percent in 1922 to 51 percent in 1970, where it remained for the next two decades.[47] The vast majority of Soviet women were engaged in employment or study, as Gail Lapidus notes: "By the 1970s over 87 per cent of working-age women were either employed or studying full-time."[48] Although the policy of integrating women into the paid labor force increased their autonomy, it did not fundamentally challenge existing gender inequalities. For example, in the sphere of production women were concentrated in "the least-prestigious and lowest-paying" sectors or jobs within male-dominated sectors.[49] Their incomes were about 65 to 75 percent that of men.[50] Women's increased labor participation was encouraged during times of labor shortages, such as during World War Two and the early 1960s,[51] and discouraged when called for by economic and demographic conditions (such as after World War Two and during the 1980s). The political sphere was similarly characterized by hierarchical gender structures. Suvi Salmenniemi notes that "women participated more actively at the local level in socio-political life, but their participation decreased strongly toward the higher echelons of power."[52] Furthermore, state policy did not tackle the transformation of unequal gender relations in the private sphere. Instead, it reinforced the notion of fundamental gender differences based on women as mothers and caregivers, and men as primary breadwinners.

During the Brezhnev period (1964–1982) policy-makers and social scientists increasingly raised concerns about the proper place of women in Soviet society. The Soviet model relied both on women's reproductive functions to renew the labor force and on their high level of integration into the paid workforce.[53] Policy-makers considered the fact that women were choosing to have fewer children a serious problem for the future supply of workers. Birth rates had fallen from 42.8 births per 1,000 persons in the population in 1913 to 15.2 births per 1,000 in 1970.[54] The population was still growing, but the rate of growth had slowed. Soviet scholars put forward two main explanations for what they regarded as a "demographic crisis." The first examined the impact of poor economic conditions on women's decisions about reproduction and considered the difficulties women faced in combining motherhood with full-time work. The second explanation posited a decline in "childbearing values" as the reason for shrinking family sizes.[55] Such arguments informed the increasingly popular view that Soviet notions of femininity required greater attention to women's role as mothers.

Debates about the demographic crisis questioned the Soviet gender order and highlighted anxieties about the size and composition of the nation's population.[56] Soviet demographic debates conform to what Nira Yuval-

Davis terms the "people as power" discourse, which she identifies as one of the key discourses informing nationalist population policies.[57] In it, the "national interest" is defined by stable or growing population sizes. As one Soviet demographer asserted, "[A] country's position in the world, all other things being equal, is determined by the size of the population."[58] The ruling elite perceived the demographic decline as a threat to the USSR's military, economic, and political status as a superpower.

Demographic concerns revealed anxieties within the Russian-led, Slavic-dominated Soviet elite about the effects of declining birth rates among Slavic women on the ethnic balance within the USSR. Statistics from 1976 demonstrated that population growth in the Central Asian and Transcaucasian republics was significantly higher than the Soviet average (up to three times higher in some Central Asian republics), whereas the Slavic (and Baltic) republics experienced below-average population increases. The Central Asian and Transcaucasian republics accounted for 30 percent of population growth in 1970, compared to 15 percent in 1959.[59] The Soviet leadership feared that the Soviet Union would eventually become a country where (Muslim)[60] non-Slavs outnumbered (Christian) Slavs, threatening the dominant position of Russians. Yuval-Davis writes: "The 'demographic race' can take place not only where there is a national conflict on a contested territory but also where an ethnic majority is seen as crucial in order to retain the hegemony of the hegemonic collectivity."[61]

The Soviet Union was an example of the latter case, as Russians were "treated as the primary nation of the USSR" despite claims of multiethnic brotherhood.[62] The understanding of who constituted a desirable mother in this demographic race exposed the contradictions inherent in the Soviet gender order and in Soviet conceptions of the nation. Slavic women were seen as "too" liberated and therefore choosing to have fewer children, whereas Muslim women's lower labor participation and higher fertility rates demonstrated the limitations of the official policy aimed at women's emancipation. This debate also highlights the unevenness of economic development across the Soviet republics, which resulted in earlier "demographic transitions" in the more economically advanced regions of the union.

Men as Workers and Defenders of the Nation

Men were expected to fulfill the roles of worker and soldier, and thus be builders and defenders of communism. Scholars have argued that the state's valorization of motherhood, involvement in child rearing, and rhetoric of women's emancipation marginalized nonelite Soviet men and undermined their authority within the family.[63] According to Sergei Kukhterin, early Soviet legislation aimed at transforming the traditional family "reflected not so much the desire of the state to destroy the bourgeois family unit, but its desire to replace patriarchal authority with the authority of the state."[64] Men's wages were set at a level that excluded the possibility of a family wage model. Instead, the average Soviet family relied on the wages of husband and wife, and on state benefits linked to women's employment.[65] While various state policies weakened men's traditional position within the family, male dominance was deeply entrenched at the decision-making levels of the state and the top management positions in the economy.

The military was defined as a fundamental institution of male socialization, which provided men a rite of passage into adulthood as well as the proper ideological preparation as citizens. At the same time, the experience of military service was one of subordinating oneself to the collective, respecting hierarchies, and following orders. Military service was fundamentally about creating individual and collective masculine identities that were politically wedded to the party-state. Soviet leaders emphasized the importance of military service to transforming "young men with little 'life experience' into responsible, upright citizens," and endowing them with patriotism and discipline.[66] Furthermore, military service was seen as a policy that could facilitate the integration of the various Soviet nationalities. Teresa Rakowska-Harmstone argues that "military service in the USSR [was] promoted as the 'School of the (Soviet) Nation' where young men of diverse ethnic origins and cultures are molded into model soldiers—and prototypes of the new 'Soviet man.'"[67] The military was considered a fundamental building block of Soviet masculinity and society, as it functioned as a school of communism, of life as well as of the nation. The state's valorization of the military and of militarized masculinity as a key plank of the gender order was one of the ways in which male power was underpinned in Soviet society.

Beginning in the late 1960s academics (primarily educational theorists and demographers) and journalists put forward the argument that Soviet policies aimed at women's emancipation had contributed to men's feminization and women's masculinization. Women's integration into the paid workforce had apparently led to the neglect of their responsibilities as mothers and to a weakening of men's position.[68] Furthermore, the dominant role of women in raising children (both at home and in the school system) was seen as creating infantilized, immature boys who did not live up to Soviet notions of masculinity. Soviet officials, commentators, and some parents viewed military service as a counterweight to men's feminization. Ellen Jones writes:

> Many Soviet parents apparently see the army as a needed maturing experience that will "make a man" out of their recalcitrant sons. Soviet military socializers concur, depicting military service as a healthy counterbalance to the feminizing effects of an overprotective home life on young Soviet boys: "[T]he soldier's life is a strong antidote against the infantilism and 'feminization' of men."[69]

This quotation illustrates the firm link between masculinity and the military in the Soviet Union and the importance assigned to military service in the formation of masculine identities. Moreover, Jones explains: "The conscript tour is generally the first sustained contact of young men with an all-male environment; and Soviet officials stress its importance in providing male role models and instilling masculinity."[70] From this perspective, the military appeared as a needed masculine space in the context of a problematic gender order and a crisis in masculinity.

The debate on masculinity and military service involved a recurring critique of the changing values of Soviet youth born after World War Two. The military elite described the younger generation as lacking the benefit of war experience and being influenced by "cosmopolitan" and "corrupt" values emanating from the West. Youth were seen as not sufficiently patriotic or self-sacrificing.[71] Some argued that these developments had led to "an upsurge of pacifism and 'political naivety' among Soviet youth."[72] Such arguments highlight the close ties between citizenship, patriotism, and masculinity in the Soviet Union, and some of the contradictions that arose alongside social modernization.[73] Nina Tumarkin explains the emphasis on military-patriotic education and the emergence of the cult of the Great Patriotic War during the 1960s as a response to these societal changes. Activities to memorialize war and prepare for war aimed at more closely binding younger generations of Soviet citizens, especially men, to the state.[74]

In addition, ethnic demographic changes led to a perceived manpower supply problem in the military and raised the question of who could be considered a reliable soldier. Male military service played a fundamental part in the construction of a Soviet identity and highlighted the intersections between masculinity and nation. The army was depicted as a tool of ethnic integration and political socialization for men. In fact, it remained a Russian-dominated institution throughout the Soviet period and reflected Russian and Slavic power in society. Russian was the language of the Soviet army, and Russians, Ukrainians, and Belorussians were over-represented in the officer corps. A survey of officers' surnames from 1976 to 1978 revealed that around 93 percent of Soviet officers were Slavic and about 61 percent were Russian.[75] It is therefore not surprising that worries about the emerging changes in the ethnic makeup of the Soviet population also found expression within the military. Anatol Lieven explains:

> From the early 1970s, Soviet generals were becoming increasingly concerned both by the growth in the number of Muslim conscripts relative to Slavic ones, and by the Muslims' supposed unreliability, low education and, above all, lack of knowledge of the Russian language.[76]

Demographic projections estimated that the cohort of Slavic men reaching draft age would decrease from 79.6 percent of the total pool in 1940–1949 to 60.8 percent in 1988, and that the numbers of Muslim men reaching draft age would increase from 5.6 percent in 1940–1949 to 20.0 percent in 1988.[77] As the Soviet military became more reliant on non-Slavs to meet its manpower requirements, the contradictory basis of Soviet conceptions of the nation became more apparent.

Militarized masculinity was a key aspect of the Soviet gender order. The official policy of women's emancipation was not applied to the military sphere, where "traditional" notions of militarized masculinity and nonmilitarized femininity were upheld. During the Brezhnev period the official policy of women's emancipation started to be revised toward a renewed focus on women's and men's "natural" roles. A number of social "problems" including demographic decline and men's feminization were blamed on the unnatural gender order promoted by state policies toward women. While these debates continued to shape public discourse, the *perestroika* period brought serious challenges to militarized masculinity and women's exclusion from the military sphere.

Challenges to Militarization during the Soviet-Afghan war

In the late Soviet period the public image of the military became tarnished and society began to reconsider obligatory military service. This was due to a combination of factors involving the Soviet intervention in Afghanistan (1979–1989), Gorbachev's reform policies (1985–1991), and the activism of soldiers' mothers (starting in the late 1980s). Relations between the military and society—and by extension between state and society—were being redefined by a growing public awareness of the high number of peace- and wartime deaths of conscripts. Soviet citizens began to publicly question the purpose of the war. Significantly, as militarism and militarization rely on notions of masculinity and femininity, their questioning involved challenges to the existing gender order. Official notions of militarized masculinity tied to Soviet men's citizenship began to be undermined in the face of the regime's growing crisis in legitimacy. The notion of motherhood that had equated patriotism with solemn sacrifice of one's son was for the first time confronted by public expressions of maternal grief and the activism of soldiers' mothers to exclude their sons from service.

The official justification given for the Soviet intervention in Afghanistan was the fulfillment of an "internationalist duty."[78] In the year and a half leading up to the invasion, the Afghan communist governments repeatedly asked the SU to intervene militarily. The objectives of the Soviet Union's 40th Army were to secure Kabul and major roads to the capital, suppress the mujahideen, and close off the Afghan-Pakistan border.[79] Over the almost ten-year period of war it is estimated that up to 730,000 Soviet citizens served in Afghanistan. The number of Soviet casualties was conservatively estimated at 14,453 dead, 49,985 wounded, and 300 missing.[80] Many of the soldiers who participated were unsure about the meaning and purpose of the war because of a lack of information and the nature of counterinsurgency warfare. As one Afghan war veteran said, "[W]hom were we defending here? and from whom? where was the enemy?"[81]

Uncertainty about the war's purpose surfaced in society more generally, yet was particularly strong among the parents of conscripts sent to Afghanistan and of draft-age men. During the first few years of the war, public debate and information on the intervention was tightly controlled by the Soviet leadership under Brezhnev. The media moved from not acknowledging the invasion to an insistence that Soviet troops were acting only in nonmilitary and humanitarian roles.[82] During the leadership of Iurii Andropov (1982–1984) and Konstantin Chernenko (1984–1985), some reports on the Afghan conflict appeared in the media, but there was no change in the official line that this was not a war and that costs and casualties were limited.[83] The government's position changed when Mikhail Gorbachev come to power. Gorbachev publicly referred to the war in Afghanistan as "a bleeding wound."[84] His philosophy of "New Thinking," which entailed a de-ideologization of foreign policy, allowed for a reconsideration of the Soviet military involvement in Afghanistan. The decision to withdraw forces was taken by the end of 1985 but not implemented until 1988–1989.[85] Gorbachev and his reformers used the policy of *glasnost'* to gain wider support for a withdrawal of troops. G*lasnost'* encouraged more open and critical media coverage and public debate on the war, which helped expose the dire conditions in which conscripts served and the growing doubts among citizens about the military deployment.[86] Remarkably, in 1989 the Supreme Soviet of the USSR passed a decree condemning the military intervention in Afghanistan both morally and politically.[87]

A number of authors have studied the effects of the Afghan war on political and social change in the Soviet Union. Rafael Reuveny and Aseem Prakash have cited four effects.[88] The war reduced the perceived efficacy of military intervention in the eyes of the leadership (perception effects);[89] tarnished the image of the Red Army (military effects); exacerbated tensions between Soviet nationalities/republics, thus undermining the legitimacy of the state (legitimacy effects); and stimulated political participation[90] and openness (*glasnost'*) (participation effects).[91] Reuveny and Prakash emphasize the Afghan war as a key factor in the collapse of the Soviet state, but that is likely an overstatement. The war exacerbated the social, economic, and political crisis of the Soviet regime but was not one of the factors causing its collapse. Rather the Afghan war helped bring to the fore the existing discrepancies between Soviet ideology and reality, and thus reinforced the need for change.[92]

Military, Masculinity, and the Nation

The prestige of the Soviet military suffered in at least three important respects as a result of the Afghan war. First of all, the fact that the Red Army could not ensure military victory and a stabilization of the Afghan regime called into question its image as victorious and undefeatable (an image cultivated from its role in World War Two).[93] As the Soviet state's status as a great power (*derzhava*) largely rested on its military prowess, the military's performance in Afghanistan helped to erode the image of the Soviet Union as a military superpower. The Soviet war in Afghanistan is often compared both by Soviet and Western commentators (and Russian citizens) to the U.S. experience in Vietnam.[94] Some of the similarities cited are the protracted nature of the wars and the constellation of forces (superior military power versus guerilla fighters).[95] While this comparison does not hold up in terms of the much larger size of the military commitment and higher casualties of the United States, it is important in another way. It illustrates the similar meaning the two conflicts had in the public discourse of their respective societies. In the U.S. and the USSR, public discussion on the wars evolved around the moral question of whether the intervention was justified at all (liberal forces) and the notion of a betrayal of the military (conservative forces).[96] Both military deployments lacked strong public support and exposed antimilitarist tendencies in U.S. and Soviet society. They led to a decrease in the military's prestige and in citizens' willingness to participate in war. The conflicts were associated with men's draft evasion and the refusal of many men and women to perform their militarized gender roles.[97]

Second, the image of the military as a pillar of society and educator of Soviet citizens suffered in the light of revelations of the abuse and violence resulting from *dedovshchina*. Mark Galeotti defines *dedovshchina* as "a seniority-based culture of 'hazing' rights that cut across class and ethnic boundaries, enlisting senior conscripts to keep newcomers in line by bullying and beating, while promising the victims eventual access to the same privileges in return for acquiescence."[98] The incidence of *dedovshchina* increased significantly in the late Soviet period. *Dedovshchina* was a common practice among the Soviet troops in Afghanistan and is believed to have undermined their fighting capacity.[99] Public discussion of *dedovshchina* during the Afghan war reduced societal support for the idea that obligatory military service was a "sacred duty" of young men. The Afghan war and the organizing of soldiers' mothers increased public awareness of the abuse conscripts experienced during service. By 1990, 43 percent of respondents in a poll conducted by the All-Union Center for the Study of Public Opinion (VTsIOM) considered military service to be morally and physically harmful to young men, while 32 percent considered military service an important preparation of young men for life; and 10 percent said they were satisfied with the situation in the military.[100] While young men had in the past "accepted the draft as an inescapable fact of life" and draft evasion had been strongly frowned upon, that changed during the 1980s.[101] The low public image of Afghan war veterans (*afgantsy*) further indicated a challenge to militarized masculinity and the link between heroism and military service. Not unlike many U.S. Vietnam veterans, many *afgantsy* felt a sense of betrayal, because of the unpopular nature of the war they had fought and the difficulties they faced in reintegrating into society and receiving state support.[102]

Finally, the military's failure to be a force that unified Soviet nationalities became more evident during the Afghan war. The war exposed the deterioration of ethnic relations within the armed forces. As came to be known more widely, in addition to *dedovshchina*, conscripts often organized along ethnic lines in a system known as *zemliachestvo* or *gruppovshchina*, which aimed at defending men of the same ethnicity against attacks from men of other ethnicities.[103] There was also controversy over which nationalities carried the burden of the war effort and whether this was a "Russian imperial war" that was being fought on the backs of non-Russian conscripts. Galeotti suggests that based on the available figures, this was a Soviet (rather than a Russian or Slav) war, with most of the casualties coming from the Slavic republics and Turkmenistan. Nonetheless, the war—together with *perestroika* and *glasnost'*—contributed to a further politicization of the nationalities issue.[104] During the 1980s antiwar protests were staged in a number of Central Asian and Baltic republics where the draft came to be rejected out of nationalist sentiment.[105]

Activism by Soldiers' Mothers

The first years of the Soviet-Afghan war were characterized by the state's imposed suppression of mothers' grief over their dead sons. This was part of a concerted attempt to keep information on casualties secret. Only with the introduction of *glasnost'* and *perestroika* could mothers' private grief find public expression and serve as the basis for activism around conscription.[106] The late 1980s saw the flourishing of civil society groups such as those of the soldiers' mothers. These women aimed to raise public awareness about *dedovshchina*, the war, and peace-time deaths of conscripts. Their efforts culminated in the founding of the Committee of Soldiers' Mothers in 1989.

Activities of the soldiers' mothers such as demonstrations, press conferences, and hunger-strikes were instrumental in bringing public attention to violence within the armed forces.[107] From 1987–1988 forward, *dedovshchina* became publicly debated.[108] Julie Elkner argues that the activism of soldiers' mothers in regard to *dedovshchina* contributed to a significant shift in the public image of the military and of military service. In 1990 the Committee of Soldiers' Mothers claimed that, largely due to *dedovshchina*, the number of peacetime deaths in the Soviet military between 1986 and 1990 was higher than combat casualties resulting from the ten-year war in Afghanistan. *Dedovshchina* raised questions regarding the military's authority: Was it an appropriate institution for the socialization of young men? Why was it not able to keep order within its ranks? Revelations about the widespread nature of *dedovshchina* challenged the twin pillars on which military service rested: that it was crucial to men's socialization and to their citizenship.[109]

Some commentators tried to link *dedovshchina* to the apparent "feminization" of Soviet society that involved "overprotective mothers" and "infantilized sons." Consequently young men were badly prepared for army life (mama's boys) and more likely to complain about the hardships they encountered during service.[110] The Soviet construction of militarized masculinity went hand in hand with a notion of motherhood that conflated the supposedly patriotic duty of sacrificing one's son with "good motherhood." Cynthia Enloe explains: "A mother who tried to hold on to her son would not only be unpatriotic, robbing the military of its needed soldiery, but would also be a bad mother, robbing a boy of his chance to achieve masculinized adulthood."[111] Thus activism by soldiers' mothers challenged notions of militarized masculinity but also prevailing notions of motherhood during the final years of the Soviet Union.

At the same time, soldiers' mothers were able to rely on the important status motherhood enjoyed in Soviet culture.[112] The Soviet state glorified motherhood and defined it as women's most important service to the state.[113] At the same time, the association of motherhood with peace was a key element of the Soviet Union's Cold War propaganda. In official rhetoric, the Soviet Union's self-portrayal as a peace-loving country rested on the notion of peace-loving Soviet mothers.[114] Both the celebration of motherhood and the association of motherhood with peace gave moral authority to the demands of soldiers' mothers.

Rather than openly tackle the problem of barracks violence, the military reacted to the activism of soldiers' mothers by either downplaying concerns or discrediting mothers. The military constructed "show military settlements" or organized its own "gatherings" of soldiers' mothers as a way of defusing the criticism of the Committee of Soldiers' Mothers.[115] Indeed, part of the movement came to work in close cooperation with the military, while more radical groups kept their distance.[116] The military also used a gendered portrayal of soldiers' mothers to discredit them and reinstate what it considered the proper boundaries between the military and civilian spheres. For example, soldiers' mothers were described as "fuelled by female hysteria," as "unbalanced ladies," or overly emotional. The military press emphasized that the proper place for mothers was outside the military, and that mothers were not legitimate commentators on military affairs.[117] Soldiers' mothers were also depicted as part of a "conspiracy to destroy the military."[118] In the non-Russian republics, conservative military commentators linked soldiers' mothers to nationalist-separatist forces, while in the Russian republic they argued that the soldiers' mothers were the creation of democrats.[119]

The first public acknowledgment of the concerns of soldiers' mothers came when Gorbachev included excerpts from mothers' letters during a Politburo session in 1985 in his arguments for a reconsideration of the Soviet involvement in Afghanistan.[120] In response to complaints by soldiers' mothers, Gorbachev set up an investigatory commission, which reported in 1991 that as many as 80 percent of the soldiers who had died in service over the preceding fifteen years had succumbed to suicide, beatings, or accidents.[121] While there was greater acknowledgment of the grief and concerns of soldiers' mothers during the second half of the 1980s, officials were aware of the potentially dangerous implications of the activism of soldiers' mothers, especially as mothers held the sympathy of the public.[122] As Elkner puts it, "Grieving soldiers' mothers symbolised the growing rift between the 'people' and the Soviet army, giving the lie to the often repeated slogan that, in contrast to the situation in bourgeois states, 'the Soviet army and the people are one.'"[123]

The struggle for greater accountability and openness of the state and its institutions was among the most important changes taking place during the final years of the Soviet Union. It included reassessing one of the key institutions of Soviet life and society, the military, in the context of the war in Afghanistan. This was a gendered process, as it involved confronting official notions of masculinity and femininity and disturbing the gendered boundaries separating military and civilian spheres.

Conclusion

The SU emerged from World War Two as an international military power, despite the great human and material losses it had incurred. The Great Patriotic War, which established the military as a key institution of Soviet life, became commemorated as the defining moment of Soviet history. *Glasnost'* opened up space for a critical examination of Soviet history and militarized socialism. The comparatively small and "insignificant" (by conventional military standards) Afghan war led to a reappraisal of the use of military intervention and of the military's status in the social and political life of the USSR. The final years of the Soviet Union were also accompanied by military retreats—from Afghanistan, Eastern Europe, and parts of the former Soviet republics—and the humiliation of having "lost" the Cold War. Thus the late Soviet period was characterized by a partial demilitarization of state and society.

The gendered subtext of these developments is often overlooked. Public discussion of *dedovshchina* and doubts about the purpose of the Afghan war undermined the image of the heroic Soviet soldier and the idea of military service as a sacred duty of Soviet men. The activism of soldiers' mothers significantly contributed to these developments, and in doing so defied Soviet notions of patriotic motherhood. At the same time, the *perestroika* period reinforced ideas of women's and men's essential gender differences. The official policy of women's emancipation became discredited, as politicians and journalists called for an end to women's high rates of labor participation and their return to the private sphere (a sentiment that was shared by many Soviet women).[124] The collapse of the communist state and the formation of a "new" state have entailed both challenges to existing gender roles and the intensification of gender inequalities.[125] The following chapters examine the extent to which militarized masculinity has been transformed, and explores the place of militarized masculinity within the broader dynamic of de- and remilitarization in post-Soviet society.

2 Militarized Masculinity and State Leadership in the Russian-Chechen Wars

> I was waiting for a new general to appear, unlike any other. Or rather, a general who was like the generals I read about in books when I was young. I was waiting.... Time passed, and such a general appeared. And soon after his arrival, it became obvious to our whole society how really courageous and highly professional our military people were. This "general" was named Colonel Vladimir Putin.
>
> Boris Yeltsin[1]

THE LINES ABOVE, from former President Boris Yeltsin's autobiography, apparently recollect the thought process that led to the selection of Vladimir Putin as Yeltsin's successor. Without a doubt the process was more complicated and calculated than described here.[2] The members of Yeltsin's inner circle (widely referred to as "the family") who ruled Russia during the last few years of Yeltsin's presidency were seeking a smooth transfer of power and a guarantee against future prosecution. To that end, firm control of the military and security structures was considered important, making Putin, who was the director of the Federal Security Service (FSB) in 1998–1999, a good candidate.[3] Yeltsin's remarks do not elaborate on these practical concerns and calculations. They do, however, tell an interesting story about the militarization of politics and the ideological function of militarized masculinity in the politics of late 1990s Russia. Why does Yeltsin invoke the generals he read about in his youth, an idealized image of Soviet militarized masculinity? How did Putin's arrival on the political scene highlight the courage and professionalism of Russia's military personnel? And why does Yeltsin insist on referring to Putin as general or colonel? Putin had left active KGB service in August 1991 and considered himself a civilian, even when he was appointed director of the FSB in 1998.[4] Yeltsin's trivial and seemingly apolitical recollections normalize militarism and help to justify gender hierarchies and inequalities. Significantly, Yeltsin was waiting for a general rather than a civilian, and by implication a man rather than a woman.

Ideas about masculinity, which inform perceptions of leadership, are often subtle and implicit.[5] Cynthia Enloe urges us to inquire into how much of the appearance of manliness that leaders seek is achieved through association with the military or war.[6] War—if successful in mobilizing the public on the basis of militarized patriotism—can confer the legitimacy of masculinity onto those waging war. War, militarism, and masculinity are also closely tied to nationalism. Joane Nagel argues that "[t]erms such as honour, patriotism, cowardice, bravery, and duty are hard to distinguish as either nationalistic or masculine because they seem so thoroughly tied both to the nation and to manhood."[7] When Enloe asks to what extent "actors [are] motivated in part by a desire to appear 'manly,'" she might just as well ask to what extent actors are motivated by their desire to appear patriotic, heroic, or brave.[8] Thus the attempt of political leaders to appear manly (and patriotic, and so forth) may militarize state- and nation-building. At the same time, a weak state and nation may become associated with a crisis in masculinity.

However, there is no straightforward connection between war and manliness. Instead, the waging of war is legitimized by various notions of militarized masculinity, including that of the soldier/warrior, patriot, hero, and enemy. The first Chechen war (1994–1996) was shaped by challenges to militarized masculinity by high-ranking officials as well as by an ambiguous image of the soldier. The war was highly unpopular and further decreased Yeltsin's approval rating. It entered national consciousness as another item on the growing list of humiliations experienced since the Soviet collapse. While Yeltsin had originally hoped to increase his popularity with a "small victorious war," his re-election campaign in 1996 promised an end to the violent conflict in Chechnya. The second war (1999–2009) saw the renewal of militarized masculinity and patriotism, and helped launch Prime Minster Putin into the presidency. The political and military leadership was united behind the war, which had the approval of much of Russia's populace. Putin's ability to exploit terrorist fears and a sense of humiliation was key to the war's popularity and his election to the presidency.

There are multiple explanations for the different way the two wars played out in national politics. Greater press freedom and inadequate military preparation during the first war, for example, help explain the lack of popular support for that war. However, feminist analysis offers additional insight by examining how different representations and articulations of militarized masculinity affected the legitimacy of the use of military force and of the Yeltsin and Putin leadership, respectively.[9]

The changing politics of militarized masculinity I describe in this chapter is linked to a broader shift in the political leadership's conception of what kind of military is appropriate to post-Soviet state and society. David J. Betz and Sergei Plekhanov explain that in the early post-Soviet period the political elite emphasized the context of a smaller state, integration into the global economy, and the domestic economic transition to argue for a smaller military and a reduced military budget. Yeltsin was concerned primarily with control over the military and with "ensuring the army's loyalty in the bitter struggles for power."[10] In contrast, after 1999 a fundamentally different understanding emerged that justified the call for a stronger military in the context of both internal and external threats, and advocated a central role for the armed forces in society and for the military and security structures in the rebuilding of the Russian state. Putin emphasized that the needs of the military had to be met, expressed his respect for the armed forces, and managed to gain the support of those in the military and security structures.[11] This shift in thinking entailed a shift in the politics of militarized masculinity, as I show in this chapter.

The Russian-Chechen Wars: A Brief Overview[12]

The Chechen National Congress, a group that included broad segments of Chechen politics and society at the time, declared state sovereignty in November 1990. The Supreme Soviet of the Chechen-Ingush Republic felt compelled to pass a similar declaration the same month. In fall of 1991, the National Congress under Dzhokhar Dudaev's leadership—which now represented the radical parts of the movement—forcibly seized power in the Chechen-Ingush Republic. The executive committee of the National Congress staged parliamentary and presidential elections to legitimate the new regime. Dudaev issued a decree asserting the Chechen republic's independence in November of 1991, shortly after his election as president. Relations between the Russian state and the separatist republic of Chechnya were fraught with tensions ever since the early post-Soviet period. They were, however, overshadowed by ongoing political struggles within Chechnya itself as well as in Moscow (such as between President Yeltsin and the Duma). Russian policies toward Chechnya were inconsistent and not informed by concerted attempts to resolve political disagreements.[13] For example, the Yeltsin government financially supported and helped arm anti-Dudaev forces within the republic, while negotiating with Dudaev. The trigger for military intervention was a failed covert operation in November 1994, in which Russian soldiers attempted a coup against the Dudaev regime. When the soldiers were captured and journalists traveled to Chechnya to interview them, the incident became an embarrassment for Yeltsin and his government, which had initially denied the involvement of Russian soldiers.[14] On December 11, 1994, about 40,000 soldiers of the Defense Ministry and the Interior Ministry moved toward the Chechen capital, Grozny. This military intervention to "disarm illegally armed formations," as it was officially termed, initiated the first Chechen war, which lasted from December 1994 to August 1996.[15]

Federal forces took control of the Chechen capital in February 1995, but fighting continued both in Grozny and elsewhere. In mid-June 1995 Chechen fighters led by field commander Shamil Basaev took 1,500 hostages in a hospital in the Southern Russian city of Budennovsk in an attempt to force a resolution to the conflict. The further course of the war was characterized by intermittent negotiations, the escalation of fighting, and attempts to undermine Dudaev's base politically. In January 1996 the Chechens staged another hostage-taking, this time in Kisliar (Dagestan) and under the leadership of Salman Raduev. As the fighting intensified, Yeltsin needed to end the unpopular war in order to improve his chances of re-election in 1996. The Khasaviurt cease-fire agreement that was signed in August 1996 amounted to a Russian defeat and postponed a resolution of Chechnya's status to 2001.[16]

The Russian-Chechen war resumed in the fall of 1999. The political leadership under President Yeltsin and Prime Minister Putin portrayed the second Chechen "campaign" as a necessary response to Chechen separatist incursions into neighboring Dagestan led by Basaev in August and the bombing of apartment buildings in Moscow and other cities in September. Some suggest the possible involvement of the state secret service in these incidents and the Russian leadership's prior plans for a renewed military campaign.[17] By the end of September the military began air attacks on Grozny and the Russian government had ordered approximately 50,000 soldiers to the Dagestani-Chechen border.[18] The Russian leadership refused to negotiate with Chechen president Aslan Maskhadov and continued the fighting.

The Chechen "campaign" officially lasted until January 2001, but a guerrilla war between Chechen separatists and federal forces continued. Increasingly, the Chechen separatists used terrorist means to bring attention to their cause. High-profile incidents were the hostage-takings in the Dubrovka Theater in Moscow (2002) and the School Number 1 in Beslan (2004), as well as numerous bombings that have occurred in Moscow and across the country.[19] After the September 11, 2001 terrorist attacks on the World Trade Center and the Pentagon, Putin justified the "antiterrorist operation" in Chechnya as part of the global war on terror.[20] Years of counterinsurgency warfare and counterterrorist policies have not led to the eradication of terrorism in Russia. The second Chechen war is typical of contemporary counterterrorist warfare, in that its ending is hard to pinpoint and contested among scholars. The counterterrorism operation was officially declared over in April 2009, but violence still plagues Chechnya and has spread to the greater North Caucasus region.

There has been a widespread cynical attitude about the state's waging of these wars, with many (including many of my interviewees) alleging that those in power were profiting from the war. Serguei Oushakine points out that official sources of information about the war are often rejected in favor of "personal narratives, rumours, contradictory testimonies, and popular culture (cinema, song, memoirs)."[21] The Russian leadership does not recognize the two military interventions in Chechnya as wars, though their participants, the public (in Chechnya and the rest of Russia), and scholars usually do refer to them as wars. The military operations in Chechnya have certainly led to a large number of casualties, though estimates vary greatly. In 2004 the Union of Committees of Soldiers' Mothers estimated Russian military deaths for both wars to be approximately 25,000.[22] The military analyst Pavel Felgenhauer cited estimates of 12,000 dead and 100,000 wounded Russian soldiers, and of 100,000 largely civilian deaths among the Chechens in early 2003.[23] Also, 35,000 ethnic Russians living in Chechnya are thought to have been killed during the two wars.[24] Widespread and systemic human rights violations against Chechen civilians and suspected combatants have been documented and include detentions in so-called filtration camps, torture, rape, disappearances, and executions.[25]

Yeltsin's Leadership and the First Chechen War[26]

Reducing state control over the economy was a central plank of neoliberal reforms implemented in Russia in the early 1990s, which had the broader effect of creating an underfunded and weakened state. The theme of nation- and state-building came to play a central role in the rhetoric of the nationalist and reform-critical opposition in the Duma. Yeltsin's opponents put forward alternative conceptions of the Russian nation—not as part of the West, but as Eurasian power or restored superpower—and criticized the president and his government for undermining the state. Yeltsin's ideological shift from reform to state-building and creation of a strong presidential system ("superpresidentialism") were strategies to defuse the opposition and consolidate his own position. State-building and the Chechen war were part of Yeltsin's efforts to strengthen his leadership.[27] George Breslauer in his book *Gorbachev and Yeltsin as Leaders* captures well the domestic context leading up to the first Chechen war:

> By late 1994—with his personal approval ratings plummeting, the economy in a precarious state after the crash of the ruble on October 11, 1994, a hostile (albeit less powerful) Duma, charges of corruption swirling around his government, powerful centrifugal forces still asserting themselves in the regions of Russia, Western assistance and investment at a small fraction of earlier expectations, integration into Western institutions proceeding at a snail's pace, and NATO expansion on the table—Yeltsin found himself severely challenged to justify the *quality of his leadership.*[28]

Peter Lentini argues that the domestic crisis, and in particular the rising popularity of nationalists, forced Yeltsin to "'get macho' in relation to the Near Abroad,[29] Chechnya and the North Atlantic community."[30] The author thus acknowledges the role of masculinity in the domestic struggle for power and how a tough stance is often associated with masculinity. Yeltsin and his advisers apparently saw military intervention in Chechnya as a means of boosting the president's dwindling popularity among the public.[31] Duma Defense Committee Chairman Sergei Iushenkov claimed that Oleg Lobov, secretary of the Security Council, told him in a personal conversation: "It is not only a question of the integrity of Russia. We need a small victorious war to raise the President's ratings."[32] Markus Soldner comments that Yeltsin and his advisers anticipated the war would help create an image of Yeltsin as a patriotic warrior.[33]

The war was officially dubbed an intervention for "the restoration of constitutional order." The state's justification for military intervention emphasized the need to secure Russia's territorial integrity, protect its citizens in and beyond Chechnya from armed extremists, and prevent a destabilization of the political and economic situation. In his first address to Russia's citizens regarding the war, Yeltsin asserted: "As President I will ensure that the Constitution and the Law are followed."[34] The theme of lawlessness and crime soon became another key justification for the use of military force against the Chechen regime under Dudaev.[35] In President Yeltsin's and Prime Minister Viktor Chernomyrdin's speeches regarding the war, Chechnya was portrayed as a place of widespread lawlessness because of illegal drugs and arms trading, crime, and corruption. The characterization of Chechnya as a center of organized crime first appeared in a speech by Prime Minister Viktor Chernomyrdin titled "For Russia We Stand and Will Always Stand," delivered at a national women's conference just a few days after the beginning of the war. Chernomyrdin stressed that illegal armed formations had already taken hundreds of lives, were threatening the integrity of the state, and were aggravating national and religious tensions. He emphasized that this state of lawlessness had allowed the growth of criminal structures that were threatening to destabilize all of Russia.[36]

In Yeltsin's second address to citizens regarding the "situation in Chechnya," he reiterated that Russian soldiers were defending the unity of Russia on the basis of the constitution.[37] However, he also quickly moved to the theme of lawlessness and crime, linking the Dudaev regime to the drug and arms trade, currency fraud, and political extremism. He spoke of the need to "clean" or rid Chechnya of "criminal elements." Despite this inflammatory language, both Yeltsin and Chernomyrdin made it a point to differentiate between the Chechen people and Chechen criminals. Chernomyrdin stated that the Chechen people are not responsible for the growth in crime—they are "not the 'notorious persons of Caucasian nationality'" (*ne preslovutye "litsa kavkaskoi national'nosti"*), alluding to widespread anti-Chechen sentiments in Russian society.[38] While Yeltsin described the Dudaev regime as criminal, he noted that Russia is not an enemy of Muslims. Finally, both politicians asserted that the intervention aimed to help the Chechen people and not to provoke war.[39]

This official discourse on the Chechen war helped construct a dichotomy of "us" versus "them" that relied both on gender and race. It can be seen as an attempt to portray the Russian leadership as the masculine protector of state and nation: Yeltsin was apparently the one who could provide order and ensure the unity of the state and the security of its citizens.⁴⁰ The notion of ordered and patriotic Russian masculinity was juxtaposed to a notion of aggressive, criminal, and corrupt masculinity purportedly embodied by (at least some) Chechen men. This depiction of Chechen men corresponded to the often racialized discourse used to describe them. Together with other people from the Caucasus and from Central Asia, Chechens are referred to as *chernye*, "blacks," in colloquial Russian. Meredith L. Roman explains that the racialization of men from the Caucasus in post-Soviet Russian society was simultaneously gendered: "[T]he man of colour was racialized as predatory and criminal (morally weak) as opposed to effeminate and physically weak."⁴¹ While the war was not officially framed in ethnic or racial terms (as it was by nationalists and some communists), Yeltsin and his allies repeatedly linked the Chechen leadership with criminality and emphasized crime as one of the main justifications for military intervention. Chechens, and especially Chechen men, came to symbolize the negative effects of Russia's postcommunist transition, such as the rise in crime or the lack of law and order more generally.⁴²

Even though more than half of the Russian population considered the Chechen fighters "bandits" and only very few thought of them as "protectors of their land" (13 percent),⁴³ the first Chechen war was deeply unpopular with Russia's citizens. In December 1994 as well as in January 1995 only 30 percent of respondents supported "decisive measures to bring order to Chechnya," and between 60 and 70 percent rejected the use of force.⁴⁴ Forty-one percent of those polled in spring of 1995 could not pinpoint the reasons behind the war. Some 22 percent suspected that the war was connected to a cover-up involving high-ranking political and military figures,⁴⁵ and 18 percent of respondents believed the war was linked to crime-fighting within Chechnya. Only 14 percent of those polled agreed that the war was about the integrity of the state, and only 10 percent thought it was about the protection of Russian citizens.⁴⁶ Clearly, the official justifications for the war had not convinced Russians and there was a wide range of opinions regarding the reasons behind the war.

While Russians did not support the Chechen separatist cause, they also did not trust their president and his justifications for the war. Against the hopes of the political leadership, the war did not help improve Yeltsin's popularity among Russians. Compared with a year earlier, Yeltsin's approval rating in February 1995 had fallen further. For each respondent who trusted Yeltsin there were almost ten who did not. A year earlier the ratio had been one to two.⁴⁷ Polls among urban Russians in mid-December 1994 showed that while 31 percent blamed Dudaev for the military confrontation, as many as 25 percent put the blame on Yeltsin.[48] In another poll, Russians were asked what position a "patriot" would take on the Chechen war. Only 19 percent of respondents associated a patriotic stance with support for the military operation, and 52 percent believed that a patriot should be against the war.[49] Thus the notion of the "patriotic warrior" was seen as an oxymoron by more than half of the population during the first Chechen war and did not serve to increase the popularity of the president. Militarized patriotism at the societal level was weak, as seen in the low popular support for the military intervention. And ambiguous notions of militarized masculinity represented by the military leadership and articulated by the president further undermined the waging of the war.

Challenges to Militarized Masculinity

Prominent members of the top military brass did not support the intervention in Chechnya. They felt that the military had not been given sufficient time to prepare, nor the necessary funding to accomplish the task successfully. Defense Minister Pavel Grachev claimed that the operation was guaranteed to lead to an easy and swift victory. However, other generals disagreed, leading to what came to be known as the "generals' crisis."[50] General Eduard Vorob'ev, first deputy minister of defense, resigned over his refusal to take command in the offensive into Chechnya in December 1994. He did not consider the use of force justifiable on the basis of the military doctrine. Vorob'ev also criticized the lack of preparation and the danger in which the military operation would put civilians.[51] The general explained: "My personal fate is not so important at this point; it is necessary to save Russia and get out of the situation that has developed in the country, in Chechnya, and in the Armed Forces."[52] Deputy Minister of Defense General Boris Gromov was another outspoken critic of the operation in Chechnya.[53] Highly regarded as commander in the Soviet-Afghan war, Gromov warned that the military intervention might turn into another "Afghanistan."[54] He strongly criticized the political leadership and the defense minister, and questioned the need to follow orders. Gromov was transferred to the foreign ministry, apparently in an attempt to reduce the political fallout that might have resulted from his dismissal.[55] Two additional deputy defense ministers had to part over their opposition to the war: Colonel General Valerii Mironov and Colonel General Georgii Kondrat'ev.[56] Furthermore, by April 1995 as many as 557 officers had refused to serve in the war.[57]

Even among those generals who participated in the Chechen war, there were many who were ambivalent about the military operation and resentful toward the politicians who had decided to send troops to Chechnya. One example of this was Major General Ivan Babichev, who commanded the westernmost group of forces entering Chechnya.[58] He ordered his troops to a halt when they encountered a group of demonstrating Chechen women.[59] Babichev stated in December 1994: "We are not going to use tanks against the civilian population. It is not our fault that we are here."[60] Although Yeltsin had personally taken responsibility for the operation, armed forces personnel were wary about using force against fellow citizens and worried about being turned on by an accusing public, as had happened in Tbilisi during the waning days of the Soviet Union.[61] The most prominent articulation of this position came from Lieutenant General Lev Rokhlin who commanded the northern group of forces in the Chechen operation and whose troops played a decisive role in the seizure of Grozny in early 1995. Rokhlin, who both opposed the war and criticized the political leadership, made a remarkable gesture when he refused all honors for his combat actions. He reasoned that this was a civil war and therefore honors should not be awarded. Rokhlin was publicly skeptical of the official reasons given to justify the war. Likening politicians to the mafia, he explained that they had pursued their own interests rather than taken any principled stance against Dudaev.[62] In Robert Barylski's view, Rokhlin's refusal to perform the role of military hero, and thus support the war and the political leadership, paradoxically resulted in his being elevated to the status of national hero:

> Lt. General Rokhlin became a national hero, a symbol of the soldier doing his patriotic duty under the most difficult circumstances. Instead of celebrating and playing the conquering hero, he refused to give the war false glamour and insisted on describing it realistically. He found it impossible to accept Yeltsin's Hero of Russia medal given his deep feelings about the war as a national tragedy.[63]

The position Rokhlin took was popular and helped him win a seat in the Duma elections of 1995.

The first war also became associated with an unheroic image of the conscript soldier as inadequately supplied, badly trained, and lacking morale. Lieutenant General Lebed, one of the Kremlin's harshest critics on the war, famously disparaged Yeltsin's and Grachev's strategy and the state of the Russian army by saying: "Russia no longer has an army—what it has is only military formations of boy-soldiers which are hardly capable of achieving anything."[64] By referring to the troops as "boy-soldiers" he implicitly questioned their masculinity and ability to wage war successfully. The political leadership failed to construct a more positive image of the soldier. In his 1995 annual address, Yeltsin emphasized the need to increase the prestige of military service, but also for citizens to conscientiously fulfill their duty in defending the fatherland.[65] This emphasis on citizens' duty rather than on the individual or collective heroism of soldiers is striking considering the context of an ongoing war. In his 1996 annual address, Yeltsin stressed the need for soldiers to target only bandits, by implication criticizing troops for using force against civilians.[66] Barylski explains the significance for the men fighting: "If Russia's soldiers expected to hear their supreme commander praising them for their bravery and the sacrifices they had made in Chechnya, they were disappointed. Instead of cheering them on, Yeltsin admonished them to target bandits and rebel fighters, not the Chechen people who are all Russian citizens."[67] Yeltsin's failure or inability to construct a heroic image of federal troops in Chechnya may not be surprising considering his own skepticism toward the military. However, this failure undermined the political leadership's ability to rally support for the war. From the very beginning, the war was associated with challenges to military professionalism, obedience, and heroism, and further reduced the military's prestige and support among the public.

The 1996 Presidential Election and the Chechen War

At the beginning of 1996, Yeltsin's approval rating was in the single digits. The main plank of Yeltsin's election campaign was the need to prevent a return to communism, pitching himself as the guarantor of democracy.[68] However, Yeltsin also realized that the unpopular Chechen war needed to be tackled, as it reduced his chances of re-election. Some 84 percent of potential voters who were surveyed before the election considered "the Chechen problem" to be the most important or one of the most important issues facing Russia.[69] Yeltsin promised to bring an end to the war and for the first time engaged in serious peacemaking efforts. At the end of March he presented a peace proposal that led to the signing of a truce two months later. During the main campaign period, between early June and early July, the fighting was limited.[70] Mikhail Alexseev writes that, according to leading opinion pollsters, "Yeltsin's campaign promise to stop military operations in Chechnya played a crucial part in his victory at the polls, helping him to increase his approval rating from a dismal 5 per cent in January 1996 to 20 per cent in May 1996."[71] Additionally, Yeltsin signed a host of decrees, such as on the payment of overdue wages and pensions, which aimed at increasing support for his presidential bid.[72] Among them was decree

722, pledging to abolish military conscription by the year 2000, and decree 723, promising to discontinue the practice of sending conscripts to conflict zones (unless they volunteer).[73] These measures were popular, because of widespread dislike for mandatory military service and parents' fears regarding the safety of their draft-age sons.[74] Not surprisingly, the Chechen war had helped increase public support for the transition to a professional, all-volunteer force. When Yeltsin signed the decree on eliminating the draft by 2000, a third of those surveyed stated that the action had improved their view of the president, including among those who would not vote for him.[75]

None of the presidential candidates received more than 50 percent of the vote in the first round.[76] A second round of voting was held between Yeltsin and his main competitor, the leader of the communist opposition, Gennadii Ziuganov. Yeltsin, who had garnered only 35 percent of the vote, needed to attract some of the nationalist vote away from Ziuganov. This led to an alliance with Lebed (by then retired from active service), who had come in third place in the first ballot with almost 15 percent of the vote and now threw his support behind Yeltsin.[77] Yeltsin in turn appointed Lebed secretary of the Security Council, made him his advisor on national security issues, and put him in charge of negotiating a peace deal with the Chechen separatist leadership. Lebed had run his election campaign on the theme of law and order as well as on the promise to bring peace to Chechnya. Although he had not served in the Chechen war, he embodied the position of high-ranking military personnel described above. He criticized the role of politicians in the Chechen war: "The people of Russia must not suffer from the political wrecks politicians make.... I am a soldier who has had enough fighting to hate war and will do all I can to make certain there is none on Russian soil."[78] As Yeltsin's representative, Lebed negotiated directly with Chechen field commander Maskhadov, with whom he signed the Khasaviurt cease-fire agreement on August 31, 1996. Lebed was chosen Russia's most popular politician of 1996.[79]

When Yeltsin decided to send troops to Chechnya in December 1994, he hoped to appeal to people's desire for order and strong leadership.[80] In reality, the war further eroded public support for Yeltsin. In his bid for re-election, the president changed his position, promising to put an end to the conflict and allying himself with Lebed. Lebed more closely resembled Russian citizens' image of a "patriot," a military general who took a stand against the Chechen war. Among the military high command that had supported or resigned itself to the conflict, Yeltsin's and Lebed's peace plans were not popular. Many of the generals who fought in the Chechen war felt that once again political goals had interfered with military affairs and the peace agreement took away their chance of military victory.[81] This sense of betrayal became an important factor in the second Chechen war.

The Second Chechen War and Putin's Presidency

From 1996 to 1999 the Chechen republic enjoyed de facto independence. In the spring of 1999, more Russians (45 percent) considered Chechnya an independent state than part of Russia (34 percent).[82] Few supported a renewal of the military operation in Chechnya according to polls conducted in autumn 1997 and spring 1998.[83] However, the events of August and September 1999 dramatically affected public opinion on Chechnya. In August, around 2,000 fighters led by Basaev entered Dagestan from Chechnya and declared the establishment of an Islamic State of Dagestan. In September, bombings targeted at apartment buildings in Moscow, Buinaksk, and Volgodonsk took the lives of almost 300 people and injured hundreds more.[84] These incidents were swiftly blamed on Chechen terrorists and formed the pretext for the second Chechen war, which was officially designated an "antiterrorist operation." In September 1999 40 percent of Russians supported sending federal forces into Chechnya and only slightly more opposed it. By comparison, the percentages had been 11 in support and 70 in opposition in February 1998.[85] By November, two months into large-scale military operations, more than 60 percent of the population favored and less than 15 percent opposed the use of military force in Chechnya.[86] This increase in support was a dramatic shift compared with just a few months earlier, as well as with the first Chechen war, when a majority of Russians had opposed the military intervention throughout the course of the war.

Another remarkable development occurred that fall when Vladimir Putin, Russia's little-known and recently appointed prime minister, saw his approval rating rise from 5 percent in September to 45 percent in November.[87] Putin became by far the most popular politician of 1999, easily taking the designation of "Man of the Year" with the support of over 40 percent of respondents in a poll conducted by the Public Opinion Foundation.[88] He became acting president at the end of 1999, and in March 2000 received over 50 percent of the vote in the first round of the presidential election.[89] The rise in Putin's popularity was closely tied to his tough execution of the Chechen war and his successful appeal to militarized patriotism. In this way, the second Chechen war made possible a smooth transition of power from Yeltsin to his designated successor, Putin.[90]

The official justification for the second Chechen war was the need to secure the state's territorial integrity and protect Russia's citizens from terrorism.[91] On October 23, 1999, the government vowed to continue to act "decisively and tough" until law and order were established throughout the Chechen territory. The government linked Chechen terrorism to international terrorism and extremism, promising to rid Chechnya of terrorist and other "bandit formations." At the same time, the government spoke out against "the persecution of people according to signs of nationality."[92] A month earlier Putin had displayed his resolve to fight Chechen terrorists in less than diplomatic language when he famously stated in a TV broadcast that "we will waste them even in the shithouse" (*i v sortire zamochim*).[93] Putin professed his willingness to take on the terrorists in his interview-based book *First Person*: "Only one thing works in such circumstances—to go on the offensive. You must hit first, and hit so hard that your opponent will not rise to his feet."[94] He also referred to the terrorists as "beasts." Talking about the capture of Raduev in a radio interview in March 2000, Putin commented: "There are still many such beasts at large. They can form themselves into packs and bite back and attack and cause us certain damage."[95] Putin represented a notion of strong, patriotic Russian masculinity, which he juxtaposed to a notion of wild Chechen masculinity, and at times animality, embodied by terrorists and Islamic fundamentalists. Later in the second war, the female suicide bomber appeared as a feminized version of the terrorist enemy, and Chechen femininity also became associated with terrorism.[96]

Opinion polls revealed that Putin's supporters saw him as "decisive, strong-willed and strict in his demands to re-establish order."[97] The polls also showed that the experience of the apartment bombings had created widespread fear of terrorism. As one poll suggests, 86 percent of people in late September 1999 feared that they or a relative might become a victim of terrorism.[98] For a while after the apartment bombings "personal safety" became more important to citizens than "social guarantees."[99] Yeltsin later reminisced that Putin had not "demonstrate[d] hatred toward the terrorists but contempt; not alarm or worry but the cold calculation of a real protector, a real man."[100] Moreover the former president concluded:

> Putin was not trying to demonize the Chechens or kindle base chauvinistic instincts in Russians. I am convinced that the reason for Putin's popularity was that he instilled hope, faith, and a sense of protection and calm. . . . Putin gave

people a guarantee of personal security backed by the state. People believed that he, personally, could protect them.... Putin got rid of Russia's fear. And Russia repaid him with profound gratitude.[101]

Yeltsin reproduced a gendered discourse of security and protection that reinforces the association of the masculinized state with protection and the feminized nation with the need for protection. There is nothing automatic about this association. Rather, the context of fear and war helped Putin *enact* masculinity and *become* perceived as strong and decisive. The fear of terrorism helped justify the need for masculinized-militarized protection and strong leadership, and generated support for the military campaign and for Putin as a leader. There was a significant shift in the public mood, as Lilia Shevtsova writes: "For the first time in many years—at least since Gorbachev came to power—Russian society had returned to the saving idea of military patriotism, which became the refuge of all in Russia who feared and who felt vulnerable."[102]

Another reason behind the renewal of militarized patriotism can be found in the humiliation that was one outcome of the Russian state's economic and military decline and epitomized in the collapse of the Soviet Union. Many Russians experienced the transition period as humiliating, both personally and collectively. In particular, the drastic decline in people's standard of living, further eroded by the August 1998 financial crisis, led to widespread disillusionment among Russians with capitalism, liberal democracy, and the West. Military defeats in the late-Soviet period (Afghanistan) and the post-Soviet period (Chechnya) were experienced as humiliating and highlighted the diminished state of the armed forces. NATO's 1999 war against Serbia (an ally of the Russian state) made evident Russia's powerlessness in the post–Cold War world and increased anti-Western sentiments among political and military leaders as well as the public.[103] According to Emil Pain: "The public, weary of economic, political and military failures, craved a victory."[104] The war became a vehicle for strengthening the state's (and by extension, the regime's) legitimacy by mobilizing society around a militarized form of patriotism. Tatiana Sivaeva explains the role of the second Chechen war in the context of regained nationhood:

> In 1999 Chechnya was turned into the symbol of the all-national enemy, a symbol that after all these years of disappointment and broken ideals managed to bring the entire nation together, made it feel strong and powerful. Russians again felt that they were a great nation that has its mission—to protect its people from enemies (here Chechen extremists or sometimes simply Chechens).[105]

The Chechen war became part of a larger patriotic agenda to strengthen the state and restore Russia's status as a great power. Shevtsova writes that "Putin, quite consciously, was appealing to that portion of society that yearned for some revival of Russia's might and glory in the Soviet style."[106] In 1999, both Yeltsin and Putin presented the situation in Chechnya as a continuation of Soviet disintegration. Putin argued: "What's the situation in the Northern Caucasus and Chechnya today? It's a continuation of the collapse of the USSR. Clearly, at some point it has to be stopped."[107] Putin made the connection between terrorism and threats to the state in the aftermath of the apartment bombings: "In blowing up the houses of our fellow citizens, the bandits are blowing up the state. They are undermining authority—not of the president, city, or Duma. But of authority per se."[108] In his *Manifesto: Russia at the Turn of the Millennium*, Putin emphasized the need for a strong state and the renewal of patriotism.[109] By February 2000, more than 70 percent of Russians expected Putin, should he be elected president, to "bolster Russia's military might."[110] Sixty-six percent believed he would be able to secure Russia's territorial integrity.[111] In his inaugural annual address in June 2000, the president stated that "the only choice for Russia is to be a strong country, strong and sure of itself," and that "the unity of Russia is strengthened by the patriotic nature of our people, by our cultural traditions, memories."[112] Enloe has theorized the concept of "masculinized humiliation" as one of the sources of nationalism.[113] The humiliation experienced by Russia's post-Soviet citizens was gendered in that it was linked to the weakening of masculinized institutions such as the state, the military, and the economy. In this context, the reassertion of power and pride necessarily relied on masculine tropes of strength. Putin used heroic and positive images of militarized masculinity as one of the planks of his program of patriotic and state renewal.

The Restoration of Militarized Masculinity

"Russia is defending itself. We have been attacked. And therefore we must throw off all syndromes, including the guilt syndrome," Putin exclaimed in early September 1999 in response to journalists' questions regarding the situation in Chechnya.[114] In his response, Putin alluded to both the Afghan and the Chechen syndromes, a shorthand for the humiliating defeat experienced in these two wars. The "guilt syndrome" refers to the guilt associated with the use of military force and the accompanying lack of pride in the armed forces. The political and military leadership formed a united front on the military operation. Both had an interest in the war and rejected society's apparent betrayal of the military during the first war. Putin argued:

You would agree that Russia's defeat in the first Chechen war was due to a large extent due [*sic*] to the state of society's morale. Russians didn't understand what ideals our soldiers were fighting for. Those soldiers gave their lives and in return they were anathematized. They were dying for the interests of their country and they were publicly humiliated.[115]

Putin thus decried the lack of militarized patriotism during the first war, and saw it as a major factor in the defeat of federal forces. Many generals saw the second war as an opportunity to undo the humiliating defeat. They also felt that victory in 1996 had been "stolen" from them for political reasons.[116] Defense Minister Grachev captured this feeling, when he stated at the end of the first war: "Yes, I deeply regret the deaths. But I also deeply regret the fact that I was prevented from defeating the remaining rebel bands."[117] From the perspective of the military leadership, the second Chechen war aimed to rectify the humiliation the Russian army had suffered in the first Chechen war, and "to restore the 'proper' place of the army in society."[118] The political leadership was in full agreement, and Putin emphasized that the survival of the state hinged on the place of the army in society: "Believe me, back in 1990–91, I knew exactly—as arrogant as it may sound—that the attitude toward the army and the special services, especially after the fall of the USSR, threatened the country. We would very soon be on the verge of collapse."[119] Militarized patriotism was central to Putin's statist ideology; he linked the strength of the state to public and political support of the armed forces. Thomas Gomart considers Putin's respect for the military genuine, but underscores that it also fulfilled practical political needs. "[I]dentifying military *prestige* with himself and his presidency" was a key tool in Putin's ability to legitimize his rule, especially as it initially lacked a political base.[120]

The image of the soldier became the personification of Putin's appeal to the prestige of the military. Conscription remained in place, despite Yeltsin's promise to abolish it by the year 2000. However, tighter control of the media coverage during the second war meant that the image of unheroic conscript soldiers was less visible than in the first war. In contrast to the first Chechen war, the Russian political leadership emphasized the heroism and professionalism of those serving in the military. In his memoirs Yeltsin captured the shift in the ideology of militarized masculinity that accompanied the second war, apparently oblivious of his own role:

The Russian soldier, the person defending the country and defending order on its territory, is being cleansed of the filth of political opportunism that was flung upon him. With each day the soldier becomes a more powerful, unifying national symbol. Russia cannot forget and betray these young men.[121]

Putin emphasized the professional conduct of the military, in an attempt to contrast it with the widespread perception of its lack of professionalism during the first war. During his inaugural annual address, he stated:

> Chechnya is an extreme example of the unresolved federative problem. The situation in the republic has progressed to that point that the territory has become a base for the expansion of international terrorism into Russia. The initial reason here was also the lack of state unity. And Chechnya in 1999 reminded us of mistakes committed earlier. And only the counter-terrorist operation was able to respond to the threat of disintegration of Russia, professional soldiers were able to preserve the dignity and integrity of the state. I bow deeply in front of them! But at what cost . . .[122]

This quotation nicely illustrates the way in which Putin employed militarized patriotism by linking state unity to the role of the soldier and expressing his respect for soldiers. Putin also acknowledged the sacrifices of soldiers and publicly honored them as heroes in a way that Yeltsin had failed to do during the first Chechen war. In his 2001 annual address, Putin asked the members of the two parliamentary chambers as well as viewers at home to observe a minute of silence in memory of the "heroes" of the war. In this group he included "our servicemen, the Dagestani militia, and Chechen police, and all those who prevented the collapse of the state at the cost of their life."[123] In contrast to Yeltsin, who during the first war had criticized the military and soldiers for their actions, Putin made public displays of deep respect for the military and acknowledged the loss of soldiers' lives.

On closer examination, however, the heroes of the second war played a more ambiguous role than the one Putin and Yeltsin describe. The generals who led the second war, all of them veterans of the first war, became known as much for their brutality as for their apparent heroism and professionalism. They advocated an especially violent approach in the pursuit of victory, one that relied on the massive and indiscriminate use of force.[124] The generals were given a relatively free hand over the military operation, as Pavel Baev explains:

> The conduct of the operation was very much left to the military, primarily the General Staff. While Defense Minister Igor Sergeev (with his background in Strategic Forces) was quite unenthusiastic about the whole enterprise, the Chief of the General Staff Anatoly Kvashnin gathered a group of combat generals

(Konstantin Pulikovsky, Gennady Troshev, Viktor Kazantsev, Vladimir Shamanov) driven hard by the desire to take revenge for the humiliating defeat in 1996. This military cabal demanded and obtained the carte blanche to proceed with victory as they saw fit. The troops moved into Chechnya rather slowly, suppressing every pocket of resistance by massive artillery fire.[125]

General Vladimir Shamanov, who commanded the western group of forces, received the Hero of Russia award for his service during the second war. Proudly answering to the nickname "cruel Shamanov," he openly admitted to not discriminating between fighters and civilians. He considered both the wife and child of a "bandit" to be themselves "bandits." As he famously stated in a June 2000 interview: "And how, tell me, do you distinguish a wife from a sniper?"[126] Shamanov and the troops he commanded were implicated in war crimes such as those committed during the seizure of Alkhan-Iurt in December 1999, during which federal troops killed and raped civilians and engaged in looting.[127] General Gennadii Troshev suggested that the "shattered city of Grozny should never be rebuilt so as to serve as a warning against treason to Russia's ethnic minorities."[128] He explained his approach to Chechen "bandits" in the following words: "This is how I'd do it: I'd gather them all on a square and string up the bandit and let him hang, let everyone see."[129] General Viktor Kazantsev, presidential envoy to the Southern Federal District, ordered that "only women, children under ten years old, and men over sixty are to be considered refugees. All others are to be detained and subjected to scrutiny."[130] General Konstantin Pulikovskii is most notorious for his actions at the end of the first Chechen war. He caused uproar during the crucial peace negotiations between Lebed and Maskhadov in August 1996 by issuing an ultimatum to civilians in Grozny and "threatening to begin air strikes and artillery bombardments."[131] These generals represented a variant of militarized masculinity that is harsh rather than humane toward civilian deaths. In contrast to the generals who had opposed the first Chechen war, these men were not plagued by concerns about the use of force toward fellow citizens, including civilians.

Putin's Policy of Chechenization

The large-scale military campaign in Chechnya was officially completed in January 2001. Command for the operation was handed over from the Ministry of Defense to the FSB, and a year later from the FSB to the Interior Ministry. In late 2002, the Putin government began to pursue a policy of "Chechenization": delegating the fight against separatists and terrorists to pro-Kremlin Chechen leaders. Three steps were central to this process. In 2003 the Kremlin organized a constitutional referendum in Chechnya, in 2004 pro-Kremlin Akhmad Kadyrov was elected president, and in 2005 the Kremlin staged parliamentary elections. The policy of Chechenization, which led to the installation of strong-man Kadyrov, largely shifted the conflict from a Russian-Chechen confrontation to an internal Chechen civil war.[132] The republic has been brutally ruled by the *kadyrovtsy*, the much feared paramilitary and security forces that took over many of the functions previously performed by Russian federal forces.[133]

After Kadyrov was killed in the bombing of Grozny's Dinamo stadium in May 2004, Alu Alkhanov was appointed as new president. Putin declared Kadyrov a Hero of the Russian Federation shortly after his assassination. His son Ramzan Kadyrov received the same award on New Year's Eve 2005, when he was first deputy prime minister of Chechnya's pro-Kremlin government. Ramzan Kadyrov, who adopted the war discourse of the federal state on fighting banditry and terrorism,[134] replaced President Alkhanov once he reached the eligible age of thirty in September 2007. In an inversion of the common Russian use of the term "syndrome" in the context of military defeat, Anna Politkovskaya coined the term "Kadyrov syndrome" to describe the gendered culture of violence that has pervaded Chechnya under Kadyrov's rule: "The main features of this syndrome are impudence, rudeness, and violence pretending to be courage and manliness . . . . The 'Kadyrovites' beat men and women in Chechnya, just as they see fit."[135] The military campaign may have officially ended, but the Chechen regime, led by an official hero of the Russian Federation, is based on the brutal and indiscriminate use of force by militarized men. Human rights activists also decry the violations of women's rights in the Chechen republic that Kadyrov has sanctioned on the pretext of Islamic tradition.[136]

Public support for the second war reached its peak in February 2000, with 70 percent of respondents in favor of continuing the military operation.[137] As the war dragged on, and a quick victory did not materialize, support decreased. By May 2002, over 60 percent of the population supported negotiations.[138] In 2002, citizens considered Putin's main failure to be the continued war in Chechnya.[139] None of this seemed to reduce Putin's popularity, however, as he was repeatedly chosen as "Man of the Year,"[140] and in 2004 won his second presidential election with over 70 percent of the vote. According to the military analyst Alexander Golts, Russians appreciated the strength of Putin: "Russian voters are just happy that Putin has demonstrated decisiveness, persistence and force."[141] While the Chechen campaign helped create Putin's credibility as leader, it also helped to solidify a highly undemocratic system. As Iris Marion Young has pointed out in another context, "[T]he logic of masculinist protection" both "justifies aggressive war" and "legitimates authoritarian power over citizens."[142] The regime Putin and his inner circle built was based on a privileged role for the power ministries, centralization of federal state power (especially in the aftermath of the Beslan hostage taking), and the weakening of civil society groups and the independent media, while being propped up by high oil prices. It also entailed a narrowing of the political field around the "party of power," United Russia, through which the Kremlin effectively controlled the Duma. While the Putin regime relied on militarized patriotism and appealed to Soviet nostalgia, this did not signal a return to Soviet times. The Russian state under Putin was also a state that pursued neoliberal policies and for the most part upheld the principles of capitalism.[143]

Masculinity, Nationhood, and State Leadership

During the Yeltsin period, the crisis of nation and state in part expressed itself in a perceived crisis of masculinity. Yeltsin began his presidency as a strong, national leader defying the putschists in August 1991 and embodying the hopes of a new Russia. However, his free market policies created economic and social havoc and disillusionment among the populace. By 1994, Yeltsin's failing health and alcoholism became defining features of his presidency. He was sick and often an absentee president during the last few years of his rule and no longer represented the image of a strong leader. During the first week of the Chechen war Yeltsin was hospitalized (the official reason given was for a nose operation) and did not address citizens with respect to the Chechen conflict until five days after decreeing military intervention. Similarly, during the Budennovsk hostage taking Yeltsin did not return home from the G8 summit in Halifax to handle the crisis.[144] The first Chechen war further undermined Yeltsin's leadership and exposed a simultaneous crisis in nationhood and masculinity. In his memoir, Yeltsin wrote of the first war: "It was then, in 1995, that Russia was infected by a new disease: a total negativity, a complete lack of confidence in ourselves and our strengths. We Russians had come to dislike ourselves. And that is a historical dead-end for a nation."[145] The crisis of the nation was reflected in a crisis of militarized masculinity: soldiers who refused to fight or to be made into heroes, and a weak and absent chief commander. While Yeltsin represented the "absent father," as Eliot Borenstein writes, Putin displayed the "image of a tough no-

nonsense 'man's man' who was sober, athletic, and decisive."[146] Putin's ability to portray an image of reinvigorated masculinity came to be conflated with an apparent renewal of state strength and national confidence. Borenstein explains:

> Where the 1990s were marked by a perceived crisis of manhood and the rise of compensatory masculinity, Putin, whose manly and martial virtues have been continually trumpeted in the increasingly submissive media, represents the restoration of long-lost vigor and confidence. The Yeltsin years considerably lowered the bar for the country's next leader: Putin's specific policies and actions arguably matter far less than his reassuring symbolic function as a "real man" who can husband the nation's resources and promise a return to greatness.[147]

Putin's masculinity gained appeal in the particular social and political context of the late 1990s. Yeltsin pinned the hope of the nation on the arrival of a general who could lead it. Putin's rise to power was intimately tied to his tough, "manly" stance in pursuing the terrorists. He took full responsibility for the military campaign and displayed decisiveness and forcefulness in his approach. Putin used the war as an opportunity to display characteristics associated with masculinity. The president furthermore played up his masculinity by publicizing images of himself fighting judo or fishing bare-chested. Putin's apparent manliness as well as his popularity among women have been the subject of much public interest in Russia.[148] Tat'iana Riabova and Oleg Riabov cite the following comment by a female voter in 1999 as typical for the public perception of Putin's masculinity:

> It is important for a woman to have a reliable, self-assured man near her on whom she would have a possibility to rely on [sic] in hard times. Then let the stones fall from the sky—it would not be terrible. Unfortunately, nowadays it is very difficult to find such men. It seems to me that Putin is a man of this kind, insignificant outwardly, but strong by spirit.[149]

In 2002, the idealization of Putin's masculinity found expression in a hugely popular pop song titled "Someone Like Putin" (*Takogo kak Putin*). The female singer tells of the disappointment with her current boyfriend and her wish for a man like Putin.[150] These examples illustrate how Putin's popularity as a leader was closely tied to notions of masculinity.

Putin's policies not only restored the association of the Russian presidency with masculinity and patriotism, but contributed to the further militarization and thus masculinization of Russia's bureaucratic and political elite. Both wars led to a privileging of the military and security structures within the state and the greater recruitment of men with military and security backgrounds (*siloviki*) into the state and into politics generally.[151] There was a steady increase in their numbers during Russia's post-Soviet transformation: they made up 33 percent of the presidential administration in 1993, 46 percent in 1999, and 58 percent in 2002, and 67 percent in 2008. These men also occupied 11 percent of government positions in 1993, 22 percent in 1999, and 33 percent in 2002, and 40 percent in 2008. Similar trends can be observed among regional elites and in parliament.[152] Valerie Sperling points to the possible gender implications of this trend:

> This fact suggests an explanation for the growing gender gap in Russia's state administration: because Russia's military and security/intelligence apparatus are so thoroughly male-dominated, if these institutions are an increasingly significant route to political power, then women's path will be limited.[153]

The growing role of the *siloviki* in Russian politics may thus be another factor inhibiting women's greater political participation in addition to institutional barriers and the prevailing gender ideology about women's primary role as mothers and caregivers. Women made up only 3 percent of Russia's ruling elite in 1993, a number that decreased to 2 percent in 2002. The representation of women in the Duma fell from 13.5 percent in the 1993–1995 Duma to 7.6 percent in Russia's third Duma (1999–2003). In the latter part of Putin's presidency there was an increase in women's representation among Russia's political elite, mostly as a result of a larger proportion of women deputies serving in Russia's relatively powerless Duma.[154] Nonetheless, the restoration of masculinity at the leadership level, supported by the waging of war, remains an important factor in relation to women's continued political marginalization in Russia.

Conclusion

During the first war Yeltsin constructed himself as the one who would restore constitutional order and portrayed the Chechen separatists as violent and criminal. The juxtaposition of ordered, patriotic Russian masculinity with anarchical, criminal Chechen masculinity was not effective in legitimizing the war. The war lacked popular support, and Yeltsin's ratings continued to fall. The war's lack of legitimacy was reflected in challenges to militarized patriotism and heroism on the part of both military brass and rank-and-file soldiers. A number of generals did not support the war and even declined to fight in it, while a prominent field commander refused the Hero of Russia medal. The ambiguous image of militarized masculinity that emerged from these events undercut public support for the war and the political leadership. Yeltsin's reelection campaign in 1996 promised to end the Chechen war and move from a conscript to an all-volunteer force.

The second Chechen war was associated with a rehabilitation of militarized masculinity linked to patriotism and (brutal) heroism. The political and military leadership stood together and exploited terrorist fears and masculinized humiliation to justify the war. The war, dubbed an antiterrorist operation, aimed to root out terrorists and undo the defeat of the first war. Putin's strong stance against terrorists was popular and helped him win the presidential election in March 2000. The war saw a "parade" of generals who proudly and brutally waged war and a president who generously expressed his support for the troops and emphasized their professionalism and heroism. Putin's "resolution" of the conflict was a policy of Chechenization that brought neither peace nor security for people living in Chechnya. The pro-Russian regime of the Kadyrovs has been characterized by the continuation of human rights abuses, brutality, and violence.

Leaders' ability to use war as a means of appearing manly depends on a complicated interplay of militarized masculinities. Despite the complex and ambiguous picture that emerged from the above analysis, both wars reinforced the privileging of militarized men and militarized institutions of the state such as the power ministries and the presidency. While this chapter focused on the politics of militarized masculinity at the state level, the next chapter adds another layer to the analysis by examining the societal crisis of militarized masculinity in regard to conscription.

3 The Societal Crisis of Militarized Masculinity

Conscription, Economic Transformation, and the Russian-Chechen Wars

THE SOVIET STATE drafted an estimated 70 to 85 percent of draft-age men during the 1970s.[1] The remainder would have received exemptions for the purposes of education or because of poor health. Draft evasion and desertion were marginal phenomena in Soviet society and emerged as serious problems only in the 1980s (as discussed in Chapter 1). The post-Soviet Russian state maintained the obligatory conscription of men, but its enforcement met growing challenges. By the mid-1990s, Russia was experiencing a breakdown of its citizen-soldier model. Conscription in post-Soviet Russia has been highly unpopular and much less equitable than during Soviet times. For much of the last decade-and-a-half the Russian state drafted only about 10 to 30 percent of men in the draft-pool. Two-thirds or more received an exemption or deferment, whether through legal or illegal means. An average of about 30,000 men annually simply failed to follow their draft summons (compared with 558 in 1990). In addition, 5,000 or more conscripts deserted their units every year.[2] This chapter examines conscription, and by extension the link between masculinity and the military, in the context of Russia's postcommunist transformation and Chechen wars. As conscription relies on and helps constitute masculine identities tied to the military, the difficulties the state encountered with its conscription policy signaled a weakening of the link between masculinity and military service.

The postcommunist economic transformation deeply affected the military and military-society relations. Underfunding and economic scarcity have plagued Russia's military, which had its budget severely cut in the post-Soviet period. The systemic violence and poor living conditions that conscripts face during military service have been some of the main reasons for widespread draft evasion and desertion. The economic transformation also resulted in the rise of notions of capitalist masculinity, which challenge Soviet notions of militarized, patriotic masculinity. The growth in socioeconomic inequality is reflected in the pool of compliant conscripts, which mostly consists of working-class and rural men. In response to societal resistance to conscription, the Russian military has aimed to attract volunteer or contract soldiers and has also more heavily relied on women to fill its ranks.

The two Chechen wars further exacerbated the problems with conscription. As an analysis of the wars illustrates, the waging of war depends on men (and women) who are willing and able to participate in the war effort. The Chechen wars did not lead to a successful mobilization of young men as soldiers, but to further draft evasion. Especially the much publicized fate of untrained conscripts sent into the battle for Grozny early in the first war destroyed the image of heroic soldiers and highlighted the plight of conscripts. The wars increased fears among draft-age men and their families, and solidified support for the transition to an all-volunteer force. The growing gap between military service, masculinity, and patriotism in post-Soviet Russia was an outcome of both the postcommunist transformation and the Chechen wars.

Obligatory Military Service in Post-Soviet Russia

While the ideological importance of military service dissipated with the end of the Cold War, the Russian state continued to define military service as a necessary component of male citizenship. Statute 59 of the Russian Constitution (1993) states that "protection of the Fatherland is the duty and obligation of a citizen of the Russian Federation."[3] The Law on Military Obligation and Service[4] obliges male citizens aged eighteen to twenty-seven to serve in the armed forces for two years,[5] but the length of service was reduced to eighteen months as of 2007 and to one year as of 2008.[6] In addition to the Ministry of Defense, conscripts serve in the forces of the other "power ministries" (such as in the Ministry of Interior Forces).[7] In Russia, there are two call-up periods per year, in the fall and the spring. The law foresees a number of reasons for which draft-age men can receive a deferment (*otsrochka*) from service, including student status, medical affliction, or having a child under the age of three. Similar deferments existed during the Soviet period, but were partly curtailed in the early 1980s.[8] The list of deferments grew to twenty-five over the 1990s, nine of which were abolished in 2005–2006 as part of a broader overhaul of military service law.[9] The 1993 Constitution guarantees the right to alternative service whether on the basis of conscientious objection or religious belief.[10] However, the law governing alternative service was only passed by the Duma in 2002, and its implementation began in 2004.[11] The law has been criticized for penalizing conscientious objectors, as alternative service lasts almost twice as long as regular service and must be carried out in state-run institutions or the military.[12] While about 1,400 men pursued alternative service during the spring draft in 2004, by the fall of 2009 the number of applicants had fallen to less than three hundred.[13]

At the end of the Soviet Union in 1991, conscripts made up more than half of the almost 4 million active duty personnel. Due to heavy personnel reductions during Yeltsin's presidency, the number of active troops fell to approximately 1.3 million in 1996 and decreased further to just over 1 million in 1999. More recently the size of the armed forces has been cut to 1 million. According to the *Military Balance,* conscripts made up about one-third of the active duty personnel of the armed forces during the 1990s.[14] However, the proportion of conscripts was likely higher during the early 2000s when the annual draft quota was nearly 400,000.[15] While the draft quota decreased over the following years, it rose again in 2007–2008 with the transition from a two-year to a one-year service period.

Only a minority of men in the draft pool end up serving in the Russian armed forces. In 2004, 9.5 percent of draft-age men were conscripted, compared with 27.5 percent in 1994.[16] The Ministry of Defense frequently complained that it was only able to draft 10 percent of young men, while human rights activists have considered the official number overblown. Liudmila Vakhnina from the human rights group "Memorial" argues that the Ministry of Defense wrongly includes all men of draft age in its calculations, including men who have already completed service, in order to push for stricter enforcement of conscription. According to Vakhnina, the figure of draftees for 2004 is closer to 30 percent of men in the draft pool.[17] Draft evasion is widespread, though the exact number of draft dodgers is hard to determine. The legal definition includes only those men who have received (and acknowledged receipt of) a draft summons and then fail to show up. The figure of 30,000 annual draft evaders was frequently cited during the 1990s and early 2000s, but there is some indication that there has since been a decline. Officially the highest absolute number of draft evaders was recorded in 1999 at 44,133, while the number fell to 28,232 in 2001 and continued to drop.[18] Often the term "draft dodging" is used more loosely to refer to men who avoid receiving their draft summons (for example, by moving to another address), though they have so far not been considered in violation of the law. In 2010, General Nikolai Markov from the General Staff of the Armed Forces claimed that there were 200,000 such draft evaders in Russia.[19] Finally, because of the flourishing shadow economy in the sale of exemptions from military service and the widespread use of corruption to evade military service, the hidden number of draft evaders is much higher than captured by the official figure.[20] The demographic situation is another factor exacerbating the problems with conscription.[21] In addition to the poor health of draft-age men, the cohort of eighteen-year-old males is expected to continue to decline over the next decade and a half, with fewer young men reaching draft age annually than required by the draft quota.[22]

In the post-Soviet period, conscription came to be disliked not just among young men and their families but also in society more broadly. The Levada Center (VTsIOM[23] prior to 2003) conducted polls from 1997 to 2007 that documented weak public support for conscription. On average 30 percent of respondents approved of mandatory service, compared with just over 60 percent who favored the transition to an all-volunteer force.[24] Opposition to conscription was even higher when respondents were asked to consider the drafting of a family member. When polled by VTsIOM in 1998, only 13 percent responded favorably to the idea of a close family member's being conscripted. The most important reasons for respondents' opposition to the drafting of a close family member included "hazing" and "violence in the army" (40 percent), the "possibility of death/injury in Chechen-type conflicts" (30 percent), and "the difficult living conditions, poor food, and health hazards" (21 percent).[25] While the state defines military service as an obligation of male citizens, these figures illustrate that there exist serious societal challenges to this official understanding. Conditions within the military, in particular the violent and poor treatment of conscripts, undermined both individual and societal support for mandatory military service.

The Situation within the Military:
Scarcity and Dedovshchina—Making or Breaking Men?[27]

During fieldwork conducted in Samara (Russia) in 2006, I interviewed young men who recounted a similar combination of reasons for their decision to evade the draft as cited in the poll above. Iurii, a student I met at Samara State University, for example, first mentioned the danger of being sent to Chechnya as the reason for his draft evasion, but then moved on to say: "I was afraid not just of the army, as much as of the fact that you have to suffer there. I was afraid of *dedovshchina* [hazing] and hunger—there was no guarantee that I would return healthy and alive."[27] These two factors within the armed forces are of particular concern to draft-age men and their families: the living conditions during service, including the lack of appropriate food and medical care; and *dedovshchina*, which literally means "rule of the grandfathers" and refers to the systemic hazing and abuse that new conscripts experience at the hands of longer-serving ones.

While these problems first emerged during the late Soviet period,[28] they became much more pronounced in the context of post-Soviet economic transformation. The cuts to the military budget,[29] and the hardships of the economic crisis during the 1990s, created a situation in which those serving in the army were often underfed and lacked basic medical care. Human Rights Watch has documented the systemic nature of violations against the right to adequate food and medical care throughout Russian military units in the 1990s and 2000s.[30] Cases of conscripts suffering from starvation or insufficient medical attention have been widely publicized by the Russian media. *Dedovshchina* interacts with this already troubling situation to produce a potentially intolerable situation for new conscripts. The high number of desertions and noncombat deaths attest to this.[31]

Dedovshchina is a more complex and developed phenomenon than is captured by the term "hazing." It is an informal hierarchy of power among conscripts based on length of service (seniority). The two call-up periods per year and two-year service create a four-tiered hierarchy with *dukhy* ("souls") at the bottom rung and *dedy* ("grandfathers") at the top. Conscripts at the lower rungs of this hierarchy live in a "state of pointless servitude" according to Human Rights Watch.[32] As one interviewee put it bluntly: "Here, the soldier is a slave."[33] *Dedovshchina* involves systemic physical and psychological violence toward newer recruits, including the exploitation of their labor. Valerii, who is in his twenties and himself avoided military service by bribing the military doctor, recounts his friend's experience: "I have a friend who served in the army for half a year. The *dedy* beat him up badly. He lay in the hospital for a number of months, then made a deal with the general and left the army."[34] Sometimes the abuse includes using soldiers as free labor such as in private construction projects. Two of my interviewees mentioned the case of officers selling conscripts' labor to a local Coca-Cola factory in Samara. The conscripts were forced to work at the plant while the officers collected their salaries.[35] The Soldiers' Mothers of St. Petersburg have described *dedovshchina* in the following way:

> The "Dedy," the elders, force the newcomers in their first months to total subordination by regular use of force. Servants' jobs, such as shoe-polishing or doing the wash, or renovations in private homes are by no means exceptional cases. These newcomers are a cheap and willing workforce to the superiors. The fustigations and floggings can sometimes cause death, but still they form an integral part of the newcomer's test.[36]

Dedovshchina includes many abuses of the rights of first-year conscripts, such as confiscation of personal belongings, salaries, and food, as well as sexual violence.[37] While the severity of the abuse will vary depending on service,[38] unit, and the individual conscript, *dedovshchina* is a central aspect of most Russian conscripts' lives. There is yet no indication whether the recent reduction of military service from two years to one has had any dampening effect on *dedovshchina*.

Hazing practices exist in both conscription and volunteer-based armies and in the armies of so-called developed, transitional, and developing countries. A number of characteristics distinguish *dedovshchina* in the Russian armed forces from hazing in other militaries. *Dedovshchina* goes much further than the initiation rituals found in most other armed forces, in that the abuse is systemically violent. In contrast to other countries, *dedovshchina* has developed so far that it deters the very manning and functioning of the armed forces and is a constant topic of media reports. In societal discourse, *dedovshchina* is not perceived as exceptional but recognized as systemic. In addition, *dedovshchina* is exacerbated by the economic and social crisis that pervades the armed forces and society at large in post-Soviet Russia. Some authors have suggested that hazing might be more severe in transitional countries where social tensions manifest themselves in army life.[39] Certainly, problems linked to the postcommunist transformation such as underfunding, scarcity, and corruption have exacerbated *dedovshchina* in Russia.

Military officials and analysts are concerned with the negative effects *dedovshchina* has on the combat readiness of the Russian military. Organizations such as the Soldiers' Mothers of St. Petersburg or Human Rights Watch and many Western scholars identify the main problem with *dedovshchina* in the multifaceted violations of conscripts' human rights. A number of explanations have been put forward for the phenomenon of *dedovshchina*. Some observers link its rise to the legacy of Soviet prison camp culture or to the decrease in the length of military service in 1967 from three to two years (from four to three years in the Navy), which created four distinct groups of conscripts (two call-up periods, two-year service). Joris Van Bladel, on the other hand, has applied Erving Goffman's concept of "total institution" to the case of *dedovshchina* and sees the latter as "a rational response from the soldiers, both as individuals and as a group, to the strange and enclosed military world."[40] He emphasizes the role of scarcity in this system: "Generally, total institutions impose a system that lacks freedom, but Russian soldiers lack even more fundamental things such as food, beverages and especially money."[41] Van Bladel further argues that the post-Soviet economic crisis increased scarcity and made *dedovshchina* more brutal.[42] Many former conscripts interviewed by Human Rights Watch during 2002 and 2003 complained about being forced to give up food and provide money and cigarettes to the *dedy*. There are also reports of conscripts having to beg or steal under the threat of violence.[43] Another factor that some scholars stress in relation to *dedovshchina* is the absence of a professional noncommissioned officer corps in the Russian army.[44] This has the effect that conscripts are left to create discipline among themselves, while officers practice studied indifference.[45]

What all these approaches and explanations fail to account for is the significance of gender in providing a better understanding of the phenomenon.[46] Forms of hazing are endemic to a host of male-dominated institutions, such as sports teams, universities, police forces, political organizations, or professional associations, to name just a few, and are found in militaries across the world.[47] Hazing practices aim to break down the individual and remake him as a member of the fraternal group, as one of my interviewees, a former conscript, put it: "You were a somebody on civvy street, you're a nobody here."[48] This "breaking down" often relies on strategies of gendered humiliation that feminize new group members. In the Russian military, weaker soldiers are referred to as "sisters" or "sissies" (*sestri*) and forced to perform menial tasks associated with femininity, such as washing the clothes or making the bed for longer-serving conscripts. In some cases, conscripts are sexually degraded, forced to imitate sexual intercourse, or become the victims of sexual assault.[49] Thus, the hierarchy among conscripts based on seniority is also a *gender* hierarchy, in which senior men feminize more junior men to establish their rule.[50] The effect is that those being humiliated want to overcome their feminized status. If physically strong enough, conscripts can fight back or are recruited by the *dedy* into the abuse of others.[51] Otherwise they have to wait until they move up in the hierarchy and can themselves humiliate newer recruits. Enduring their feminization is a phase that conscripts must pass through on their way to achieving "manhood."

Informally, it is exactly these types of hazing practices that are seen as necessary to the transition to manhood. In one case investigated by the Soldiers' Mothers of St. Petersburg and Human Rights Watch, the abusers argued that violence was required to "maintain discipline in the company" and also to turn conscripts into men.[52] The men I interviewed acknowledged the role of gender in *dedovshchina* but in a way that naturalizes masculine violence. In the view of one former conscript, Anatolii, the "male collective" is always violent and brutal.[53] Iurii similarly argued that the separation along age and experience is inherent in any male collective. But he also linked *dedovshchina* to men's nature: "Maybe it's male nature, physiology, and deep in their souls men like to torture—cats, women, soldiers . . . . In the depth of every man a sadist is hiding."[54] Igor', a twenty-five-year-old construction engineer who had dodged the draft, argued that "[it's] just stupidity. When a couple of guys get together and they're bored, they begin to entertain themselves." He went on to recount the story of a friend who, for refusing to wash a fellow conscript's socks, was so badly beaten that he spent more than a month in the hospital.[55] Thus, *dedovshchina* relies on a gendered ideology that helps justify, or at least explain, abuse and violence. However, the brutality of these practices and the many deaths they cause made it increasingly difficult to maintain the gendered myth that strategies of humiliation and abuse are necessary to turn conscripts into "men." Over the 1990s, *dedovshchina* undermined the very acceptance of the idea that men should serve in the military. As one conscript, who deserted because of constant abuse, stated: "I had thought it was every man's duty to serve the Army. But I would not have signed up if I had known the conditions. Joining the Army was the biggest mistake of my life."[56] Widespread media reporting on the conditions draftees encounter and anecdotal evidence of military service from friends and relatives changed societal views on conscription and the army. Sarah Brown commented in 1997: "Stories of starvation, disease, and cruel hazing in the barracks have replaced tales of the past glory of the Soviet army."[57] A poll conducted in 1998 found a majority of respondents (61 percent) express the opinion that healthy young men need not serve in the army but should be provided the opportunity to perform alternative nonmilitary service.[58] In post-Soviet Russia, conditions within the armed forces linked to the hierarchical hazing of soldiers and aggravated by the economic crisis undermined the gendered notion of military service as a duty of male citizens. Broader socioeconomic changes, including the introduction of a market economy and the emergence of new notions of masculinity, also contributed to this development.

Market Economy and Class: New Notions of Masculinity

During Soviet times completion of military service did not conflict with a man's working life. On the contrary, it was often considered a critical phase in a young man's development. The economic transition has profoundly affected men's identities and societal notions of masculinity, also in relation to military service. In the context of a market economy, absence from the labor market is viewed as a serious disadvantage. Rebecca Kay captures this idea when she refers to the "contradictions of conscription in a market economy."[59] Many young men interpret military service as conflicting with the demands of a fast-paced market economy. Valerii explained to me:

> I am probably not the first person to tell you that in order to have some prospects in life, you need to avoid the army. Today everything is developing at a rapid pace; in two years it is possible to lose all contacts and no one needs you anymore. I personally think that I need to study, not serve in the army.[60]

Today many men feel that military service will disrupt their life and decrease their career chances. In addition, men fear the effects of military service on their mental health and development, which in turn will impair their ability to reintegrate into the labor market. Igor' mentioned these points:

> For me, the most important argument against serving in the army is the degradation. A person who goes there, simply throws out two years of life. During these years he has no possibility to develop—he becomes stupid. In addition, his psyche is ruined. I don't need that. I completed college, am working in my field of specialization, and earning good money. I am not

convinced that if I join the army today, anybody will need me in two years' time.[61]

Both Valerii and Igor' emphasized the pressures of the labor market as reasons for not wanting to serve in the military. Nikolai also brought up the problem of "losing time" as one of the main reasons for men's draft evasion (after *dedovshchina*) and explicitly linked it to competition: "Time in the army is time during which you could have done something. Army is like prison. During his service the person falls out of society. It is hard to return. People of your same age have *moved forward* during this time and it's hard to *catch up* with them."[62] The reasons mentioned by these young men such as wasting time, not being needed, and falling behind have gained greater significance alongside Russia's transition to a market economy, and are out of sync with the state's continued definition of military service as a duty of male citizens. The concerns mentioned by the draft evaders I interviewed are borne out by Marina Ilyina's research into men's employment. Her interviewees struggled to find or regain their footing in the labor market or follow through with plans to return to school upon their completion of military service. She concludes that military service is one of the major events that can negatively affect men's labor market trajectory.[63]

Generational differences are a key factor determining attitudes toward the military and conscription. In polls, older respondents have higher levels of trust in the military and consistently show greater support for conscription.[64] In part, this is connected to the fact that the older generation was socialized entirely during Soviet times. As Valerii commented in relation to the idea that a real man is one who has served in the military: "That myth already no longer exists. It exists in the heads of our parents' generation, into which they 'drove' it. For the majority of people, the myth is absent."[65] However, the different generational perspectives on militarized masculinity are also linked to a perception among young men that the situation in the armed forces has gotten much worse. For Igor', the military might have once been a source of masculinity, but no longer is:

> You said that many think that every man should serve in the army. It seems to me that in the past people used to think that way. Today, we have a completely different life and completely different conditions. If in the past you could really go serve and become strong in the army, become a man, then today things are different.[66]

In Soviet society, dominant notions of masculinity were more closely tied to military service than they are today. The chair of one of the committees of soldiers' mothers in Samara argued that previously completion of military service was part of a man's appeal for many heterosexual women, but that this has changed. Ol'ga T. said: "In my generation, if a man did not serve in the army, then all thought that he had some kind of defect, that he was sick. Girls tried to avoid such a man: 'Oh, you know, he didn't serve in the army!'"[67] Igor' pointed out that while the older generation might frown upon his draft evasion, among his peers everyone has the exact same view of military service as he does.[68] Valerii underscored that he has not encountered any prejudice as a result of his draft evasion:

> I never met a single person who judged me. It seems to me, if a person wants to go to the army and ends up going, his family condones it. We have a different relationship to life and all related well to my decision. I didn't encounter any reproaches. My parents helped me money-wise, they didn't want me to serve.[69]

Similarly, Nikolai felt that draft evasion did not carry with it negative social connotations: "Nowadays, society does not view your refusal to serve as a sign that you are a bad person."[70] In postcommunist Russia, a significant number of young men no longer see military service as central to their life stories or identities as men, but more likely as an obstacle to succeeding in the market economy. Additionally, they do not feel any social pressure to serve, as draft evaders are more often met with compassion than disapproval although generational differences persist. For example, 40 percent of all respondents declared their sympathy for draft dodgers in a national survey conducted in 2003, but only 34 percent of those aged sixty and older did.[71]

Another way to appreciate the effects of the economic transformation on militarized masculinity is through an examination of new notions of masculinity. The introduction of market reforms and the emergence of class distinctions have promoted class-based definitions of masculinity.[72] Anatol Lieven notes the attraction that capitalist masculinity has among young men in postcommunist Russia compared with traditional notions of militarized masculinity:

> Today, Russian youth culture is overwhelmingly non-militarist and indifferent or hostile to the idea of self-sacrifice and military discipline. The admired figures among most young Russians today are some version or other of the

"New Russians"—bankers or mafia-type "businessmen," with their luxury cars, ostentatious lifestyle and strings of "girlfriends." Poor old Captain Maxim Maximovich doing his duty in the Caucasus simply doesn't get a look in.[73]

I think Lieven underestimates the extent to which the mafia-type "New Russians" are disliked by ordinary Russians and therefore are unlikely to serve as a new model of masculinity for young Russian men. However, he is right to argue that class has become a defining feature of masculinity in post-Soviet Russia. Elena Meshcherkina's research shows that men within the new capitalist class were most able to protect or regain their sense of masculine identity during the transformation period.[74] In interviews she conducted with Russia's new capitalists, they often contrasted their liberated position after the fall of communism with their subordinate status vis-à-vis the Soviet state. She explains:

> [S]uch men are now embracing the values of risk, independence and individualism. This is part of a wider rehabilitation of entrepreneurialism in contemporary Russian society—a rehabilitation which links entrepreneurship with values which are being culturally defined as masculine.[75]

Private business has developed as a primarily male sphere of activity. Thus, dominant notions of masculinity are increasingly tied to capitalist values and the prototype of the businessman.[76] Most of my interviewees defined their identities as anchored in the market economy, but expressed them in more humble terms, defining themselves as breadwinners or professionals.

The importance of class-based notions of masculinity also becomes evident when we look at the social makeup of the Russian military. Men from economically privileged backgrounds and from urban centers are more likely to have the resources, such as bribes, connections, or student status, that allow them to find legal or illegal means of evading service.[77] Military conscription exerts a disproportionately high social cost on poor households. Michael Lokshin and Ruslan Yemtsov's study shows that "rich households ... are at least three times less likely to have their sons enlisted in the army than the poor."[78] Konstantin Bannikov rightly states that "[t]he armed forces provide a tale-telling picture of the growing social stratification of the Russian society."[79] Sergei, an antidraft activist in Samara, underscored that draft evasion has become a sign of social status. He explained: "Nobody wants to feel that they are socially limited, and military service today is a sign of low social status. If a person has low social status, that means he serves in the army, because he can't 'buy his way out.'"[80] Men from economically disadvantaged backgrounds may lack the resources necessary to avoid military service. As class differences correlate with the urban/rural divide, young men from Russia's rural regions are more likely to serve than their counterparts from Moscow. While Russian men increasingly reject the notion of militarized masculinity tied to compulsory military service, whether or not they can evade the draft largely depends on class and regional location.

Iurii, one of my interviewees, argued that it is mostly rural and working-class men who hold on to the myth of the military as a "school of manhood" and see military service as offering social mobility and opportunity (*sotsial'nyi lift*).[81] This observation holds some truth as a result of the deep social crisis afflicting Russia's depressed rural regions. Polling results show that the idea of military service as a school of life is more common among rural and less-educated respondents.[82] However, I believe it is important to avoid classist and elitist assumptions that discussions of the class makeup of Russian conscripts tend to reproduce. Dale R. Herspring, for example, emphasizes the poor "quality" of conscripts both in terms of lack of education and bad health. He states that by 2004 it was evident that "[t]he quality and character of those who were being drafted was at 'rock bottom.'"[83] The draft evaders I interviewed often shared this opinion of those who served in the military and referred to them as having "few brains" or as mostly "bad people."[84] Valerii expressed the view that

> the army itself is a terrible place. To go there only ruins a person's life. Your life in the army depends not only on how the army is organized, but on the people you come across. And the majority of people there are bad people: people who couldn't realize themselves, couldn't get their act together in time. It seems to me that the majority of people who go there, do it consciously. These are people who have nothing to occupy themselves with (*nechem zaniat'sia*) here.[85]

The fact that the majority of Russia's conscripts are from socially disadvantaged backgrounds *is* a problem, but it is primarily a problem of justice and indicative of the massive rise of social inequality that has resulted from the transition to a market economy. The losers in the process of Russia's economic transition are more likely to find themselves serving in the army today, which has contributed to the negative societal image of the military and of conscripts. This social context has been used to explain violence and abuse in the military as the outcome of the behavior of particular men rather than as inherent to the construction of militarized masculinity.[86] Military service in post-Soviet Russia has become disassociated from a hegemonic masculinity defined by citizenship and is increasingly tied to a marginal masculinity differentiated by class.

While the state's attempt to define men as citizen-soldiers has lost much of its appeal in post-Soviet Russia, the economic transition has given rise to new forms of militarized masculinity. There has been an explosion of private security firms (often staffed by former soldiers) that quickly moved in to fill the vacuum in security provision left by the post-Soviet state. As Vadim Volkov has documented, the number of private security and private protection firms in Russia, which was zero in 1992, grew to 11,652 in 1999. These private agencies employed 850,000 people in 1999, almost 200,000 of whom were licensed to carry a weapon.[87] That the market economy reproduces militarized masculinity is also evident in the brisk sale of military uniforms, soldiers' magazines, and films that celebrate violent masculinity.[88] The link has become weaker between masculinity and military service—and by extension—between militarized masculinity and the state. Yet, militarized masculinity in post-Soviet Russia is taking new marketized forms rather than disappearing. Contract-based service is one of these new marketized forms of militarized masculinity.

Contract-Based Service and Women's Recruitment

The Law of Military Obligation and Service regulates not only mandatory military service but also contract-based or volunteer service (*kontraktnaia sluzhba*), for which men and women can apply.[89] The transition to a professional military made up solely of volunteers serving on a contract-basis (*kontraktniki*) has been a recurring topic in discussions about military reform since the early post-Soviet period. From the state's perspective, contract service is seen as a way of dealing with societal opposition to conscription. Military officials have resisted the transition to an all-volunteer force, in part arguing that the financial cost related to a contract versus a conscript soldier is greater (more than twice as much).[90] A military strategy that continued to demand superiority of numbers in a conventional war was also a factor in their reluctance to abandon conscription.[91]

The men who serve as *kontraktniki* are former conscripts or conscripts who have completed the first six months of service. In post-Soviet Russia, the number of contract soldiers rose to approximately 170,000 but was still short of its target.[92] In 2004, the recruitment of contract soldiers reached 17 percent of the target in the Moscow Military District, 45 percent in the North Caucasus Military District, and 25 percent in the Volga-Ural Military District.[93] Contract soldiers' low pay, relative to what they can earn in the private sector, has meant that the military is not a particularly attractive employer for Russian men.

Women make up more than half of the total volunteers and almost 10 percent of the overall armed forces personnel. In view of the challenges women have faced on the labor market, some women see military employment as an attractive option. Women suffered disproportionately (especially during the early reform period) as a result of the gendered effects of market reforms such as high rates of female unemployment and poverty.[94] Therefore, women were drawn to military service by economic necessity. Surveys indicate that female volunteers are "seeking, at the very least, a period of stable employment and financial security."[95] Other female volunteers have family members in the military or live in the vicinity of a garrison.[96] Since the early 1990s a growing number of women have joined the Russian armed forces. There were only 10,000 women volunteers in the Red Army at the dissolution of the Soviet Union. In the post-Soviet period the number of female volunteers increased to approximately 100,000.[97]

The military has been careful not to depict military work as a career for women, but rather to emphasize the continued "femininity" of military women. Women's increased presence is emphasized to be the result of exceptional and temporary staffing shortages. As Christine Eifler notes: "Women are needed to maintain the functioning of the military. But at the same time women are not to disturb the masculinity of the institution."[98] It is assumed that, once the personnel shortage is overcome, women will return to the private sphere and the "natural" gender order will be restored.[99] Women have been concentrated in areas such as administrative, medical, and clerical work. They have been restricted from combat duty, although some women did see combat in the Chechen wars.[100] In one report written by a researcher with the Federal Security Service (FSB), the author states that the Russian military can still increase the number of women volunteers without undermining its combat readiness. The implication is clearly that women's full integration into the military would conflict with the priority of combat readiness. Combat is defined as the prerogative of men, and following this logic women's role in the military needs to be kept in check.[101] Cynthia Enloe has argued that this approach—recruiting women in a way that does not question the masculine culture of the institution—is often considered important from the perspective of militaries that want to continue to attract men.[102] In a similar vein, the Russian state has arguably tried to downplay its reliance on women in order not to further undermine the already weakened link between masculinity and the military.[103]

Russian media reporting on female soldiers generally reproduces the military's position. A typical article on the topic, which appeared in the *Moskovskii komsomolets* in 2007, was dedicated to Russia's only female battalion commander, Ol'ga Mal'tseva. The author of the article was careful to emphasize the commander's untarnished femininity. The following question illustrates the gist of the story line: "Your whole life you're commanding men. Who rules at home?" Mal'tseva responds: "Of course my husband, he's the head of the family."[104] While the female commander disturbs the military's gender order, she makes sure to emphasize her subordinate (feminized) status vis-à-vis her husband in the private sphere.

The state's increasing reliance on female soldiers represents a significant change in the military's gender order. However, both the military and media depict female soldiers in a way that reinscribes the link between masculinity and the military. The increase in women's participation in the military has not brought about a reconsideration of the gendered nexus between citizenship and military service epitomized by the image of the male citizen-soldier. The influx of female volunteers has gained little public attention. The men and women I interviewed during my fieldwork did not regard the issue as particularly important. Most argued that it was fine for women to serve in the military, but not in combat positions, which reflects the military's official line.[105] It is also noteworthy that the Russian women's movement has not considered gender equality in the armed forces a pressing issue.

Nonetheless, changes within the military and within society undermined the success of the state's conscription policy and challenged the link between masculinity and military service in post-Soviet Russia. The two Chechen wars further undercut support for conscription, and were one of the main reasons contributing to the high amount of draft evasion. The wars witnessed increased public debate and criticism of mandatory service, especially as conscripts, often poorly trained, were sent to the war zone.

Conscription and the Chechen Wars

At the beginning of both the first and second Chechen wars the state had difficulty assembling the necessary troops. In 1994 the state was forced to call up units from across the country. During the second war it took a month to get troops ready, although preparations for a renewed military campaign had begun months earlier. Putin later noted in regard to the beginning of the second war: "There was nobody to send to war."[106] Besides availability of troops, the other main problem was the lack of preparation of conscript soldiers who were sent into battle.[107] This became starkly obvious in the early days of the first Chechen war, when hundreds of untrained conscripts died in the attempted storming of Grozny. As one observer put it: "The first Chechen campaign represented the nadir of Russian combat readiness. When the troops entered Grozny, they were slaughtered."[108]

One of the draft evaders I interviewed, Nikolai, was a student in his early twenties whom I met through my contact with a local antidraft activist. Nikolai mentioned the high casualty rate among conscripts during the first war as reason for not heeding the draft call: "It was a true 'meat-mincing machine' there, into which they threw untrained new conscripts. For many, that severely damaged their trust in the army. Nobody wanted to go to the army and die for no good reason."[109] Similarly, the mother of a son who was nearing draft age told me: "The most important and most scary thing is that my child could find himself in one of the 'hot spots' and get hurt there. If a child goes to war, his mother can even lose him completely!"[110] The high casualty rate was one factor that undermined young men's willingness to serve and their families' and the public's support for the war. The media coverage was thorough in its depiction of both the plight of Russian soldiers and of civilians across the ethnic divide.[111] During the second war, the military switched its strategy from trying to reduce "collateral damage" to the massive use of force through air and artillery bombing to avoid federal troop casualties and, as one military analyst wrote, to "compensate for the low quality of . . . fighting units in Chechnya."[112] The second war had more military success because of the massive use of force and not as the result of improvements in the military's personnel situation.[113] This strategy increased the number of displaced persons compared with the first war and also resulted in high numbers of civilian deaths.[114] The official slogan characterizing the second Chechen campaign as a "low-casualty war" had to be abandoned eventually, as the battle for Grozny once again led to many casualties.[115] During the first war the media had exposed the dire situation among the Russian federal forces and the civilian population, while coverage of the second war avoided pictures of dead soldiers and mention of civilian casualties. Instead television coverage showed the precision bombing of Chechen targets by the Russian air force. It was reminiscent of the Western media coverage of the Persian Gulf war and the NATO war against Serbia.[116] This was the result of the government's and military's public relations campaign and the tighter control of the media during the second war.[117] However, by early 2000 some media outlets such as the (still) independent and government-critical NTV were reporting on "Russian setbacks on the battlefield, and the grief of mothers whose sons have died, while allowing officers on the ground to contradict the positive message emanating from their commanders."[118]

Conscripts serving in the war faced many of the hardships of regular conscripts in addition to being in a combat situation.[119] *Dedovshchina* was widespread among troops in the conflict zone, according to Arkady Babchenko, who served as a conscript during the first war and a volunteer during the second war.[120] Two Russian scholars claimed in 2004 that "[m]ore than half the casualties in the second Chechen campaign (and up to 80 percent in some units) are the result of hazing, violations of safety regulations, and other non-combat situations."[121] *Dedovshchina* had a negative effect on the combat readiness of federal troops in Chechnya both materially and in terms of morale. Babchenko notes that soldiers were at times forced to sell their weapons and ammunition to get money to pay off their *dedy* and other harassers.[122] He explains how the war experience exacerbated the use of violence: "Our older conscripts have already killed people and buried their comrades and they don't believe they'll survive this war themselves. So beatings here are just the norm. Everyone is going to die anyway, both those doing the beating and their victims."[123] There were also reports of soldiers killing their abusers in the conflict zone.[124]

In the fall of 1995 the official number of draft evaders reached a new high, at 31,000. A report from the first war cites as the main reasons for draft evasion "the war in Chechnya, the risk of being killed in a war that is unpopular with the people, hazing, and the lack of clear-cut state guarantees of social protection" for servicemen.[125] The problems the state encountered in mobilizing young men persisted during the second Chechen war, despite its greater initial popularity. Officials stated that the number of draft evaders had decreased during the years following the first war but rose to 38,000 at the beginning of the second war in the fall of 1999.[126] Polling results from the early phase of the second war (2000 and 2002) show that the danger of death or injury in a Chechen-type conflict was the number one reason Russians would not want to see a family member or close relative serve in the army. Opposition to the draft went hand in hand with greater support for an all-volunteer force. For much of the post-Soviet period, there was roughly twice as much support for moving to an all-volunteer force as for maintaining the draft.[127] Already in February 1995, 68 percent of respondents considered the transition to a professional military the most important factor in strengthening the military's combat readiness.[128] There was also solid acceptance of draft evasion and desertion. A poll conducted in 2002 indicated that 54 percent of the population relate to draft evaders with understanding and empathy; a significantly smaller number, 35 percent, condemned their behavior. Similarly, deserters were supported by 53 percent and judged negatively by only 28 percent of respondents.[129]

Resistance by draft-age men took a private not public form: instead of public protest, they used "social networks and individual strategies" to evade the draft.[130] It was the mothers of conscripts and draft-age youth who played a more public role in opposing both the wars in Chechnya and mandatory service. The Committee of Soldiers' Mothers of Russia supported young men seeking to evade the draft as well as deserters. Amy Caiazza argues that desertion and draft evasion increased as a result of the activities of soldiers' mothers.[131] Although Yeltsin during his presidential campaign in 1996 had signed a decree promising that conscripts would be sent to conflict zones only on a voluntary basis, conscripts found themselves in Chechnya once again during the second war. In early 2000, promises were made by the Ministry of Defense that conscripts with less than six months of training would not be expected to serve in the conflict zone.[132] In addition, President Putin declared that starting in 2005 the forces in Chechnya would be composed entirely of contract soldiers.[133] These announcements were responses to widespread draft evasion and attempts to allay public fears about the dispatch of conscripts to the war zone. The Committee of Soldiers' Mothers questioned the voluntary nature of contracts in the case of conscripts, who may agree to sign a contract without being told that they will be sent to Chechnya.[134] There were reports in 2006 of conscripts still being used in combat roles in Chechnya.[135] As discussed in the previous chapter, Putin attempted to construct a heroic image of the Russian soldier as part of his broader agenda of strengthening the state and renewing militarized patriotism. In my interview with Nikolai, he was skeptical of Putin's policy and underscored its societal limitations: "They said that 'the Russian soldier is being reborn,' although there were also enormous losses [in the second war]. It seems to me that despite the massive 'brainwashing,' there are even fewer who wanted to serve in the second war—nobody wants to join the army and die."[136] This quotation speaks to the gap between the mobilization of the population in support of the war and men's continued lack of willingness to participate in the war.

In order to deal with insufficient manpower, the state found coercive ways to increase the pool of conscripts. During the first war (1995) a law was introduced that increased the length of obligatory military service from eighteen to twenty-four months.[137] In the second war, the state took even more coercive measures by employing aggressive recruitment methods that Human Rights Watch has referred to as "conscription by detention." This led to the rounding up of draft-age men off the street and the conscription of men who do not fit medical or age requirements or who might be eligible for deferment.[138] In addition, there was a stricter enforcement of the draft through cooperation between the local police and draft boards.[139] A national survey conducted in 2003 found that a majority of Russians do not "approve of the practice of arresting men for draft dodging."[140] Moreover, the list of deferments was cut back, which resulted in the conscription of a greater percentage of draft-age men.

The second way in which the state attempted to deal with its manpower problems and mitigate societal and media criticism was to attract more volunteer or contract soldiers. Already during the first war there was an attempt to recruit contract soldiers.[141] However, the military had difficulty retaining them, and many broke their contracts to leave service early.[142] The share of contract soldiers among federal troops in Chechnya rose from 7 percent at the outset of the second war to 20 percent by the fall of 2000, according to official figures.[143] In spring 2000, the Ministry of Defense started to actively recruit volunteers to fight in Chechnya, attracting them with promises of high material compensation. However, the government's inability to pay on time and in full led to protests and lawsuits by contract soldiers.[144] The greater use of contract soldiers placed an economic burden on the Russian state that it was unable or unwilling to fully meet. On the other hand, Stephen Shenfield writes that "[e]specially for Russian officers and mercenaries (professional soldiers on contract), service in Chechnya, for all its dangers and inconveniences, came to be valued as an opportunity for personal enrichment."[145] The wars presented opportunities for some to make money by collecting bribes at checkpoints, kidnapping Chechens for ransom, selling arms, and engaging in other corrupt activities.[146]

To increase its success in recruiting contract soldiers, the Russian state would have needed to improve the financial incentives of volunteer service. Nikolai Poroskov explained in 2004: "[T]hese days there aren't all that many people who want to become professional soldiers. Even in Chechnya, men who face death on a daily basis receive only 15,000 rubles a month, while those serving under ordinary conditions get just over 6,000."[147] Increasing the wage of contract soldiers, however, not only is a burden on the state coffers but challenges the official conception of militarized masculinity in terms of an obligation of citizenship rather than a market relation. To make contract service more attractive, the state will also have to contend with the negative societal attitude toward contract soldiers, which exists despite solid societal support for an all-volunteer force. The Chechen wars highlighted the problems with conscription but showed that contract service is far from becoming a legitimate and attractive profession among young men. In the interviews I conducted, I often encountered the following view, expressed here by a Russian journalist: "As a rule, those who become contract soldiers are men who cannot find anything to which to apply themselves in the civilian sphere, are unemployed, or are thrill-seekers."[148] This attitude underlines the crisis in notions of militarized masculinity in post-Soviet Russia: often men who evade the draft receive sympathy, while those who volunteer for service are considered socially inept or deviant.

The Russian state's ability to wage war in Chechnya suffered because of the many problems associated with conscription. The wars further weakened support for conscription among young men and society at large. However, the wars also highlighted the fact that despite Russians' support for an all-volunteer force, contract-based service is plagued by financial difficulties and a negative societal attitude toward contract soldiers. Men's willingness to serve in the military and participate in war was also impacted by changes in the meaning of patriotism.

Patriotism in a Postmilitary Society?

Post-Soviet Russian society has a contradictory relationship with the military. Levels of trust in the military decreased during the first Chechen war, but were not negatively affected by the second war.[149] The military remained one of the most trusted institutions in post-Soviet Russia, after the presidency and the Russian Orthodox Church.[150] Yet a large number of young men have not been willing to serve in the military, much less participate in a war. Not only has the link between masculinity and military service weakened, so has the link between military service and patriotism. Draft evasion is common and more often socially condoned than frowned upon. This is a remarkable development considering how closely militarism and patriotism were intertwined in the Soviet era.

When we compare post-Soviet Russia to Western societies, the situation I am describing does not appear unfamiliar at all. Stephen L. Webber and Alina Zilberman use the term "postmilitary society" to theorize the changing nature of militarization in Russian society. The term was introduced by Martin Shaw in 1991 to describe the decreasing role of the armed forces politically, economically, and socially in Western European societies at the end of the Cold War.[151] One of the key factors in a postmilitary society is the "revision of the relationship between individual citizens and their obligations and rights, with regard to what we can see as the *military component of citizenship*."[152] Russia may quite possibly be moving toward becoming a postmilitary society, even though at a rhetorical level there has been increased support for the military and militarized patriotism since Putin's rise to power. The fact that militarism still holds appeal at the rhetorical level also indicates similarity to Western postmilitary societies. Some authors have used concepts such as "spectator militarism" to describe the less participatory aspects of militarized citizenship. Here it is not the figure of the citizen-soldier, but of the citizen-spectator, who becomes militarized.[153] This should caution us against joining the growing chorus of observers who see a return of Soviet militarism. Instead, if we put developments into the context of Russia's postcommunist transformation we see the specific characteristics, including gender characteristics, of post-Soviet militarization.

The economic and social transformations of the post-Soviet period have increased the tension between patriotism and individualism that began to emerge in the late Soviet period.[154] The weakened link between military service and patriotism is related to a breakdown of the social contract that informed Soviet state-society relations. The introduction of a market economy has affected social attitudes about the relationship between the individual and the state. Igor' captured this shift in the following way:

> Military service is not at all connected to patriotism. Previously that was not the case. Previously the state educated people in such a way, that *first came the common, then the individual*. Today everyone looks out for themselves, and only afterwards for society. At the same time, previously the state provided social guarantees, housing, and today it doesn't do any of that. Then why should we do anything for it?[155]

The liberal economic transformation has shaped state-society relations in a way that undermined societal acceptance of men's obligatory military service and of its link to patriotism. In addition, the Chechen wars and societal perceptions of them as unnecessary and politically motivated contributed to this change in military-society relations. Even though in the early phase of the second war a majority of the population supported military intervention, this war also soon lost favor with Russians. The Chechen wars are not recognized as a clear-cut case of aggression that would justify Russian men to follow their "patriotic duty." This became evident in my exchange with Valerii:

> It's a different question if suddenly a war started. Then I would go right away, without any discussion. There is some patriotism in me.
> "And the Chechen conflict? Don't you consider it a war?"
> I don't know—that conflict was far away.... No, I wouldn't have gone there. I consider it an "excessive" war: we were not invaded, we were intervening. I consider that our politics were wrong.[156]

During my interviews one argument kept recurring: men would be willing to fight in a "real" war, epitomized by the Great Patriotic War. Valerii explained his position by reference to his grandfather: "My grandfather fought in the Great Patriotic War. I watched movies and read books about the Great Patriotic War. I think, I wouldn't ponder for long, if a Third World War broke out and the fatherland was in danger. I would right away go to defend it."[157] It is noteworthy that someone who evaded the draft still holds on to a notion of patriotic duty, and it highlights the central place World War Two continues to hold for Russian identity.[158] Another draft evader, Iurii, on the other hand argued that he would have considered serving if the situation in the armed forces was better. As he explained by reference to the German military: "If I lived in Europe, for example, in Germany ... it's totally possible that I would have completed my service.... But in the Russian army which is undisciplined, criminal, and corrupted, of course, it's scary to serve, because anything can happen to you."[159] These statements show that men who evaded the draft are not necessarily antimilitaristic and that their identities may become remilitarized if the circumstances change. It is therefore important to keep in mind the particular context of the Chechen wars and of the post-Soviet armed forces when considering whether Russia is becoming a postmilitary society. The quotations indicate that there might be potential for men's mobilization on the basis of wars perceived as more just than the Chechen wars and for men's recruitment into reformed and well-funded armed forces.

Under Putin the state began to take an active interest in restoring the link between military service and patriotism. As part of the president's emphasis on renewing patriotism, the Russian government introduced a program of patriotic education in which the military took center stage. The first state patriotic education program (2001–2005) identified the lack of patriotism as a key problem for state and society in post-Soviet Russia. It stated that the postcommunist transition had given rise to economic crisis, social divisions, and the depreciation of spirituality, which diminished patriotism. The apparent result was "indifference, egoism, individualism, cynicism, unmotivated aggressiveness, and a disrespectful attitude toward the state and social institutions."[160] The program outlined a system of patriotic education that aimed at societal consolidation and strengthening of the state. The program included courses, conferences, cultural events, exhibitions, and military-sports games, and also aimed at raising the profile of patriotic themes in the media and cultural sphere. Militarization has been a key component in this effort to increase citizens' patriotism. Many of the activities and events focused on Russia's military history, especially its role in World War Two. Indeed, one of the explicit goals of the program was to prepare young men for military service and instill in them a sense of duty to serve. The second state patriotic education program (2006–2010) reiterated the need to strengthen patriotism in order to ensure citizens' loyalty to the fatherland and willingness to fulfill their constitutional duties.[161]

Opinion polls indicate that there has been an increase in support for conscription over the last few years. In 2010, 34 percent of respondents (in contrast to only 13 percent in 1998) supported the idea of a close family member following the draft call. For those opposed to the idea, *dedovshchina* rather than "a Chechen-type conflict" was the number one reason, as had been the case before the start of the second Chechen war. A greater number of Russians still supported the transition to an all-volunteer force in 2010, though the margin of difference between them and those in favor of a conscription army has been decreasing.[162] The official number of draft evaders has also declined, though draft evasion remains a problem for the Russian state. The political and military leadership has been encouraging young men to follow the draft call, and also threatened more punitive measures against draft evaders. Judging by opinion polls, the idea of military service as an obligation of citizenship has gained some support. In 2004, more respondents than previously (60 percent versus 51 percent in 2002) thought that young men were obliged to follow the draft call.[163] While societal support for conscription increased, a poll conducted in 2004 found that 87 percent of respondents held the view that most young men did not want to serve in the army, in comparison to 6 percent who thought they did. In fact, a majority of respondents thought men's willingness to serve had further fallen over the preceding few years.[164] Putin rather dramatically linked the fulfillment of military service to the survival of the Russian state, when he commented in 2006: "We must explain to the entire generation of young people that the question of whether or not to serve in the army should not even come up for a young person to begin with. We must all realize that without the army there would be no country. Nobody should have the slightest doubt on this score. No army, no Russia."[165] Whether young men will be any more willing to serve remains questionable, especially if conscripts are sent to war, considering that the decline in draft evasion coincided with the scaling back of the second Chechen war and the increased use of contract soldiers and police officers to wage war in Chechnya.

Conclusion

The situation within the military, the rise of new notions of masculinity in society, and the Chechen wars challenged acceptance of military service as a duty of male citizenship in Russia. The media and human rights groups have well documented the many dangers conscripts encounter during service. *Dedovshchina* and the lack of food and medical attention are the main reasons, in addition to the danger of being sent to a conflict zone, that young men and their families search for ways to avoid conscription. For the men drafted, the situation within the military may push them to desert or, worse, commit suicide. The postcommunist economic transformation encouraged the demilitarization of masculinity as anchored in military service. Many young men in post-Soviet Russia no longer consider military service as central to their transition to manhood. In the context of a market economy, military service is more likely to be seen as a waste of time and a career obstacle. New notions of masculinity tied to capitalism and individualism undermine the link between patriotism, masculinity, and military service. The political leadership, however, has attempted to re-establish this link by encouraging young men to heed the draft call.

The Russian-Chechen wars highlighted the problems with conscription and society's faltering support for a conscription army. They also made evident the difficulties of moving toward contract-based service, as the military had difficulty retaining contract soldiers because of financial problems. The Russian state has been no more successful in attracting contract soldiers as the war in Chechnya scaled down. Despite the many promises made over the past decade and a half that conscription would be abolished, the transition to an all-volunteer force seems out of the question in the near future. Policy under the current defense minister, Anatolii Serdiukov, indicates that conscription will continue alongside attempts to reform and modernize the armed forces. While the length of service has been reduced to one year, some commentators fear that obligatory military service will need to be extended once again in order to meet the personnel needs of the armed forces.[166]

The Russian state's ability to wage war in Chechnya was severely affected by the many problems that plague conscription and contract service. The Chechen wars illustrated the difficulties of mobilizing the population for war in the post-Soviet period. While a majority of Russians initially supported the second Chechen war, neither of the two wars indicated a rise in men's willingness to serve as soldiers. Draft evasion declined only as the second war was unwinding. This raises the question of the future of state-society relations in the military sphere. How will the relationship between state, citizenship, and soldiering develop in Russia? While the link between masculinity and the military has weakened, gender differences in the military sphere are still strongly maintained. Women are not seriously considered as soldiers, though their numbers significantly increased in the post-Soviet period. The state defines military service as a duty of male citizenship and considers draft evasion as unpatriotic. It has so far failed to seriously reassess the military component of male citizenship, and instead holds on to Soviet ideals of militarized, patriotic masculinity. However, young men, society, and prominent civil society actors continue to challenge the association of citizenship and patriotism with military service, even while there has been an increase in militarized patriotism at the societal level. The next chapter explores how this tension has played out in the movement created by soldiers' mothers.

4 The Soldiers' Mothers Movement
Contesting and Reproducing Militarized Gender Roles

THE RUSSIAN SOLDIERS' mothers movement emerged during the late 1980s. The Soviet-Afghan war as well as Gorbachev's reform policies spurred the development of soldiers' mothers groups across the Soviet republics. These women soon had a significant impact on Soviet policy. In 1989, soldiers' mothers successfully protested the drafting of students in postsecondary institutions, leading to the return of 176,000 students from military service.[1] Soldiers' mothers also demanded information on peace- and wartime deaths during military service, and were instrumental in uncovering the widespread abuse of conscripts through hazing (*dedovshchina*).[2] This chapter offers a detailed examination of the activities and ideologies of soldiers' mothers in post-Soviet Russia. It investigates the role of soldiers' mothers in relation to the policy of mandatory military service for men and the Russian-Chechen wars. More specifically, the chapter asks: in which ways have soldiers' mothers contested but also at times reinforced militarized notions of motherhood and masculinity?

Feminist International Relations scholars have shown how militaries rely on particular notions of femininity and masculinity (for example, women in need of protection, women as patriotic mothers; men as soldiers and protectors). These articulations of women's and men's roles are not static. They may be redefined according to the needs of states and militaries, or contested by societal forces. I begin from the assumption that there is no given relationship between motherhood and pacifism or militarism. Motherhood can be used to oppose conscription and war, yet it can also serve in support of military and state agendas. In fact, Soviet and post-Soviet leaders recognized that motherhood was a powerful tool that, if not harnessed, could potentially damage the legitimacy of the government and undermine the functioning of the military. From the inception of the independent soldiers' mothers movement, the state tried to undermine the popular movement and co-opt it by founding similar progovernment organizations. In 1989 the Soviet Defense Ministry created the Council of Mothers and Widows of servicemen killed in Afghanistan.[3] Two years later the Council of Servicemen's Parents was founded, a soldiers' mothers group that is attached to the Russian Ministry of Defense.[4] The independent soldiers' mothers activists refer to this organization and its regional affiliates as "twin committees" or "pocket committees."[5] These committees are not so much concerned with defending conscripts' and servicemen's rights as they are with encouraging men to serve and mothers to support their sons' service. It is therefore important to distinguish different currents within the soldiers' mothers movement in Russia. There are independent and co-opted soldiers' mothers organizations as well as ones that fall in between these two poles.

This chapter compares the independent soldiers' mothers groups in Russia's two largest cities with two regional groups in Samara, which are formally independent but rely on local power structures for support.[6] The Union of Committees of Soldiers' Mothers in Moscow and the Soldiers' Mothers of St. Petersburg have challenged notions of patriotic motherhood and militarized masculinity by publicly opposing conscription and the wars in Chechnya. Their ability to act publicly was linked to a motherist approach that emphasizes women's responsibility for their children. While all soldiers' mothers groups assist draftees and their families, not all groups disrupt militarized gender roles. Soldiers' mothers in Samara avoided taking a public stance against the war and have reproduced a patriotic, militarized gender discourse that celebrates "defenders of the fatherland" and their mothers. The analysis of these different soldiers' mothers groups illustrates the complicated politics of motherhood and militarization in post-Soviet Russia.

Motherhood and Militarization

An essentialist view of gender roles posits that men are inherently militaristic and women naturally peaceful. While most feminist scholars reject such a view, it is often associated with feminism by those with a superficial knowledge of feminist arguments. At the same time, the notion of women as pacifists and men as warriors has retained a position of "common sense" across many societies, despite changes in societal gender orders and in the gender makeup of militaries during the twentieth century. Cynthia Enloe's work shows that the association of men with war and women with peace is overly simplistic, as militarization relies on both men and women, and on notions of masculinity and femininity. Women have been militarized both inside and outside of the military, as soldiers, military wives, prostitutes, nurses, rape victims, mothers, and feminist activists.[7] To assume that women are naturally peaceful overlooks the complexity of women's experiences.[8]

Mothers may be mobilized in support of, or in opposition to, war and conscription. The militarization and potential demilitarization of motherhood depend on state and military "maneuvers" and women's actions.[9] A mother's militarization is evident in the extent to which she raises a "good" soldier, and gains pride and social recognition from her son's military service. Throughout history there are examples both of women who have encouraged their sons to join the military and of women who have withheld approval for their sons' actions.[10] The Spartan mother and the *mater dolorosa* represent two historical archetypes of the relationship between motherhood and war/militarism. In contrast to the Spartan notion of patriotic motherhood, the medieval Christian Madonna image (*mater dolorosa*) evokes, in Jean Bethke Elshtain's words,

> the more pacific figure of the mother as beautiful soul, who embodies verities and virtues at odds with the clamor and killing of war. This is the mother who laments and protects and regrets and mourns. Finding in the paths of peace the most desirable way of being, she exalts a pacific alternative. Ironically, of course, she does so from a stance that has historically been civically denuded. Absent from the ranks of warriors and leaders, she had to exert her influence in other ways and through other forms, often religious, sometimes sentimental.[11]

Differentiating between patriotic and suffering mothers helps advance our understanding of the relationship between motherhood and war/militarism. However, women's experiences cannot necessarily be slotted into one of these categories. Instead, each individual case deserves its own investigation to uncover the complex, and often contradictory, politics of motherhood during war. The context of war can reinforce patriotic motherhood and militarized masculinity but can also undermine the militarization of gender roles. Protest against war may be expressed by men's refusal to fight and women's organizing against war.[12] Women's opposition to war is often grounded in motherhood and emphasizes the role of mothers as child bearers, protectors of life, and peace lovers. This fact does not validate essentialist arguments about women's peacefulness, but rather tells us about prevailing notions of femininity within the particular gender order.

Challenging Militarized Patriotism and War: Soldiers' Mothers in Moscow and St. Petersburg[13]

This section discusses the activities of the two best-known soldiers' mothers organizations in Russia: the Moscow-based Committee of Soldiers' Mothers of Russia (CSMR), renamed the Union of Committees of Soldiers' Mothers of Russia in 1998, and the independent human rights organization Soldiers' Mothers of St. Petersburg (SMSP).[14] The Moscow Committee serves as an umbrella organization for dozens of regional committees.[15] According to the committee, up to 50,000 people per year seek help at its Moscow office or at one of the regional offices.[16] The group in St. Petersburg was set up in 1991 by Ella Poliakova and has no formal ties to the Moscow CSMR. The SMSP claim to have offered legal advice to more than 65,000 people over the 1990s and to have helped around 59,000 draftees receive exemption from military service.[17] Both organizations have received international recognition and financial support from Western donors.[18] The SMSP and the Moscow CSMR are the most studied of Russia's soldiers' mothers groups, and are the subject of much Russian and Western scholarship.

The main goal of these soldiers' mothers groups is to protect the rights of draftees, conscripts, and their families in the face of human rights violations during the conscription process,[19] as well as during military service.[20] Some of their key demands have been the recognition of the systemic nature of *dedovshchina*, more accountability from the military in respect to missing recruits (whether or not they are combat casualties), and an end to illegal conscription practices. A major part of the groups' day-to-day activities is to legally advise and assist men seeking to evade the draft or those who have left their units on account of maltreatment. The soldiers' mothers also offer help to families who have been unable to get information on their conscript sons' whereabouts from the military.[21] The activists contact military authorities, visit military units, and submit complaints on behalf of parents. They also collect evidence of human rights violations and fight court cases. The SMSP moreover see their role as educational; their members hold lectures and seminars in which they inform young men and their families about the laws and tutor them in filing their own claims for deferment or exemption from military service. The larger objective of both organizations is to subject the military to the rule of law and to create a military they consider appropriate for a democratic society. The soldiers' mothers have sought to transform the nature of military service in Russia by lobbying for the legal implementation of alternative service as well as the abolition of obligatory conscription. They view the transition to a professional military as key to reducing human rights violations in the armed forces.[22]

These soldiers' mothers groups pose a serious challenge to the Russian state's policy of mandatory conscription. Their activities counter the state's definition of military service as a citizenship obligation for men. In defiance of notions of patriotic motherhood, these mothers support young men who evade the draft or desert the army. The activism of soldiers' mothers has been both a manifestation of the crisis of militarized masculinity *and* a force transforming societal views on military service in Russia. The mothers organized to address the very real problems faced by their sons and other young men. Their concerns were initiated in the private sphere, but took on public expression as their work created societal awareness of the dangerous conditions of military service and the need for military reform.

Soldiers' Mothers and the First Chechen War

The CSMR and the SMSP were the most vocal opponents of the Russian government's military intervention in Chechnya and called for a political settlement of the conflict.[23] The CSMR states that it was the first Russian NGO to take a public position against the war.[24] The start of the Chechen war in 1994 led to a further mobilization of soldiers' mothers and the founding of new groups. In addition, their concerns and forms of collective action expanded on account of the war.[25] Their antiwar activities included pickets, demonstrations, petitions, and letters to the media and policy-makers.[26] The leaders of the CSMR and the SMSP spoke out against the use of conscripts in military conflicts and demanded their return from the war zone.[27] The war led to a radicalization of the ideology of soldiers' mothers, as Russian sociologist Elena Zdravomyslova explains: "Pacifism became the prevailing ideology in the radical branch of the movement."[28]

The soldiers' mothers challenged the official "war story," the state's justification of war, by offering an alternative interpretation of the threat facing Russia. Eva M. Hinterhuber writes in regard to the SMSP: "The government and the military leadership were specified as offenders, and the 'simple' soldiers (on both sides), the civil population and the families of those affected were specified as victims."[29] The soldiers' mothers identified the actions of the military rather than the threat of Chechen separatists as a source of insecurity. In fact, the mothers laid the blame for the war at the foot of the Russian government; they were critical of the government's scapegoating of Chechens and suggested that "the source of evil might well be the Russian state itself."[30] In order to hold the government accountable, the soldiers' mothers collected their own information on casualties.[31] In October 1995, the CSMR opened a hot line to receive information on the deaths of service personnel in Chechnya,[32] and parents of conscripts also increasingly turned to the organization for information.[33]

The activism of the CSMR and the SMSP shook one of the very foundations of war and militarization. It undermined notions of militarized masculinity and patriotic motherhood that are central to the state's ability to wage war: that military service is a man's duty and that "good" mothers support their sons' soldiering. The women challenged these gendered assumptions on the grounds of the Chechen conflict and the violence conscripts faced during military service. In February 1995, the CSMR held a congress titled "For Life and Freedom," at which participants from forty-four Russian cities supported an appeal that concluded: "We will not give our sons over to a criminal war."[34] Representatives of the committee actively encouraged young men to evade serving in the war.[35] Members of the SMSP advised parents to protect their sons from the military: "If the army is dangerous to the lives and the health of our sons, we have to hide them from the military service in all possible ways."[36] The CSMR was successful in lobbying the Russian Duma to pass a law that guaranteed amnesty to Russian soldiers who deserted or evaded the draft during the war.[37] However, the CSMR was unable to prevent the passage of a law that extended military service from eighteen to twenty-four months in 1995, or have it amended.[38]

Soldiers' mothers' activism went beyond lobbying, as the mothers inserted themselves into the conflict zone. Activists helped individual mothers travel to Chechnya to bring their sons home and cooperated with Chechen mothers to organize exchanges of prisoners of war.[39] Through their cooperation with Chechen mothers, these women espoused a conception of motherhood that crossed national and ethnic boundaries.[40] They rejected the image of the "hero's mother," and instead used motherhood as a platform from which to voice their critique of the military and the war.[41] The CSMR delivered humanitarian aid to wounded Russian conscripts as well as Chechen civilians.[42] On March 8, 1995, soldiers' mothers undertook a peace march, the "Mothers' March for Life and Compassion." The march embarked from the Tomb of the Unknown Soldier in Moscow and ended in the war zone, with approximately 300 mothers from fifteen cities taking part.[43] Zdravomyslova explains: "The concept of the March was both symbolic and instrumental: it aimed to demonstrate antiwar attitudes, to collect reliable information about those killed and injured, and finally to stop the war in Chechnya."[44] Participants were harassed and the march was delayed by military authorities on numerous occasions. Although the mothers did not end the war, they drew public attention to their cause and the dire situation in Chechnya, and helped strengthen antiwar sentiment and organizing in society.[45] According to one poll conducted in February 1995, the soldiers' mothers had the support of three-quarters of the Russian public.[46] Political and military leaders accused the soldiers' mothers (in particular, the CSMR) of being unpatriotic, undermining the army, conspiring with the West, and of being bad mothers.[47]

Soldiers' Mothers and the Second Chechen War

During the second war, the CSMR and SMSP once again spoke out against the war and called for a peaceful resolution of the conflict. Members of the CSMR participated in antiwar demonstrations, organized conferences, wrote open letters, and repeatedly challenged the official casualty figures.[48] During its second congress, "For Life and Freedom," which brought together dozens of regional committees of soldiers' mothers in 2000, the CSMR adopted a resolution that stated in part: "Soldiers' Mothers never will agree that the annihilation of peaceful inhabitants and young soldiers, the destruction of cities and villages can serve as a basis for the well-being and spiritual rebirth of Russia."[49] In 2002, members of the CSMR declared that they had "lost their faith in the state power of Russia" and that "the so-called anti-terrorist operation in Chechnya is, by itself, a powerful stimulator of state and non-state, transnational terrorism."[50] The CSMR was skeptical of the revival of militarized patriotism that accompanied Putin's rise to the presidency and once again provided an alternative to the official justification of the war.[51] Together with other civil society groups the SMSP held weekly pickets to protest the war, which they characterized as genocide against the Chechen people. These activists carried signs with slogans such as: "Forgive us Chechnya," "Cleansings of Chechens and conscripts is a disgrace for our country," and "We say no to conscription slavery." They condemned the human rights violations committed against both Chechen civilians and Russian conscripts.[52] In doing so, the SMSP challenged the ethnic divide and tensions that had become more pronounced as a result of the ongoing conflict.

Both organizations faced more restrictions and received less media coverage and societal support than in the first war.[53] Ida Kuklina, member of the CSMR, explains the main differences between the first and second war from the perspective of the committee. The first difference was that the state "closed the conflict zone completely," which affected both the ability of the media to report on the conflict and of NGOs to operate in the war zone.[54] Second, the war took place in the context of greater public support for the war. While the CSMR had been at the forefront of antiwar mobilization during the first war, it was not able to play that role effectively during the second war. The members of the CSMR participated in antiwar demonstrations in the early phase of the war, but concluded that they were not effective in shaping public opinion against the war. Kuklina notes that the CSMR focused on a campaign to expose the true extent of casualties, which it estimated were twice as high as state officials acknowledged. Members of the CSMR maintained contacts with Chechen women and Chechen organizations, but were restricted in their actions because of the tight military control of the conflict zone. The CSMR was no longer able to influence policy to the degree it had during the first war, as it lacked allies within the Duma.[55]

As a result of the state's tighter control over the media, reports on activities and positions that were critical of the war became less frequent. Observers agree that the soldiers' mothers received limited press coverage during the second war.[56] Tatiana Sivaeva notes that the activities of soldiers' mothers were more likely to be covered when they fit the image of "caring mothers" than when they made political statements. The CSMR and the SMSP were negatively affected by the clampdown on government-critical NGOs under Putin's presidencies. Civil society groups that resisted government co-optation increasingly encountered harassment, intimidation, and difficulties with funding.[57]

In an attempt to increase its political influence and bring about the reforms for which it had lobbied over the past decade and a half, the CSMR founded a political party in November 2004, the United People's Party of Soldiers' Mothers.[58] The CSMR also attempted to participate in the resolution of the conflict, meeting with representatives of the Chechen leadership in London to discuss the conditions for peace.[59] The committee was not successful in these political ventures. Furthermore, official criticism of the CSMR increased during the second war, according to Larisa Deriglazova. Defense Minister Sergei Ivanov referred to the organization as the "so-called" soldiers' mothers and was critical of their support for draft evaders and their cooperation with Chechens.[60] Nonetheless, the CSMR remained one of the highest-profile human rights organizations in Russia, and continued to engage and lobby the government and military structures. Members of the CSMR have also been invited to participate in state bodies, such as the Presidential Commission on Human Rights.[61] The leader of the CSMR, Valentina Mel'nikova, is one of fifty members of the Social Chamber of the Ministry of Defense, which is a consultative body that was set up in 2006 to improve relations between the Ministry of Defense and civil society.[62] These examples show that while the CSMR has been under attack, it has also established itself as an organization that the state cannot discount.

The CSMR and the SMSP continued to challenge notions of patriotic motherhood during the second war, but found it increasingly difficult to gain public attention for their antiwar stance. Motherhood as a platform for dissent, represented by the image of Russian and Chechen mothers opposing the first war, lost some of its legitimacy in the context of Putin's strengthening of the state and revival of militarized patriotism. The image of soldiers' mothers opposing the war and reaching out to Chechen mothers was marginalized during the second war by the juxtaposition of caring Russian mothers opposite Chechen female suicide bombers.[63] Such a dichotomy reinforced the war on terror rhetoric and its construction of a civilized "us" versus a barbaric "other."

The Politics of Responsible Motherhood

Russian and Western observers have both been quick to make sense of the activities of soldiers' mothers through an essentialist understanding of motherhood. The Russian press has depicted these women as maternal heroines who have a special duty as mothers. The soldiers' mothers themselves often explain their actions in essentialist terms, as they portray a mother's right and duty to protect her child as linked to biology or nature.[64] The press secretary of the CSMR commented: "[T]he first person who reacts to a threat to the life of a son, it is a mother. It is this way because of the biology of women; for women these issues are intimately important."[65] The chair of the SMSP made a similar point in reference to the name of her organization: "It sounds better than any other [name], and it is the basic truth—mothers are responsible for their sons and for life in general."[66]

Feminist scholars view motherhood as a strategy of the movement rather than as an essential gender identity of its activists. Zdravomyslova argues that motherhood forms the basis on which these women justify their activism and mobilize supporters.[67] Amy Caiazza identifies the "exploitation—whether consciously or not—of traditional ideas about women and motherhood" as one of the strategies of the CSMR.[68] Hinterhuber considers what she calls the "dramatization of motherhood" as a key strategy of the SMSP.[69] The appeal of essentialist notions of motherhood is deeply rooted in the Soviet Union's and post-Soviet Russia's gender orders.

As discussed in Chapter 1, the Soviet state took an active interest in motherhood while pursuing a policy of gender equality that brought large numbers of women into the workforce. During the 1960s and 1970s the political and societal debate shifted toward an emphasis on women's roles as biological reproducers.[70] Social scientists and education theorists asserted women's essential maternal functions and their "responsibility towards society and the child."[71] The importance assigned to women's responsibility as mothers became even more pronounced during the 1980s and in the post-Soviet period.[72] Zdravomyslova writes: "The model of responsible motherhood is at the core of the femininity construction of contemporary Russian gender culture."[73] At the same time, the difficult conditions of postcommunist transition have undermined "the ability of women to adequately care for or protect their children."[74] This has spurred many women into activism based on their identity as mothers.[75] The mothers who aim to protect their sons from the dangers of military service are a prime example of this development.

The Soviet state also espoused women's civic duties, although women's participation was limited to the lower echelons of power.[76] In the post-Soviet period women's participation is no longer publicly promoted, and the emphasis of women's maternal role goes hand in hand with their return to the private sphere. The soldiers' mothers may rely on a notion of femininity defined by motherhood, but their activism defies the idea of women's redomestication and political passivity that informs post-Soviet gender ideology.[77] Soldiers' mothers challenge women's exclusion from the highly masculinized sphere of military and security policy.[78] They engage in this sphere from a position that is constructed as "private" (motherhood) and adheres to prevailing notions of femininity. As a number of authors point out, the ability of soldiers' mothers to voice their critique of the military is closely linked to their motherist approach, which emphasizes women's responsibility for their children. Speaking and acting as "mothers" gives them the moral authority that other actors lack in relation to the military and the state as well as society. The fact that the identities and actions of soldiers' mothers conform to dominant ideas of womanhood arguably helped increase their legitimacy among Russians and made it more difficult for the state and military to neutralize them. The ability to use motherhood in a political way is paradoxically due to its perception as natural and private. The emphasis on motherhood depoliticizes the actions of soldiers' mothers by making them seem natural, which in turn is what allows them to engage publicly and politically.[79]

The ability of soldiers' mothers to use motherhood as a legitimate form of political expression was furthered by their nonfeminist stance. Feminist ideas are unpopular in Russia, in large part because they are associated with the Soviet regime and its rhetoric of women's emancipation.[80] While these mothers work to save lives and challenge the state's illegal practices, they are not involved in the overthrow of masculine dominance. Indeed, they do not see women's oppression as a relevant political issue.[81] As Mel'nikova from the CSMR stated: "Nobody in this organization thinks that women are particularly oppressed."[82] The committee does, however, make a claim for women's equal participation in politics, including in questions of war and peace.[83]

Lisa Sundstrom argues that the success of soldiers' mothers was also a result of their primary focus on the "bodily harm" done to their sons. The focus on the image of the suffering son (and suffering mother) elicited more public sympathy than an antimilitarist, pacifist, or human rights discourse. While they protested the wars and advocated for the rule of law in the military sphere, the women did so in behalf of their sons.[84] They did not make a claim as political actors in their own right. Antimilitarist and anticonscription organizations such as the Antimilitarist Radical Association (ARA) were less successful. Caiazza argues that as an organization made up by men, ARA lacked the "gendered opportunity structures" that made possible the success of soldiers' mothers: "Ideas about gender turned out to be a defining factor determining groups' policy successes."[85] Gender and, in particular, the construction of responsible motherhood were crucial to legitimizing the activities of soldiers' mothers organizations such as the CSMR and the SMSP. Soldiers' mothers in Samara also rely on a notion of responsible motherhood to defend soldiers' rights, but at the same time promote militarized, patriotic notions of femininity and masculinity.

Soldiers' Mothers in Samara: Reproducing Militarized Patriotism while Defending the Rights of Soldiers

Soldiers' mothers began to organize in Samara in the early 1990s. The local committee (founded in 1991) split during the first Chechen war into the Samara Oblast' Committee of Parents of Servicemen[86] *Sodeistvie* ("Assistance") and the Regional Voluntary Organization of Parents of Servicemen *Synov'ia* ("Sons"). The split seems to have occurred because of a clash of personalities, but other reasons not revealed to me may also have contributed. The distrust continues as the leaders of both groups expressed their criticism of each other to me. Despite this rivalry, the two groups espouse a strikingly similar ideology and partake in similar activities. The groups receive financial support from the municipal and regional administrations and maintain close contacts with government and military officials. Both *Sodeistvie* and *Synov'ia* have moved away from the "soldiers' mothers" name in order to be inclusive of all servicemen (not just soldiers) and of fathers (not just mothers). Yet in reality they are typical soldiers' mothers groups, made up overwhelmingly of middle-aged mothers fighting for the rights of their sons and other conscripts. At the time of my fieldwork, each group had only one male participant in the core group of a dozen activists. Five of the six activists I interviewed had joined because they and their sons had received the group's support in the past. All the women—again, except for one—had sons who had served in the military, and most sons had fought in the Chechen wars.

Sodeistvie defines its main goal as the "defense of life, health, honour, and dignity of servicemen and their family members, as well as military-patriotic and moral education of pre–draft age youth."[87] The group has offered legal help to conscripts and organized seminars in schools on conscripts' rights, such as the right to deferment on account of illness. Maria, an energetic member of the group in her late forties, explained: "For example, if a boy is sick and not in agreement with the decision of the draft commission, we explain to him how he can receive a deferment on the basis of the law."[88] At the same time, much of the group's work has been directed toward the support of veterans of the Chechen wars and their families. The slogans of the group's activities between 1997 and 2004 reflect the combination of rights-based and patriotic ideologies it employs: "We defend the defender of the fatherland," "A soldier also has rights," "I am still alive," "Into the third millennium without conscript slavery," "I serve Russia."[89] *Synov'ia* has pursued a similar two-pronged approach, with a focus on soldiers' rights as well as support for the troops. The main goals of the group, as defined by its leader, are to convey a minimum of legal knowledge to parents of conscripts, involve parents in the organization's work in military units, and "for our kids to serve under normal, dignified conditions—and not get killed."[90] The group's activities have included trips to Chechnya to deliver aid to the troops and assistance to veterans and deserters.[91]

Visits to military units make up a significant part of both groups' activities. Members participate in oath-taking ceremonies, military holiday festivities, and birthday celebrations that take place in military units. *Synov'ia* conducts surveys during its visits that inquire into conscripts' experiences, such as whether they have witnessed hazing, want to transfer from their subunit, have received their monetary allowance, or have any problems.[92] The goal is to help resolve any problems conscripts might face or help arrange for transfer to another unit. During the "Defend the Defender of the Fatherland" action, *Sodeistvie* members organized concerts and celebrations in military units and gave gifts of books, cassettes, and pictures to conscripts. When *Sodeistvie* visits military units to attend an oath-taking ceremony, the focus is on boosting the morale of soldiers and reinforcing the idea of military service as male duty.

Military Service and Masculinity

Sodeistvie is chaired by Ol'ga T., a pensioner who still works to make ends meet. She grew up in a military family and has two sons who completed military service. In our conversations, Ol'ga T. often replaced the words "sons" or "conscripts" with the phrase "defenders of the fatherland." This is an interesting semantic choice, as it indicates a hold-over of militarized Soviet gender ideology, which defined men as the defenders of the fatherland and military service as man's sacred duty and as an act of patriotism. Ol'ga T. considered it wrong that women have had to get involved in military affairs: "I consider the Committee of Soldiers' Mothers a black mark on the conscience of Russian generals, because not mothers but the Minister of Defense Ivanov and the generals should bring order into the army, so that our children could go there not to die, but to become men."[93] This quotation shows that the chair of *Sodeistvie* favors a traditional gendered division of civilian and military spheres, where mothers do not deal with military issues and sons can achieve manhood in the military. At the same time, she challenged militarized masculinity as she supported the abolition of conscription and the transition to an all-volunteer force. Ol'ga T. argued that individuals should have the right of choice: everyone has a different calling in life and should therefore be able to choose whether or not to join the military. As she put it: "Life is so short, and we have the right to decide how to spend it."⁹⁴ She also addressed the issue of systemic hazing conscripts face and saw professionalization as a way to resolve it: "It's more difficult to offend a professional, a professional can stand up for himself, a professional respects himself."⁹⁵ Here Ol'ga T. expressed a hope that the transition to an all-volunteer force may reduce the violations of soldiers' rights and rehabilitate militarized masculinity.

Other members of the group were less radical in their rejection of obligatory service. They strongly held on to Soviet notions of militarized masculinity that posited military service as an obligation of male citizenship and as central to male socialization. Liudmila first approached *Sodeistvie* when her son was conscripted and sent to fight in the first Chechen war. She found comfort in sharing her worries with other mothers, and has been active ever since. Liudmila considered military service as both men's duty and a rite of passage: "I believe it is the duty of men to defend us." And later she added: "The army gives the boys more independence, teaches them to take independent decisions in difficult situations. In the end, the boys get to know themselves as men. They learn to defend themselves, their relatives and close ones."⁹⁶ Liudmila argued that men should at least receive basic military training, if not be obligated to military service.⁹⁷ Another member of *Sodeistvie*, Maria, thought that "[t]he army shows a boy to what extent he is prepared for life." She referred to military service as "a big school of life," which echoed the famous Soviet slogan.⁹⁸ Maria's views on military service were linked to an essentialist definition of men's identities: "In every man there is a bit of war. I think that's programmed at a genetic level."⁹⁹ Maria moreover criticized mothers for failing to prepare their sons for the military. She described herself as patriotic and took pride in having raised a son who had willingly served. Maria commented that young men evade the draft because they are scared of *dedovshchina*, but also because they are anxious about leaving home. It is the role of mothers to prepare their sons for service: "If a boy arrives in the army and he doesn't like anything, doesn't know how to do anything, doesn't want to do anything, if he's a 'mama's boy'—of course, he'll find it hard. I consider that to be the fault of the mother. It would have been necessary to prepare the boy .... She had eighteen years to raise him into a strong, sporty young man, who would be prepared for service in the army."¹⁰⁰ Her argument recalls late-Soviet debates on the "feminization" of Soviet society, in which "overprotective mothers" were blamed for producing "infantilized sons" unfit for military service.¹⁰¹ Maria considered obligatory military service for men necessary, but conceded a place for an additional volunteer force.

Tat'iana N., in her sixties and in poor health, is the leader of *Synov'ia*. She believes that the professionalization of the military is very unlikely. In particular, she problematized the tensions between military service as a patriotic duty and as a source of income. As she argued: "A person who serves must have a feeling of responsibility and an ideology. A person who serves and receives money for it must serve not only for the money—he must have a feeling of the motherland in him and an understanding that money doesn't resolve everything. That's why I doubt that the draft will be abolished some day."[102] Tat'iana N. thus held on to the idea of military service as a duty of citizenship and an act of patriotism and was skeptical that it could be replaced by a market relation. Iulia, a member of *Synov'ia*, supported the idea of an all-volunteer force but also considered it unlikely. She had first turned to the group when her son went missing during his tour of duty in the second Chechen war. Iulia emphasized that people need to be given a choice whether or not to join the military and identified the lack of order in the military, rather than the military itself, as the main problem. At the same time, she stressed that military service is important to men's socialization: "There needs to be some kind of service: boys really do grow up in the army."[103] Another member of the group, Irina, has a son who had not yet reached draft age when I interviewed her. She joined the group because she wanted to support its cause. Irina spoke in favor of a professional force, because it would allow for better trained forces. She too emphasized the significance of military service to boys who want to become men: "And the army attracts guys who want independence, who—excuse me—have had enough of their mother's apron-strings and their mother's caring." Irina furthermore placed the value of military service in the context of fathers' absence and the high number of households headed by mothers.[104] Despite their acceptance of the need for a volunteer force, Iulia and Irina reproduced the idea that the military provides boys with a rite of passage to manhood.

As these examples show, the Samara soldiers' mothers embrace notions of militarized masculinity. They define men as patriotic defenders and military service as men's duty. These women also see the experience of military service as central to men's transition to adulthood. Nonetheless, they acknowledge the need for—or even support—moving to an all-volunteer force, but except for Ol'ga T. do not strongly oppose conscription.

Supportive Motherhood

The Samara soldiers' mothers rely on two notions of motherhood: responsible and supportive. The notion of responsible motherhood is much like the one employed by the CSMR and the SMSP. As the chair of *Sodeistvie* put it: "If I gave them life, then I must fight for that life and save my children."[105] This is the advice she gives other mothers: "Except for you, nobody needs your child. If you gave him life, then you have to fight for that life as best you can, with whatever means."[106] Here again we find the argument that women's reproductive abilities make them natural protectors of life. At the same time, notions of supportive (and patriotic) motherhood have an even more important place in the ideology and activities of *Sodeistvie* and *Synov'ia*. Tat'iana N., chair of *Synov'ia*, emphasized the support role that in her view mothers should perform for their sons:

> Mothers must help their sons. On the day of oath taking I always tell mothers: "You must not write your sons in the army letters about how everything is bad at home, how you're sick and don't have enough money . . . . Write him that everything is fine. The main thing is that he should serve calmly these two years, and it is precisely you who must help him in this respect. The mother is a foundation for her son, and he puts all his hope in you.[107]

In this quotation women's role as caregiver becomes implicitly militarized, because Tat'iana N. defines "good" motherhood as support for a son undergoing military service. This reflects a traditional patriarchal understanding of gender roles, in which women are assigned primarily to take on support roles. Tat'iana N. herself has two sons, both of whom served in the military and one of whom fought in Chechnya. Both her sons were apparently unfit to serve, but talked the military doctors into declaring them fit for service, because they strongly believed in their duty to serve. Tat'iana N. explained that she did not want to get in the way of her children's choices, but rather supported them in their decisions.[108] However, the chair of *Synov'ia* goes beyond supporting her conscript sons; she actively encourages young men to follow the call of duty. She described the following exchange:

> When they take the oath, I tell them: "Kids, you don't take the oath for one day and not for two years of service—you swear an oath to the motherland for your entire remaining life! Because, if necessary—even if you're in the reserve—you can at any moment go to defend the motherland."—They say: "And what's that—the motherland?" And I say: "The motherland—it's a mother, a house, a

piece of land on which your house stands, it's a father, children, brothers, and sisters. That's our Motherland."[109]

Tat'iana N.'s construction of the nation, "the motherland," is imbued with an ideology of domesticity and family often found in nationalist imagery. What is particularly interesting for the analysis of militarized masculinity, however, is the apparent disconnect between her understanding of patriotic duty and the confusion of young conscripts. While Tat'iana N. confidently reproduced a discourse of militarized patriotism, the conscripts she described lack clarity about the meaning of the motherland as a source of patriotism. This lack of clarity reflects the broader ideological crisis of state and society in post-Soviet Russia. It is in this context that the state has encountered serious challenges to its policy of conscription in the form of widespread draft evasion. As the above quotation illustrates, even those who serve might be less than certain about their role as "defenders of the motherland."

The crisis in the gendered ideology of patriotism is found not only in young men and their confused relationship to the motherland. Ol'ga T. pointed out that it is also present in how women think about themselves as mothers and about the relationship to their sons. In the words of the chair of *Sodeistvie*:

> Every mother is in shock. Well, I am a mother of two sons. I believe that when the boys grow up, the parents should truly experience a feeling of pride: the sons have learnt to stand on their own feet, have matured, have acquired manly professions. There should be pride in the fact that you brought up a defender of the fatherland. And our mothers experience fear, nothing but fear. I have already told you how people speak in our birthing centres: "I gave birth to a girl—she won't go into the army!"[110]

Ol'ga T. addressed the pride and social recognition that militarized patriotism promises and the lack thereof in post-Soviet Russia. Mothers may experience a sense of relief when giving birth to a daughter, knowing that she will not be conscripted. The situation within the Russian military deteriorated so far in post-Soviet Russia that it was hardly able to serve as a source of pride and patriotism. When conscripts ask, "[W]hat's that, the motherland?" and mothers are relieved to give birth to a girl rather than a future conscript, it reflects an inability to "consummate" the gender roles prescribed by militarized patriotism. In recognition of this very crisis, *Synov'ia* engages in activities centered around patriotic motherhood. The group organized a Mother's Day event, "You serve and we wait for you!" that took place in the House of the Officers. Mothers were awarded with certificates and plaques that acknowledged their role as "Mother of the Defender of the Fatherland." The chair of the group acknowledged that the goal of such activities was to shore up mothers' morale.[111]

While members of the CSMR and SMSP encourage mothers to keep their sons out of military service, the Samara soldiers' mothers encourage mothers to support their sons during military service and think of themselves as mothers of defenders of the fatherland. Instead of opposing the military, they decry the demise of militarized patriotism. Both Ol'ga T. and Tat'iana N. see the lack of patriotism and of prestige for the military as major problems for contemporary Russia. The women expressed this problem, at least partly, by reference to what they considered disrupted gender identities.

The Chechen Wars

The Samara soldiers' mothers did not publicly oppose nor support the wars in Chechnya. Instead they were opposed to their sons being sent to war. Irina, a member of *Synov'ia*, explained the organizing effort at the beginning of the first war. She corrected herself, when she was about to say that the group formed to oppose the military campaign (the Chechen war) to point out that the women were against the sending of children to war:

> It all began when Tat'iana N.'s son, younger son, served and fought in Chechnya. And she, who is a very patriotically inclined woman, gathered a meeting of women . . . parents, whose children were being sent to Chechnya in a regiment. She appeared on the radio and on television, simply as a voluntary organizer, without any kind of registration, she simply initiated . . . yes, initiated such a meeting that said, let's be against this camp[aign] . . . , against our children being sent to serve in Chechnya.[112]

This subtle differentiation is significant. In the case of the CSMR and SMSP discussed above, the private concern over sons' well-being translated into a public antiwar position. In the case of *Synov'ia*, opposition to the war was publicly expressed only in the form of opposition to the use of conscripts in the war. The speaker noted the patriotism of the group's leader, underscoring that it is not unpatriotic to be against the participation of one's children in war. As she continued her recollection, Irina acknowledged the leader's apparent fragility and femininity, and her inability to prevent that conscripts from Samara region were sent to fight in Chechnya: "Well . . . it didn't quite work out. In short, she [Tat'iana N.] put everything on her fragile womanly shoulders. And later, after that, she was in Chechnya more than once, she herself traveled to the places of military glory [*mesta boevoi slavy*]." Interestingly, Irina chose to speak of the places of "military glory" instead of the places of "military actions" [*mesta boevykh deistvii*], which is the phrase more commonly used in reference to the conflict zone. In doing so, she redefined the meaning of the conflict zone as a place of military glory. Irina used her recollection not to express opposition to the war, but rather to interpret the war through the lens of militarized patriotism. This is a semantic choice similar to the one discussed above, where Ol'ga T. repeatedly referred to defenders of the fatherland rather than to sons or conscripts.

However, the use of such discourse is not simply an unconscious reiteration of militarized patriotism. Instead, it fulfils two important functions for soldiers' mothers in Samara. First, it gives legitimacy to their demands when addressing state and military officials. A letter sent by *Sodeistvie* to a Duma deputy requesting better social protection for conscripts who are orphans serves as a good example. In the letter, the soldiers' mothers emphasize the difficult social situation these men live in after having "fulfilled their duty to the motherland."[113] They justify their appeal to the state for help on behalf of the men with a discourse of patriotic duty. Yet the use of patriotic discourse by the Samara soldiers' mothers must also be understood as an attempt to give meaning and value to the participation of their and other mothers' sons in the wars. This is particularly important considering the ideological crisis of the transformation period, which made it harder to justify the wars and citizens' sacrifices for them. As well, weak societal support for the wars created a difficult situation for those who had fought. Soldiers' mothers in Samara attempted to address the lack of support by both state and society by engaging in activities in support of the troops and veterans.

When conscripts from Samara were sent to fight in Chechnya, the soldiers' mothers focused their energy on delivering humanitarian aid to soldiers in the conflict zone, on helping veterans receive benefits, and on burying and memorializing the soldiers who were killed in the wars. *Synov'ia* delivered care packages to the soldiers in Chechnya with books, note pads, pens, razors, shampoo, soap, toothpaste, food products, and more.[114] *Sodeistvie* delivered humanitarian aid to the troops in Chechnya, set up a hot-line, and supported wounded soldiers returning from Chechnya. The chair of the group, Ol'ga T., was especially proud of her success in having a section of the main Samara cemetery designated for graves of soldiers who died in the Chechen wars (*chechenskii "kvadrat"*). She also lobbied the regional parliament to pass a law on compensation for parents of fallen soldiers, and helped arrange for financial support for local wounded soldiers.[115] The two groups cooperated with local organizations of veterans and families of fallen soldiers to have a town memorial erected in remembrance of servicemen who died in Chechnya. For some regional soldiers' mothers groups, the memorializing of dead sons has become the focus of their work, as Serguei Oushakine documents in his study of soldiers' mothers in Barnaul (Siberia).[116]

Despite their lack of public opposition to the wars and their support for veterans and their families, the Samara soldiers' mothers were critical of the war and felt a cross-ethnic commonality with Chechen mothers. With one exception, the interviewees did not blame the Chechens for the war. On the contrary, the chair of *Sodeistvie* argued:

> All these wars start from above.... Our sons died for these interests. I don't know anything about the men, but I met with the women, when we tried to pull the boys out of captivity. The women there fed our kids, tried to save them in the hospital. A mother always and everywhere remains a mother. If she kills someone else's child, she is no longer a mother, but a she-wolf, some kind of beast. A mother's heart will quiver no matter, it is not important who is bleeding—a Chechen or Russian.[117]

Ol'ga T.'s description of caring Chechen mothers is based on an essentialist notion of maternal responsibility for life. She asserts a universal motherhood that is rooted in biology and crosses ethnic and national lines. According to this logic, mothers everywhere act according to their "nature"; a mother who kills can no longer be considered a mother. That Ol'ga T. moreover considers mothers who kill not to be human recalls the Russian war discourse about Chechen fighters and suicide bombers as "beasts."[118]

Tat'iana N. saw mothers on both sides as the victims of the wars. Rather than viewing the Chechen wars as an ethnic conflict, the chair of *Synov'ia* insinuated that political or economic interests fueled the war:

> I have acquaintances in Tol'iatti who are Chechens, women and men, they are great people. They have absolutely no connection to the war. Women and children in Chechnya—what do they suffer for? Who needs this? Our mothers don't need this, the Chechen mothers don't need it. Our sons don't need this. But somebody needs this, somebody stirs it all up and sponsors it.[119]

Tat'iana N.'s question "Who needs this?" was echoed by the chair of *Sodeistvie,* who also questioned the purpose of the war: "I ask myself just one question: For what—so many deaths, so much grief, pain, broken families? This war sowed so much hate and many years will be needed for it to go away. It's not clear—what for?"[120] Both Ol'ga T. and Tat'iana N. agreed that political and economic interests were the true cause of the conflict, but rejected publicly speaking out against the wars.

In the end, both *Synov'ia* and *Sodeistvie* understand their work as a social service rather than as a political act, which is typical for the less radical branches of the soldiers' mothers movement.[121] *Sodeistvie* is affiliated with the Union of Committees of Soldiers' Mothers of Russia in Moscow. However, Ol'ga T. did not support the founding of the United People's Party of Soldiers' Mothers and disliked the fact that the CSMR was involved in electoral politics. Instead, she thought soldiers' mothers should focus on the kind of practical work that is needed to help military servicemen and their families.[122] *Synov'ia* is not a member of the CSMR, but rather maintains close relations with the Council of Servicemen's Parents, which is a state-sponsored organization under the leadership of Galina Shaldikova aimed at undermining the independent soldiers' mothers movement.[123] The ability of the Samara soldiers' mothers to take a critical political stance was also restricted because of the financial and other support (for example, office space) they received from the local and regional governments. Their politics were shaped by close cooperation with organizations of veterans and families of fallen soldiers (rather than human rights groups, as is the case with the CSMR and SMSP). Their agenda was moreover determined by the fact that a relatively large number of conscripts from the Samara region, including their own sons, fought in the wars.

Conclusion

To a certain extent, the soldiers' mothers groups in Moscow, St. Petersburg, and Samara have pursued the same agenda: the defense of soldiers' rights and opposition to the use of conscripts in the Chechen wars. Yet the effects of these groups on the politics of militarization in post-Soviet Russia were quite different. The independent soldiers' mothers in Moscow and St. Petersburg have contributed to the demilitarization of Russian society. They took on a leading role in opposition to the Chechen wars and demanded a political settlement of the conflict. The CSMR and the SMSP have argued for a new arrangement of military-society relations characterized by the rule of law, transparency, and civilian control. Both organizations reject military service as an institution of male citizenship and campaign for the abolition of obligatory service.

The Samara soldiers' mothers, in contrast, are more difficult to place on the spectrum of de- and remilitarization. In part, their activities support the process of demilitarization, such as when they defend the rights of conscripts or demand accountability from the military. Yet their morale-boosting of conscripts and their mothers, support for the troops, and memorializing of fallen soldiers contribute to the militarization of society. The Samara groups employ a gendered discourse of militarized patriotism that centers around men as the defenders of the fatherland and women as the supportive mothers of militarized men.[124] The Samara activists use this militarized, patriotic discourse to legitimize their demands, but also to give meaning to their sons' participation in the wars that they and many other Russians have considered senseless and needless. However, their politics also bolster the renewal of militarized patriotism and patriotic education that accompanied the second Chechen war. *Sodeistvie* mentions the military-patriotic education of predraft youth as one of its goals, even though it is an affiliate of the Union of Committees of Soldiers' Mothers of Russia, which is critical of militarized patriotism and opposes conscription. The leader of *Synov'ia* encourages young men to serve and their mothers to support them during military service. *Synov'ia* and the national Moscow-based Council of Servicemen's Parents with which it is affiliated deliver the very same message as the Russian state: that young men should follow the draft call. They work to convince individual men and their mothers to comply with the policy of mandatory military service. By this logic, responsible motherhood is not only about protecting the rights of draft-age sons but also about preparing sons for military service.[125]

The chair of the Council of Servicemen's Parents, Shaldikova, has polemically commented on the difference of her organization with the CSMR: "We do not exist in order to bring down the armed forces, but to restore understanding between families and the troops, to increase the significance of military service in society."[126] If we do not pay attention to mothers, we miss a crucial piece of the puzzle of militarized masculinity in post-Soviet Russia. Mothers have been at the forefront of the struggle to transform the relationship between the military, masculinity, and citizenship. Mothers have also been central to the state's efforts to increase draft compliance. As the analysis of the four groups shows, there is no straightforward relationship between motherhood and militarization. Rather, the soldiers' mothers movement is itself part of the gendered terrain on which militarization is contested *and* achieved in post-Soviet Russia. The next chapter, which explores the identities and representations of veterans of the Chechen wars, shows that veterans have a similarly complicated relationship to processes of de- and remilitarization. While veterans often uphold the link between masculinity and the military, their experiences during and after the wars expose the many challenges to militarized masculinity in post-Soviet Russia.

5 Veterans of the Chechen Wars
Questionable Warriors or a Model of Masculinity?

THE CHECHEN WARS were not popular among Russians.[1] Only during a brief phase early in the second war did a majority of Russians support the military operation. Not unlike the U.S. war in Vietnam, doubts about the wars expressed themselves in questions regarding the role of Russian troops in Chechnya. As Anna Politkovskaya eloquently put it during the second Chechen war: "We all tried to make sense of these soldiers and officers who, every day, were murdering, robbing, torturing and raping in Chechnya. Were they thugs and war criminals? Or were they unflinching champions in a global war against international terrorism using all the weapons at their disposal, their noble aim justifying their means?"[2] Representations of the men who fought on the side of Russian federal forces in the Chechen wars (*chechentsy*) often diverged from the ideal of the heroic warrior that is central to waging and justifying war. This chapter examines how society and the state in post-Soviet Russia have regarded and treated the *chechentsy*, and also explores what these men think about their war and postwar experiences.

While the ideology of militarism links men with the military and war and women with the need for protection,[3] there is no straightforward relationship between masculinity and war. The warrior remains a "key symbol of masculinity," and men's participation in war reproduces militarized masculinity in myriad ways.[4] However, war also exposes the challenges to militarizing men's identities as seen in draft evasion and the difficulties many countries face in recruiting soldiers. Some men struggle with their role as a warrior, and high rates of combat-related stress experienced by servicemen underscore the inherent fragility of militarized masculinity.[5] As the analysis in this chapter shows, contradictory processes of de- and remilitarization shape men's identities and notions of masculinity, both during and after war.

In the Soviet Union, veterans of the Great Patriotic War were revered as heroes and exemplary citizens. In contrast, Russians largely have not viewed the participants of the Chechen wars—estimated at 1.5 million in 2003[6]—as heroes or role models. More often, Russian soldiers fighting in the Chechen wars have been portrayed as questionable warriors and as men who upon their return do not sufficiently conform to hegemonic notions of masculinity. Multiple representations of the men who fought in Chechnya emerged as a result of soldiers' experiences and actions, societal perceptions, and state policy. The ideal of the heroic warrior was contested by four representations of the Russian serviceman: unwilling warrior, excessive warrior, fragile warrior, and unrecognized warrior. These representations contributed to the state's difficulties in waging war and mobilizing the population for war. Attempts to improve the image of the *chechentsy* during the second war focused on representing them as patriotic heroes and male role models that could inspire a new generation of soldiers.

Military Service and Male Identity

As previous chapters have shown, the idea that military service is a key component of male socialization and citizenship lost its currency for many in post-Soviet Russia. It is noteworthy that the importance of military service for male socialization retains its value among people who have worked or served in the military. The male veterans whose stories inform much of this chapter all considered military service to be central to their identities as men. I met these men through veterans' organizations in Samara, local soldiers' mothers groups, and other individual contacts.[7]

The adventure and romanticism of military life and the desire to protect the country had attracted some of the men to the military.[8] Others were drawn to the military because of a fascination with war games and military equipment that began in childhood.[9] The veterans stressed the role of the military as a key institution of male socialization, which helps men grow up, mature, and take on life's challenges. In particular, they linked military service to male independence and responsibility. Aleksei S. is a former regiment commander in Chechnya who retired because of a wartime injury and is serving as a member of a local draft board. He remarked about the part military service plays in the transformation of the conscript into a man:

> When he arrives in the army, he is pulled into the system—into the daily schedule, the military preparation ... and when he returns home after two years, he arrives as a man, prepared for any difficulties. He is able to take decisions, to understand tasks, and carry out any job. He left for the army as a boy after school, and there [in the army] they instilled independence in him.[10]

This view was echoed by conscripts who stressed the importance of the military for a man's development. One of the conscripts I interviewed, Anton, supported mandatory service explicitly for its role in forming men's character:

> [T]he army setting itself is a purely male collective, where a person for the first time in his life encounters serious, responsible things. In the army setting a person has the possibility to develop his character, to form his character. All in all, after the army people differ from their peers who did not serve. They relate to things with more responsibility.[11]

Even those men who considered an all-volunteer force as more effective for Russia's defense insisted that the military remains crucial for male socialization. As one Afghan war veteran put it, society requires an institution for the socialization of men: "The army instills in a man necessary male qualities: warrior qualities and survival techniques."[12] Vadim, who had been a conscript in the first Chechen war, said that the experience of military service radically changed him and was the key event in his transition to adulthood. He supported mandatory service, not only because it helped socialize men but also because it endowed men with the role of defender: "It is necessary that every young man feel his significance as defender of his motherland. That, in coming to serve in the army, he realize that he came here in order to protect his relatives and close ones. If you pay money for the defense of the motherland, that changes the goal of service."[13] Interestingly, Vadim acknowledged that the role of defender gives men a particular significance, and that it helps constitute their very identity as men. As these examples show, men who have served in the military are still influenced by notions of militarized masculinity regardless of the negative experiences they may have had as a result of hazing or participation in combat.[14]

Family ties play an important role in men's (and women's) decision to join the military. The veterans I interviewed who were professional soldiers all came from military families and had spent their adult life in the military. Two of the conscripts considered male family members who had previously served to be role models. Dmitrii, a shy and thoughtful man in his mid-twenties, acknowledged this: "Maybe what also influenced me was that my father was a military man, and my grandfather had served during the war [Great Patriotic War]."[15] Anton also mentioned his father's service as a factor in his own decision to heed the draft call, and pointed out: "The people I admire all served, why should I be different from them?"[16] These men saw their military service as part of an intergenerational family connection based on male kinship bonds.

Sometimes, however, men serve in the military or go to war not because of a male role model but because they need to "measure up" to other men. This dynamic played itself out among the police officers of the Interior Ministry forces who served in Chechnya. The Demos Center in Moscow conducted a survey among these veterans of the second Chechen war. The head of the center, Tanya Lokshina, commented on the machismo that drove new police personnel to Chechnya: "[G]oing to Chechnya is part of an initiation or compulsory socialization process for new police personnel. New rookies are surrounded by older police officers who had been to Chechnya. So, they don't want to fall behind, they want to be seen as tough."[17] Among these police officers, combat experience was an important step in being recognized as a "real man" (and a real police officer).

Military service and especially combat experience create new male bonds, as Anton commented: "I think that, from the guys who served with me, nobody regretted that he joined the army. It's been already ten years that I came back from the army, but we meet to this day, because we are a brotherhood, and these people became like family to me."[18] The military and combat reinforce separate gender spheres, in that they bring men together in a setting from which women are largely absent.[19] In some cases, fellow soldiers become closer to each other than they are to their own family, especially female members of their family. One conscript I interviewed (who had not served in Chechnya) underscored that he could not share his army experience with his mother. When telling me about the hardships and brutality of military life that bonded him to his fellow soldiers, he stopped to say: "I never told my mother any of the things I've told you, because she simply wouldn't understand. No woman could understand it."[20] For these male veterans, military and combat experience initiated them into manhood, reinforced old male bonds, and created new ones.

Unwilling Warriors: Soldiers' Morale and the Morality of War

The Russian-Chechen wars became associated with a representation of the post-Soviet Russian serviceman as unwilling warrior. The first war in particular revealed men who did not want to participate in the war and men who were morally opposed to or morally unprepared for war. When men do not embrace the masculinized task of soldiering and soldiers do not want to fight and kill, militarized masculinity itself and the state's ability to wage war are called into question. The unwilling warrior epitomized the diminished combat readiness of the armed forces in post-Soviet Russia.[21]

Militaries are essentially about training men (and some women) to kill other human beings. To be a soldier means to be prepared to commit extreme physical violence on behalf of the state.[22] Training men for war involves ideas of masculinity such as courage and bravery as well as the suppression of traits stereotypically associated with femininity such as emotion and compassion. "Suppressing emotions" and "mastering fear," as Joshua Goldstein explains, are key components in ensuring men's ability to fight.[23] Men who refuse to participate in war or are reluctant to kill risk being seen as cowards and failed men.

A significant number of officers did not willingly participate in the first Chechen war, which started in December 1994.[24] One of the veterans I interviewed is an example of an officer who fought despite his skepticism toward the war. Mikhail R. served as a commanding officer in the first war but was troubled by the moral dilemmas of his participation. He commanded troops in the storming of Grozny on New Year's Eve 1994–1995, during which his forces suffered huge losses, with 62 men dead and 147 wounded.[25] He described the night of December 31, 1994 as the worst day of his life and was especially distressed at having to hand over the bodies of dead soldiers to family members. Mikhail R. viewed the war as politically motivated and a result of the failure of the Russian and Chechen leadership to come to an agreement. He emphasized that he did not harbor negative feelings toward Chechens, whom he considered to be "like us." In his opinion, the war was "unjust" in that "every people should decide its own fate." He therefore considered it "morally impossible" to fight a war against fellow citizens and regarded the casualties on both sides as a "senseless loss." Mikhail R. also pointed out that the servicemen who participated in the New Year's Eve storming of Grozny did not have a desire to fight, but that it was more apparent the next time they entered Grozny.[26]

Military analysts linked the poor performance of Russian federal forces, especially in the first Chechen war, to inadequate military preparation and soldiers' lack of training.[27] The military and state leadership also had to contend with the low morale of soldiers.[28] As Lt. General Nikolai Tsymbal noted in February 1995: "Soldiers and even officers[,] that is, professional military men, are surrendering by the dozens. One can judge the morale of our troops from this alone."[29] At the early stages of the first war, conscripts were not properly informed about the mission and did not understand for what they were fighting.[30] One paratroop major expressed his doubts in the following way: "If it is a question of Chechen bandits, that would be a different matter . . . . But still, I don't know why we are here."[31] The second war had greater support among the general population than the first war, but morale among the troops was nonetheless low. To illustrate this point, Pavel Felgenhauer cites the example of troops who refused to follow their commander during the second Chechen war. In January 2000, troops of the Ministry of Internal Affairs abandoned commander General Mikhail Malofeev, who was killed as a result.[32]

The soldiers' lack of desire to fight was one of the main issues also mentioned by Aleksei S. He served as a regiment commander during the first Chechen war, and when asked about his war experience focused on the insufficient "moral" preparation of his soldiers. Aleksei S. described the soldiers under his command as fearful and overly concerned with the loss of human life, which undermined their ability to wage war. He acknowledged that experiencing fear is part and parcel of being a soldier and at times can be useful in war, but he emphasized that overcoming fear was crucial to a soldier's ability to carry out his task, which is to "defeat the enemy."[33] In regard to the issue of civilian deaths, Aleksei S. stressed that "good" soldiers must follow orders and leave the question of responsibility to the state. Soldiers should not worry about whether civilians might find themselves in the line of fire: "A prepared soldier must not think like that, he must fulfill his task. The state who sent the soldier there, must be responsible for that."[34] According to this officer, a soldier's role is simply to follow orders and not to ponder the morality of his or her actions.

A well-trained soldier will be able to commit physical harm when ordered.[35] According to Aleksei S., the Chechen wars signaled a change in the Russian soldier's ability to kill:

> Another important moral aspect is that a person who goes to war must be morally prepared for it. In which way? When he fires at a target, that is one thing. But when you have to fire at the enemy, at living people, that's a different matter. In Afghanistan our guys were prepared, but in Chechnya, unfortunately, they weren't.[36]

The contrast with the Soviet-Afghan war is significant. It draws our attention to the superior combat capability of the Soviet military and its soldiers compared with the post-Soviet period; it also underlines the different ideological contexts within which the two wars were fought. The Soviet-Afghan war took place during the final years of the Soviet Union, which was still a time of ideological certainty compared with the ideological crisis of the postcommunist years. As Dmitrii Pisarenko points out, soldiers fighting in Afghanistan generally believed the official reasons given for the war.[37]

In the Chechen wars the state was not able to impose a hegemonic interpretation of the wars, and societal uncertainty about the true reasons for the war translated into moral uncertainty for the soldiers fighting.[38] The following quotation from Arkady Babchenko's memoir of the wars captures this feeling of uncertainty: "We don't know what we are fighting for. We have no goal, no morals or internal justification for what we do. We are sent off to kill and to meet our deaths but why we don't know."[39] Justification of the wars was complicated by the fact that "the enemy" lives within the territory of the state. Chechens are citizens of Russia just like the members of federal forces fighting them. Babchenko quotes a fellow soldier who expressed this dilemma in the following way: "What I don't get is this: are Chechens citizens of Russia or enemies of Russia? If they are enemies then we should stop messing around and just kill the lot of them. But if they are citizens, then how can we fight against them?"[40] When the purpose of war is unclear and the enemy is ambiguous, soldiers' ability to fight and commit physical violence is in jeopardy.

The lack of certainty about the reasons for killing (and dying) makes evident the ideological, including gender, crisis surrounding these wars. The representation of Russian soldiers as unwilling warriors is part of the broader crisis of militarized masculinity in post-Soviet Russia. Significantly, the Russian public was sympathetic toward the men who refused to participate in war. In a poll conducted in early 1995, 74 percent of respondents thought that it was unfair to prosecute servicemen who had refused to serve in Chechnya.[41] Polls conducted during the second war show that a majority of the public supported draft evaders and deserters.[42] The state's waging of war in Chechnya was challenged by the men who dodged the draft, resigned from service, or showed emotions such as fear and empathy while serving, as well as by the public sympathy that these men held.

Excessive Warriors: Killing the "Other"

Running parallel to the unwilling warrior we find the representation of Russian servicemen as excessive warriors. International law and more specifically the Geneva Conventions outline the humanitarian treatment of prisoners and noncombatants, and set limits on the use of violence in war. Both Chechen wars saw widespread violence against civilians, as documented by journalists, scholars, and human rights activists. During the second war, however, there was an increase in its scale and systematic use.[43] The representation of the excessive warrior called into question the justness of the wars and of the actions of Russian servicemen in Chechnya, especially during the first war. The justification of the second war as a war against terrorism created greater acceptance of the excessive violence carried out by some Russian servicemen in Chechnya.

When soldiers commit violence against civilians rather than combatants, state and society may interpret their violent acts as excessive rather than heroic. Feminist scholars, however, argue that excessive violence perpetrated by soldiers is not incidental, but grows out of the very processes that help construct militarized masculinity. Sandra Whitworth notes that military training "involves selecting for and reinforcing aggressive behaviour."[44] Furthermore, the exaggerated ideals of manhood that are inculcated through military training often rely on the devaluation of (gendered, raced, and/or homosexual) "others." Excessive violence vis-à-vis the "other" is an outcome inherent to the making of soldiers.[45] "The other" is central not only to the making but also to the reproduction of militarized masculinity. For example, a clear-cut picture of the "other" in war helps justify more aggressive behavior toward the enemy.[46]

The close connection between militarized masculinity, excessive violence, and the construction of the enemy was borne out in my interviews. Dmitrii, who served as a volunteer during the second war, was critical of the excessive force used by some servicemen in Chechnya. He stated in regard to the war: "It left an unforgettable imprint. But I don't feel hatred towards the Chechen people. I think that a soldier should not do everything in cold blood. If it is necessary, then he must fulfill his task, but without pouring out negative emotions."[47] While he rejected excessive violence, he considered a certain level of force necessary for a soldier to carry out the task he has been assigned.

In contrast, my interview with Anton illustrated a less restrained approach. A conscript during the first war, Anton was displeased with what he considered an inadequate execution of the war by his commanding officers. He favored a more violent approach toward the Chechen fighters:

> Early on, I think it would have been necessary to do everything differently. It would have been necessary to be more tough, more brutal, simply to kill everyone, well, I don't mean to kill them all, but encircle the whole territory ... and announce, that whoever considers themselves a peaceful civilian should leave, we won't touch you ... and everyone who remains in the city, we'll consider a fighter.[48]

Anton blamed the military commanders for not permitting the soldiers to fight more brutally. He complained that the approach to the military operations in Chechnya was inconsistent. What bothered Anton most was the fact that federal forces lost the first war: "It hurts (*obidno*) that we weren't more brutal. War is war. People die."[49] Anton clearly was prepared to kill and commit the physical harm necessary to win the war. While Anton was careful to distinguish between Chechen combatants and civilians in the interview with me, a later conversation with him and his friends revealed that he held negative stereotypes toward Chechens, referring to them as "criminals" and "inferior beings."

Although Anton supported a more violent execution of the war, he was disappointed with the media portrayal of Russian federal forces as excessive warriors. In contrast to the many young men who have evaded the draft in post-Soviet Russia, Anton willingly embarked on his military service. He contrasted the voluntary nature of his service (despite being conscripted) with the media's negative depiction of his service:

> I went voluntarily, I did everything I was told, I fulfilled all the tasks. My help was really needed there, I could tell, I spoke to the local population. I was really needed. ... And what did I receive in turn? What did they show on TV? That we are invaders. Especially NTV. ...[50] That we were killing everyone .... That we were unhappy fighters wandering about. The information flow was such ... as if I was in the wrong. As if it hadn't been the country that sent us there, but we ourselves had decided to go. That of course was not easy. ... The state wants to forget about the war as quickly as possible. It will all come out eventually.[51]

In Anton's view, the media betrayed the soldiers. It represented them as excessively violent, did not acknowledge their sacrifice, and blamed them rather than the state for the violence in Chechnya. The public depiction of the first Chechen war deeply affected Anton's sense of identity regarding his wartime role. He felt that the war was important and his role in it necessary, but he did not see this publicly recognized. Framing relations to society and state in terms of betrayal is common among veterans, as was also seen in the U.S. war in Vietnam[52] or the Canadian Somalia affair.[53]

The Case of Colonel Budanov: War Criminal or Military Hero?

The themes of the "enemy" and of "betrayal" also appeared in the case of Colonel Iurii Budanov, a prominent example of the excessive warrior in the context of the second Chechen war. Colonel Budanov fought in both Chechen wars and received two Orders of Valour. On the night of March 26–27, 2000, Budanov, commander of the 160th tank regiment in Chechnya, entered the house of the Kungaev family in Tangi-Chu (southwest of Grozny) and seized eighteen-year-old Elza Kungaeva. She was taken back to the military unit for interrogation, during which Budanov strangled and killed her. A few hours later Colonel Budanov ordered three of his subordinates to bury the body outside the military's premises. Budanov was arrested the next day and later charged and tried in a court case that dragged on for over three years. In December 2002 the North Caucasus Military District Court acquitted Budanov on the grounds of temporary insanity. The Russian Supreme Court declared the verdict illegal,[54] and in July 2003 retried and sentenced Budanov to ten years' imprisonment for the abduction and murder of Kungaeva. Budanov was also stripped of his military rank and decorations. While there was strong evidence of Kungaeva's rape, this charge was dropped because of contradictory interpretations of whether the rape had taken place before or after her death.[55]

Budanov claimed to have arrested Kungaeva on evidence of her being a sniper and member of separatist forces in Chechnya. Budanov stated that he went into a rage and killed her during the interrogation after apparently realizing that she was responsible for the recent death of some of his subordinates.[56] While evidence for Kungaeva's involvement with separatist forces was never found, Budanov's supporters emphasized his status as military hero and constructed an image of Budanov as the victim of the state and court system. Demonstrations outside the court in Rostov-na-Donu were organized in support of Budanov, with placards reading such slogans as "Freedom for the heroic officer!" Polls conducted by local media found that 70 to 80 percent of local residents rallied behind Budanov.[57] Members of the far right and, to a lesser extent, the far left vocally demanded Budanov be set free. He received prominent support from Governor Vladimir Shamanov, a former general of the Chechen wars and previously Budanov's military superior: "I responsibly declare that Budanov is not guilty and it will in no way be possible to prove his guilt. I do not say this out of some feeling of corporate solidarity, but because there is hope for an unbiased court."⁵⁸ Shamanov interpreted Budanov's trial as "an ideological intervention of Western countries against Russia" and described him as "a true officer, commander, [and] the dignity of Russia."⁵⁹ Budanov also received support from the Committee of Soldiers' Mothers of Briansk and officers in Volgograd. The latter summed up the argument made by Budanov's supporters in the military: "[In] the person of Budanov they are judging the entire army for the fulfillment of its duty in Chechnya."⁶⁰ For his supporters, Budanov became a symbol for the military's place in society and its role in the Chechen wars. If Budanov was on trial, so was the military, and if his reputation was tarnished, so would be that of the military.⁶¹

The Putin administration and sections of the military leadership, however, wanted to use the Budanov case to improve the reputation of the armed forces in Chechnya. The chief of the Army's General Staff, Anatolii Kvashnin, commented after Budanov's arrest that "bastards like him have to be torn out of our Armed Forces by the roots."⁶² Arkadii Baskaev, a Duma deputy for the progovernment United Russia party who had served as a general during the first Chechen war, reacted to Budanov's sentencing in the following way: "It is because of people like Budanov that many started to say that all [of the servicemen] going through Chechnya are like this. I don't want to be added to that list. Therefore it's best that Budanov be fully held responsible for his actions."⁶³ Presidential aide Sergei Iastrzhembskii similarly reacted to Budanov's sentencing by stating: "The army is being cleansed of the people who have blackened its honor."⁶⁴ These prominent political and military figures were primarily concerned with the reputation of the armed forces and those who had served in the wars, and not with a deeper reflection on the use of violence against civilians in Chechnya.⁶⁵

Budanov's case is one of the few legal cases that the Russian state has brought against armed forces service personnel in Chechnya for crimes against civilians. As Usam Baysayev notes, the massacres in Alkhan-Iurt (November–December 1999), Grozny's Staropromyslovskii district (January–February 2000), Novye Aldy (February 2000), and many more war crimes remain to be investigated.⁶⁶ Budanov's strongest critics came from human rights groups, liberal-oriented journalists (such as Anna Politkovskaya), and the Chechen administration. Many observers have commented on the political reasons for Budanov's arrest and conviction, considering the lack of prosecution of other war criminals. Amandine Regamey argues that the charges against Budanov must be understood in the context of Putin's attempts to restore Russia's image abroad after his election in March of 2000.⁶⁷ Others have argued that Budanov's conviction was an important tool in increasing support among Chechens for the pro-Kremlin regime in Grozny.⁶⁸

Public criticism of Budanov was muted, and there were few public calls for his conviction. While public opinion was generally supportive of Budanov, Regamey points out that it is hard to distinguish public indifference from compassion for Budanov.⁶⁹ A VTsIOM poll conducted among 1,600 Russians in 2002 found that 32 percent thought that "the Budanov case was spun with the goal of compromising the Russian army," and 24 percent agreed with the statement that "Budanov killed the Chechen girl when he found out that she was a sniper."⁷⁰ Only 14 percent of respondents thought that "Budanov raped and killed the Chechen girl."⁷¹ As one observer writes, it is striking that more than two-thirds of respondents were able to pick a position, despite the fact that little information on the case was making its way into the public realm.⁷² Only 15 percent claimed to have heard nothing about the case, and an equal share had difficulty picking one of the versions. Public opinion was divided on whether Budanov's actions were a "random act, committed in a state of nervous break-down" (44 percent) or "a typical occurrence, which reflects the situation and morals of participants in military actions in the conditions of the terrorist war in Chechnya" (36 percent).⁷³ At the same time, 29 percent of respondents thought that Budanov's sentence should be reduced under consideration of the war context and his military service, and 19 percent felt that he should be "acquitted, because in the fight with bandits all means are justified."⁷⁴ Only 15 percent of those polled favored the harshest possible sentence for Budanov.⁷⁵

In general, more compassion was extended to Budanov than to the victim, and this was achieved by falsely portraying the young Chechen woman as a combatant. The misrepresentation of the victim fit well into the dominant "war on terror" discourse during the second Chechen war.⁷⁶ Mikhail Sokolov argues that people's ability to decide on a true version of the case was a result of grafting the story onto existing stereotypes of Chechens.⁷⁷ Budanov came to represent the military and with it the Russian nation, while Kungaeva was linked with the Chechen fighters despite the lack of evidence. The war on terror frame was powerful enough to marginalize more important questions such as the victim's and her family's rights or the application of the Geneva Conventions. The debate instead focused on the meaning of Budanov's conviction to the national psyche in the context of a war on terror. As one participant in a Russian-language BBC online forum commented: "If the motherland sends a soldier to war and then judges him for [his participation in] this war, then it stops being a motherland."[78] In this view, the state's loyalty toward its soldiers is elevated over the state's obligations to enforce domestic and international law. The Budanov case came to be seen as one of the state's betrayal of its soldiers rather than what it really was about—namely, human rights and war crimes.

The issue of Kungaeva's rape, and of sexual violence in war more generally, was sidelined in the public debate on Budanov and dropped from the legal case. However, the fact that Budanov went after a young woman might not have been a coincidence. Sergei Markelov, the Kungaev family lawyer, explains:

> And did Budanov go looking for a female sniper, or was he just looking for a pretty girl? . . . If so, then the idea that Budanov was a hero . . . all that ideology, is completely beside the point. It's no good the psychiatric report basing all its conclusions on his "heroism" and "vengeful feelings towards the sniper." The more so since there are tell-tale references in the file to numerous earlier "women of the colonel." "The Commander has brought a woman back again" is a quote from the testimony of one of the soldiers at the preliminary investigation.[79]

While Budanov was sentenced for the abduction and murder of Kungaeva, the rape of a civilian by a military man was not problematized. This can be interpreted in a number of ways. Either rape was seen as a "normal" part of men's excessive violence in war, or the issue was seen as too damaging to the Russian military and/or to Russian-Chechen relations. That the problem of sexual violence was not put on the agenda is also likely a result of the weakness of the contemporary women's and human rights movements in Russia, as Politkovskaya notes the lack of protest from women's or human rights groups when rape charges against Budanov were withdrawn.[80]

Feminist scholars and international and nongovernmental organizations have documented the greater insecurity civilian populations and especially women face during military conflicts, and that sexual violence is endemic to war.[81] While there are numerous causes for the higher incidence of rape during war,[82] the masculinized military culture itself contributes to men's sexual violence. Cynthia Enloe has suggested that the pressures soldiers experience "to conform to the standards of 'masculine' behavior" and to prove their manhood among fellow soldiers may encourage men to commit, or participate in, rape.[83]

In the case of the Chechen wars the documentation of sexual violence against women has been hampered by two factors, according to Andy Knight and Tanya Narozhna: the Russian government's suppression of this information, and the taboo and stigma attached to rape in Chechen society. One of the few available surveys, based on interviews with thirty-five Chechen asylum seekers in England (nineteen female and sixteen male), documented that sixteen of the women and one of the men reported to have been raped during the war. Thirteen of the rapes were allegedly committed by Russian soldiers, three by Russian police officers, and one by Chechen separatist forces.[84] While this represents just one survey, the fact that sixteen out of the nineteen women interviewed reported to have been raped indicates a staggering level of sexual violence in Chechnya.

Representations of the excessive warrior have the potential to destabilize militarism, as they highlight the violence and brutality of war. The excessive warrior contributed to the fact that the Chechen wars were generally not popular or considered just, especially during the first war. In the second war, arguments about the terrorist enemy, betrayal, and a "few bad apples" sidelined the important issue of war crimes and sexual violence perpetrated by Russian servicemen in Chechnya. Neither of the wars led to a deeper public reflection on the excessive violence of militarized men.

Fragile Warriors: The "Chechen Syndrome" and Masculinity

The prevailing representation of the Chechen war veteran is of a person who suffers from the "Chechen syndrome." The media, society, veterans' and soldiers' rights groups, and sometimes veterans themselves use the term to describe a cluster of problems associated with the transition from combat to civilian life of armed forces personnel who served in Chechnya. As in other wars, many veterans experienced extreme levels of fear and stress during combat that led to post-traumatic stress disorder (PTSD). The Chechen syndrome entails psychological and medical problems such as depression, anxiety, insomnia, as well as alcohol and drug abuse.[85]

Whitworth has examined the specifically gendered aspects of PTSD. She argues that there are inherent contradictions in militarized masculinity between the warrior image and men's actual identities that contribute to PTSD. The emotions some men experience in war such as anxiety, shame, and pain lay bare the contradictions and inherent fragility of militarized masculinity. Such emotions are usually associated with femininity and seen as contrary to the image of the tough military man.[86] On the other hand, men suffering from combat stress often deal with their condition by engaging in practices that Tracey

Xavia Karner has called "toxic" masculinity: alcoholism, drug abuse, and aggressive behavior.[87]

The Chechen wars increased academic and societal interest in PTSD in Russia, as Russian troops who fought in the Chechen wars were seriously affected by combat-related stress. There are no available statistics on the overall number of Chechen war veterans suffering from the stress-related effects of combat, although the results of various medical studies indicate that as many as two-thirds of service personnel may have experienced combat-related psychological problems. Timothy L. Thomas and Charles P. O'Hara summarize the results of a Russian study conducted among 1,312 servicemen four months after the start of the first Chechen war:

> [Some] 28% were healthy and the other 72% had some type of psychological disorder symptoms, such as insomnia, lack of motivation, high anxiety, neuro-emotional stress, tiredness, and hypochondriacal fixation (when a soldier is primarily concerned about cardiovascular functioning. Frequently, this is expressed as concern about heart attacks, difficulty in breathing, and may be diagnosed as a panic attack).[88]

Another study, which followed 453 veterans of the first Chechen war, concluded that only 16.6 percent of servicemen did not develop signs of combat-related stress. The rest of them suffered from varying degrees of "maladaption," ranging from psychological stress reactions, pathological psychological reactions, post-traumatic stress disorder, to pathological psychic disorders.[89] Media reports indicate that a majority of veterans from the second war have also suffered from the Chechen syndrome.[90] While there are no conclusive numbers on PTSD among veterans, it is evident that a large proportion of veterans experienced psychological problems as a result of their participation in combat.

The abuse of alcohol is one of the main ways soldiers in Russia as elsewhere dealt with the fear and stress of combat.[91] As one lieutenant colonel put it during the first war:

> Only alcohol helps relieve the tension. We drink before we go into combat, during the fighting and afterwards. There's no other way to ease your state of mind. But the most intense moments of the fighting stay in your memory anyway. A mine explosion, a pile of maimed soldiers. Trees looking like New Year's trees, only hung with scraps of clothing and blown-off arms and legs.[92]

Alcohol has long been used by soldiers during war, whether to deal with the stress of combat, the pain of being away from home, or to socialize with fellow soldiers. In his memoir, Babchenko describes the importance of sharing alcohol (and cigarettes) among his group of fellow soldiers. He also underlines the constant and exhausting fear soldiers in the combat zone experienced.[93] While alcohol helps deal with fear and homesickness, the experience of fear manifests itself in sickness after return from combat: "Sickness starts later, when you get home. Your fear leaves you in screams and insomnia at night, and the tension ebbs. Then war crawls out of you in the form of boils, constant colds, depression and temporary impotence, and you spend six months coughing up the recon's diesel soot."[94] Both quotations illustrate the fragile figure of the warrior, dependent on alcohol and unable to cope with the effects of combat.

My interview with Anton made evident the tensions between the tough warrior image and combat-related stress. He began his recollection of returning home after serving as a conscript in Chechnya like this: "I wouldn't say that I lost my mind ... or that I saw some things. Nothing especially bad ... but of course, it affected me."[95] Anton emphasized that he did not suffer from combat-related stress. On the contrary, he argued that the war made him realize that he was well suited to deal with extreme situations. After making this assertion, he suddenly recalled: "I can't at all watch war movies, not one. Before the army, I greatly enjoyed watching war movies. Now, as soon as the movie starts, I'm in tears, I'm crying."[96] Although Anton viewed his own identity in terms of a tough version of militarized masculinity, he had almost forgotten to mention the more "feminine" emotional side of his postwar life. The denial of combat-related psychological problems is not uncommon among veterans. In part it is linked to notions of masculinity that encourage men to be strong and handle their war memories stoically rather than seek help.

Another interviewee openly acknowledged his experience of combat-related stress and the difficulties he experienced in adjusting to civilian life. Mikhail R., a commanding officer during the first war, framed the effects of the war on his own life in terms of the Chechen syndrome. This is how he explained its meaning:

> After a person has found himself in an extreme situation such as war he psychologically views life differently. Everything is divided into black and white, into true and false. The person develops a feeling of special justice and others no longer understand him. He turns inward and this process often involves the abuse of alcohol. This person now feels the need to speak the truth about anything he perceives as unjust, which creates conflict with others.[97]

This quotation speaks to the estrangement veterans experience when returning to civilian life, and the perceived incompatibility between military and civilian values. Veterans argue that civilian life is less sincere and truthful and that those who have not served in war can never truly understand them.[98] Not unlike other veterans, such as U.S. Vietnam veterans, Chechen war veterans describe their psychological difficulties as linked to the lack of understanding they encounter upon their return home.

The rejection veterans feel from society has a gender and sexual aspect. The social conflicts that arise from combat-related stress are most intimately experienced by family members, especially the wives of veterans. A study conducted by the Demos Center in Moscow among policemen who had served in the second Chechen war and their spouses illustrates some of the problems that arose after men's return from the war. These included the estrangement couples experienced and the need to get accustomed to each other once again, especially if the tour of duty lasted longer than three months. Some men's newly acquired or increased abuse of alcohol and other intoxicants led to conflicts within the family. Relationships became aggravated when men felt that their spouses could not understand what they had gone through in Chechnya. At least one woman mentioned that her husband had become more aggressive since his tour of duty. Another interviewee observed that it is often the wife who had to compensate for the lack of medical and psychological rehabilitation her husband received from the state.[99] Another woman commented that her husband had turned inward and cut himself off from the family: "He sits in front of the TV for hours, looks in front of himself, doesn't talk to anyone, doesn't move. And at night he twitches! In the beginning I would jump in front of him and try to distract him . . . . And nothing helps, as if he doesn't see me. I then scream: 'I'm also a human being! You don't even talk to me!'"[100] Divorce rates are especially high among policemen who went on multiple tours of duty to Chechnya. One employee at a social rehabilitation center noted that in his experience men in the special forces (such as SOBR and OMON) were married three or four times and that "the families of OMON officers fell apart 80% of the time."[101] On the other hand, the Demos Center study found that some men began to value their families more after their tour of duty.[102] As a result of the study, the center recommended shorter tours of duty, a consideration of a man's family situation in the decision to post him to Chechnya, and an inclusion of family members into rehabilitation programs.[103]

Veterans experience problems readjusting to family life, but also in establishing new relationships. Unmarried veterans complain that it is difficult to find a woman who will put up with a Chechen veteran. As Vadim puts it in a documentary on the Chechen syndrome: "If you turn up in company, girls in particular are very wary. They think that people who have come back from Chechnya are really messed up, that we are grenades waiting to explode. But then, when they get to know us better they realized we are ... real men."[104] This quotation points to the fact that Chechen war veterans are generally not seen as desirable men, although Vadim insinuates that he is more of a man than someone who has not fought in war.

PTSD furthermore poses problems for veterans who try to enter or re-enter the workforce and perform the "masculine" role of breadwinner. As masculinity in post-Soviet Russia has become more closely tied to a man's success in the market economy, veterans' economic marginalization makes it difficult for these men to live up to prevailing notions of masculinity. Difficulty finding a job after returning from combat service is a frequent complaint among veterans of the Chechen wars. Mikhail R. argued that veterans' strong sense of right and wrong makes it difficult for them to fit into a collective such as a workplace.[105] However, most veterans describe the problem as one of potential employers' prejudice against them. This prejudice consists of labeling Chechen war veterans as being psychologically not in order.[106] As one veteran who is featured in a documentary on the Chechen syndrome remarks: "When they find out you've served, they say you're not suitable. That happened to me. Because I was in combat in the North Caucasus, people say I'm psychologically disturbed."[107] Soldiers' mothers in Samara complained that veterans were not treated fairly on the job market and were forced into criminal structures or the drug trade.[108] Finding work for former soldiers was one of the areas of activity of the Samara soldiers' mothers group *Sodeistvie*. Maria, a member of the group, explained:

> After the first Chechen war guys had a hard time adapting. Nobody wanted to hire them: they had seen blood and had nightmares.... It was considered that they are still at war and can't think of anything else.... Then societal organizations such as ours began to raise the issue that veterans of armed conflicts need to be hired. Otherwise what happened is that such guys would "lose" themselves after returning from the army: there's no work, no money. They began to drink and take drugs.... We helped them find work. Some special security firms were created for them.[109]

In Russia's postcommunist economy militarized skills are in demand, and the security sector seems to be one niche into which veterans can break. While former soldiers may find work in the private security industry, the state security sector is more likely to reject them.[110] A survey conducted in 1996 among veterans of the first war found that more than 50 percent were intent on working in a private security firm or the state security structures.[111]

Another way veterans have responded to the difficulties of adapting to civilian life is to find comfort within a community of brothers-in-arms or to return to the war zone. One survey among veterans of the first war found that 75 percent of them expressed a desire to return to Chechnya or another war.[112] Babchenko writes about his decision to volunteer in the second war after having served as a conscript during the first war:

> There were many thousands of us, ex-soldiers, who returned to that second war after the first. I have no answer to why I went there again. I don't know. I just couldn't help it. I was irresistibly drawn back there. Maybe it was because my past was there, a large part of my life. It was as if only my body had returned from that first war, but not my soul. Maybe war is the strongest narcotic in the world.[113]

The nostalgia for combat is also linked to the belief that men at war share a close community and comradeship not found in civilian life.[114] As Andrei Grebennikov, research psychologist at the North Caucasus Military Institute, explains: "They share the same bowl, the same mug, the same roof over their heads, and the comradeship of brothers-in-arms. But out there, in civilian life, it's every man for himself."[115] Significantly, the return to war and a community of military brotherhood also offers an opportunity for recognition of veterans' masculinity by fellow soldiers. In contrast, veterans' experiences of postwar civilian life demonstrate the difficulties of living up to notions of masculinity, whether to the militarized ideal of tough and heroic warrior or the market-based ideal of male breadwinner.

The Chechen syndrome may well be aggravated by the ambiguous nature of the Chechen wars in Russian society. As Whitworth notes, U.S. studies have found that "the incidence of PTSD appears to be higher among soldiers who participated in armed conflicts that resulted in an ambiguous military outcome, or in which they faced a less appreciative societal homecoming at the end of the hostilities."[116] Writing toward the end of the first war, Pisarenko argued that the Chechen war would create a more serious "syndrome" than the Soviet-Afghan war.[117] He linked this to the fact that for those fighting in

Afghanistan "the sense of the war still held—propaganda still worked."[118] The author viewed societal opposition to the Chechen war as the main factor aggravating the Chechen syndrome. He asked how a young conscript would perceive his situation upon return: "Either he must consider himself wrong that he fought in Chechnya, or he must stand in opposition to society itself."[119] While only 5 to 7 percent of Afghan war veterans kept their service in Afghanistan a secret, this is apparently more common among Chechen war veterans according to the author. In addition, the Chechen syndrome is aggravated by the fact that the soldier is "fighting on the territory of his own country."[120] And finally, Pisarenko noted that soldiers were returning to a society undergoing postcommunist transition and racked by instability itself, which "appears as a mini-model of a war situation."[121] Afghan war veterans in contrast returned to a relatively stable and calm society that facilitated their transition to civilian life, with the exception of those who came back in the late 1980s.[122] Thus the extent to which servicemen can recover from the combat experience depends not only on proper rehabilitation but also on the societal context, which includes societal views of militarized men.

Military psychologist Aleksandr Kucher is critical of what he sees as common societal perceptions of Chechen war veterans as "murderers, rapists, looters, sexual perverts, [and] the psychologically abnormal."[123] In 1997 he argued that such attitudes make it harder for veterans to readjust to civilian live. He therefore called for a change of attitude toward veterans: "A decisive factor is the moral atmosphere in society in relation to those returning from war. What is required is universal attention, respect, and recognition."[124] While such treatment might help veterans, it also does not allow for a critical engagement with the role federal forces played in the wars.[125]

During the second war, greater support for military action in Chechnya was not enough to turn around the prevailing societal view of veterans. As one journalist put it in early 2000, "[S]ociety subconsciously expects the return not of heroes, but of potential criminals, homeless, [and] alcoholics—in one word, of people living on the fringes of society (*marginaly*)."[126] The association of veterans with the Chechen syndrome continued, and the state's reluctance to grant these veterans official veteran status further aggravated their social and economic marginalization.

Unrecognized Warriors:
Respect and Benefits for Militarized Men?

Chechen war veterans had a difficult time being legally recognized as veterans and are still not recognized as veterans of *war*. The state called the first war a campaign for the restoration of constitutional order and the second war a counterterrorist campaign. While the state refuses to recognize the Chechen campaigns as wars, it is important to note that those who fought on the side of federal forces refer to them as wars.[127] Chechen war veterans fell between the cracks, as the law "On Veterans" (1995) recognized only veterans of the Great Patriotic War and "participants in combat operations on the territory of other countries" such as veterans of the Soviet-Afghan war.[128] A letter written by V. Kotliarova inquiring about benefits for her son who fought in the second Chechen war was typical of people's confusion about the status of Chechen war veterans: "My son fought in Chechnya and returned home broken. He can't work, and we don't have a father. I went to the various authorities, so they would help us to at least survive. But it turns out, he has no right to in-kind benefits.[129] They say that what is going on in Chechnya is not a war. How is that to be understood?"[130] In 2002 the law "On Veterans" was finally amended to give Chechen war veterans the status of "veterans of combat operations." In line with the amendments, veterans of the Chechen campaigns became entitled to a number of special benefits such as 50 percent discounts on social housing, free prescription drugs, free public transit, and more.[131] The new law went into force in January 2004, but veterans report that it is hard to access the benefits.[132] That the masculinized task of soldiering and fighting in war is not valued by the state and backed up by a functioning and well-funded benefits structure is one aspect of the broader post-Soviet crisis of militarized masculinity.

Among Chechen veterans the view is widespread that the state has not sufficiently acknowledged their service through social welfare provisions.[133] All my interviewees complained about the lack of adequate benefits for veterans and linked it to insufficient respect for militarized men in today's Russia. Anton, who had served as a conscript in Chechnya, remarked: "I wouldn't say that people relate negatively to those who served in the army. But I think that people who served are worthy of more attention, are worthy of more respect and I would like this to be reflected in a concrete way."[134] A similar point was made by Dmitrii, a former contract soldier in Chechnya, who commented:

The state did not treat my service with the worth it deserved. I am not only talking about myself, but also about many other people. People who choose service in the army for their whole life go for many deprivations, and the state should relate to them with respect. The minimum should be the allocation of housing, and there are big problems with this. I'm not even speaking of vacations, sanatoriums, and other things.[135]

Both men argued that to show respect to former service people means to provide them with adequate social welfare.[136] They underscored the necessary material basis for a revival of militarized masculinity in post-Soviet Russia.

In order to address these socioeconomic challenges, veterans of the Chechen wars have followed in the footsteps of previous generations of veterans and created organizations to promote their specific interests. Mikhail R. is the chair of one of the veterans' organizations in Samara, the Regional Oblast' Organization of Participants of Combat Operations in Chechnya and Dagestan *Pamiat'* ("Memory"). The organization was founded in 1997 to address the economic problems families face resulting from the loss of a breadwinner, who has either been killed or is unable to work. Mikhail R. described his own socioeconomic challenges managing on a military pension that pays only for his apartment rent but is not sufficient to cover living costs. As he pointed out, it is very difficult to find a job when all you have is a life of military service, even with his two diplomas of higher education. Veterans and their families have turned to *Pamiat'* for material assistance and psychological support. The organization's attempts to influence state policy toward veterans were unsuccessful, according to Mikhail R. This was in part due to the financial crisis of the local government itself, and the fact that these issues of social policy needed to be resolved at the federal level. He also mentioned that while many Chechen veterans' organizations existed in Samara, none of them had any real effect or influence. Attempts to unite the various organizations in Samara apparently failed, and the movement remained fragmented.[137]

Another Samara veterans' organization was founded in 1999 to address the social challenges of veterans and invalids of local wars and retired servicemen. The main issue this organization deals with is the lack of social housing and benefits. Its chair, Pavel, asserted that the rights of servicemen have been completely violated. He linked the fact that Russia's younger generation does not want to serve in the military with the social problems facing servicemen. He framed the problem as one of dignity: "The problem is the lack of pension provisions, which do not allow a retired officer to live in dignity."[138] He argued that the demands of former armed forces personnel are within the frame of their legal entitlements, but that the state has not responded to them in a positive way. That militarized men are no longer valued as they were during Soviet times also affects their status as head of the family. Pavel contrasted the lack of response from the state with the Soviet era:

> The Soviet government made many mistakes, but at the same time it cared about us professional officers. It provided us with housing and our wives, whenever possible, with work. Our kids always went to kindergarten or school and we knew that they had the possibility of receiving free higher education.[139]

Pavel underlined the importance of a material basis for a functioning ideological structure: "When I defended my country [in Soviet times] I had ideas in which I believed. But I don't understand how one can believe in any ideas today. We cared about our soldiers, and the state cared about our homefront."[140] Pavel was decrying the breakdown of the social contract between the state and armed forces personnel that had previously endowed militarized men with a privileged position.

Women's status as the wives of militarized men also suffered as a result of the lack of recognition and state support for veterans. Valentina is the chair of the Samara Committee *Chechnya*, an organization of widows and families of fallen soldiers founded in 1996. The organization began to take shape when she lived at the garrison town located outside of Samara after her husband's death in the first Chechen war. There were twelve widows and one set of parents who had lost their husbands/son in Chechnya. She recalled: "Come on, I said, let us get together, let us support each other, resolve our problems."[141] The group started to address the local administration and request its assistance. The Committee *Chechnya* aims to improve the lives of families of fallen soldiers in three primary ways: by securing housing and health benefits for the families and education for the children. In addition, the committee works on legal reform to ensure that widows and family members of fallen soldiers who fought in Chechnya are entitled to benefits. Valentina also tied the question of benefits to the issue of dignity: "The laws have not yet been brought to the level, at which families of the deceased can live with dignity. Why, for example, do widows get married for a second time? Because it is very difficult to raise kids by oneself."[142] In her opinion, all problems arise due to the lack of adequate laws, and she sees legal reform as the most suitable approach to resolving the difficulties that members of her organization encounter. However, even legal recognition has not necessarily brought Chechen veterans the economic benefits they believe they deserve, as claiming benefits involves a complicated bureaucratic process.

Representations of Chechen war veterans as fragile and unrecognized warriors are indicative of the crisis of militarized masculinity in post-Soviet Russia. Neither of these representations is useful to a state waging war. The Russian state has only in limited ways provided the resources needed to address the many problems Chechen war veterans face. The state has, however, taken an active interest in countering these negative representations of fragile and unrecognized warriors as part of its broader agenda of militarized patriotism.

Chechen War Veterans:
Role Models of Patriotism and Masculinity

During the second Chechen war, the political and military leadership as well as some veterans' groups attempted to improve the image of the *chechentsy* by portraying them as patriotic heroes and male role models. The government's emphasis on militarized patriotism led to the introduction of a state patriotic education program, as discussed in Chapter 3. One of the goals of the patriotic education program is to prepare children for military service and the defense of the country. Elisabeth Sieca-Kozlowski argues that the patriotic education program employs a pedagogy that "glorifies the soldier-hero and the feats of strong and courageous men, but also close friends and relatives, and fathers."[143] The state has actively encouraged Chechen (and Afghan) war veterans to participate in the program, in order to replace the dwindling number of World War Two veterans.[144] Veterans are seen as an integral part of the patriotic education classes and clubs that have sprung up across Russia, and are invited to give lectures and teach basic military skills.[145]

The celebration of male veterans as heroic warriors and teachers of patriotism reinforces militarized citizenship and its gendered assumptions. When veterans serve as a model of masculinity, there is usually not much room to question militarism or the myth of protection that posits men as the militarized protectors of women. Through their involvement in military-patriotic education, Chechen (and Afghan) veterans serve as a model for the younger generations, just as veterans of the Great Patriotic War served as a model to their parents.[146] A documentary on the Chechen syndrome features a Chechen war veteran, Vadim, who was not able to find work after his return from Chechnya but now leads the patriotic education program in a local school in Yaroslavl'. The gendered nature of the program becomes evident when the (female) principal of the school remarks on the positive influence Vadim has on the children, especially considering that many of them are brought up by single mothers and lack male role models.[147] This remark again harks back to late Soviet debates that emphasized the importance of military service to male socialization in the context of the apparently growing "feminization" of Soviet society.[148] The incorporation of Chechen war veterans into patriotic education helps both to rehabilitate the image of *chechentsy* and to revive the link between masculinity, military service, and patriotism in society more generally. It does not offer a space for critical reflection on Russia's recent wars, but rather replaces the complexity of veterans' experiences with the more straightforward task of preparing Russia's youth for the event of another war. The possible disruption of militarized masculinity through the experiences of Chechen war veterans is negated when veterans participate in the reproduction of militarized patriotism.[149] Sieca-Kozlowski argues that veterans' integration into military-patriotic education can also be seen as a state tool to better control veterans, in particular in view of their involvement in violent and criminal acts upon their return from the war zone.[150]

During my fieldwork in Samara, I found that veterans' groups emphasized a representation of veterans as patriotic heroes and defenders of the motherland. This entailed a focus on veterans' sacrifice and the memorializing of fallen soldiers. By the end of 2008, 250 citizens of Samara Oblast' serving in the Chechen wars had been killed.[151] Both the Committee *Chechnya* and *Pamiat'* were instrumental in having a memorial erected for the fallen soldiers. The memorial is dedicated to Samara veterans who died in local wars, including the Chechen wars. Other veterans' groups and the soldiers' mothers were also involved in this process. Mikhail R. named the construction of the memorial as his organization's main success, considering the lack of success it had in gaining improved financial benefits for veterans. To a certain extent, memorializing fallen soldiers and acknowledging the sacrifice of veterans took the place of the struggle for adequate socioeconomic recognition. However, veterans' groups also used the representation of Chechen war veterans as patriotic heroes in order to further their goal of improved benefits. They hoped to secure better material support for their members by appealing to what veterans had done for the state and framed the issue in terms of a social contract between servicemen and the state. The chair of the Committee *Chechnya* said about the

Representations of Russian Veterans of the Chechen Wars

Representation	Description
Unwilling Warriors	Resignations and draft evasion; low morale among troops
Excessive Warriors	Violence, including sexual violence, against civilians, perpetration of war crimes
Fragile Warriors	Experience of post-traumatic stress disorder, difficulties reintegrating into society ("Chechen syndrome")
Unrecognized warriors	State policy does not recognize veterans until 2002, lack adequate benefits
Patriotic Heroes	Male role models, participate in military-patriotic education

soldiers who had served in Chechnya during the memorial celebrations of the fourteenth anniversary of the start of the first Chechen war: "They all worthily fulfilled their duty and we, their close ones, have nothing to be ashamed of in front of the state. We hope, it too will not forget us."[152] Thus, the practice of memorializing serves not only to integrate the memories of fallen soldiers into the memory of the nation but also as a basis for claims on the state.

Significantly, the memorializing of dead soldiers and celebration of veterans relies on a reinterpretation of the Chechen wars, in which doubts about the wars' necessity are replaced by a new certainty. Aleksandr Iaroslavets, commander of the 81st Motor-Rifle Regiment during the first war, commented at the same memorial celebration:

> Much time has already passed since our regiment left Samara for Chechnya, but the pain of loss has not gone. Often I am asked: were these sacrifices necessary? In the beginning we ourselves did not know whether we did the right thing to go there. But afterwards, when we saw the suffering of the civilian population, of children, all these horrors, our doubts disappeared. We were obliged to defend our citizens. Our memory will be eternal. Nobody will forget what was done.[153]

This newly constructed memory of the war is also one from which the war crimes committed by federal forces and the memories of those who served unwillingly are obliterated. The memory of the war is not used as a basis for antiwar activism, but rather works to remilitarize society. Attempts to reinterpret the memory of the Chechen wars and reinvent Chechen veterans as role models of patriotism and masculinity may reshape how Russian society conceives of the wars and its veterans. However, they do not resolve the material challenges that continue to weaken militarized masculinity in post-Soviet Russia.

Conclusion

Militarized masculinity continues to hold meaning for those men who have worked or served in the military. They view their military service as a central component of their socialization as men and argue that men have an obligation to defend the country. However, the first Chechen war revealed not only many men's lack of willingness to serve but also the serious problems with morale among those fighting. At the same time, some federal servicemen in Chechnya represented excessive warriors who used undue violence and commited war crimes. Importantly, neither of these masculinities was ideologically useful to the waging of war and to increasing public support for the war. The representation of the unwilling warrior demonstrated the diminished state of the armed forces in post-Soviet Russia compared with the Soviet Union. The representation of the excessive warrior cast doubts on the justness of the war and the military's actions in Chechnya. While the men who hesitated to kill often held a neutral or ambiguous view of Chechens, Colonel Budanov justified his killing of Kungaeva on his belief that she was an enemy sniper. Militarized masculinity and the legitimacy of the actions of militarized men are reinforced by a clear-cut definition of "the enemy." The ambiguity of Chechens as both the enemy *and* citizens of the Russian Federation is precisely what made these wars so complicated both for society and armed forces service personnel.

The Chechen wars were not officially recognized as wars, and service personnel who fought in Chechnya were not legally recognized as veterans and thus not entitled to state benefits until 2002. Their ambiguous status and society's lukewarm support for the wars made it difficult for male veterans to define their postwar identities. Many faced the negative psychological effects of combat experience, which further hindered their social and economic reintegration into society. Veterans often did not conform to the ideal of tough and heroic warriors, but also found it difficult to live up to nonmilitarized notions of masculinity such as breadwinner and desirable husband. Some veterans have attempted to shape public perceptions and state policy by promoting the symbolic recognition of veterans and fallen soldiers as patriotic heroes, which goes hand in hand with the state's renewed emphasis on militarized patriotism during Putin's presidencies. This entails an uncritical view of the wars and its participants that silences the many contradictions of militarized masculinity that the Chechen wars exposed.

While the representations of masculinity discussed in this chapter were present in both of the wars, it is worth noting some differences between the two wars. The representation of federal forces in Chechnya as unwilling warriors was more in evidence during the first war than the second. While low morale (and draft evasion) remained a problem during the second Chechen war, that war was increasingly fought by men who embraced their role as warriors (as discussed in Chapter 2). The representation of the Chechen war veteran as patriotic hero emerged during the second war, and was not possible to the same extent during the first Chechen war because of the skepticism Yeltsin showed the military and its service personnel. During the second war Chechen war veterans became recognized by the state as veterans of combat operations, which improved their status, though they were not recognized as veterans of war. There was also a greater societal recognition of the need to address veterans' problems such as post-traumatic stress syndrome during the second war. The representation of excessive warriors committing crimes against civilians was present during both wars, though excessive violence became more easily justifiable in the context of the second war, which was waged against terrorism and had greater support in Russian society.

Many of the contradictions of militarized masculinity described in this chapter are not unique to the Russian-Chechen wars but linked to the very construction of the ideal soldier as tough and heroic warrior. Some men's hesitancy to kill, excessive use of violence by others, and soldiers' experience of post-traumatic stress are more common than states and militaries want to acknowledge. What makes militarized masculinity such a salient issue in the Russian case is the context of postcommunist transformation and crisis. Despite President Putin's representation of the heroic Russian soldier fighting in Chechnya and other attempts to reshape the image of war veterans, the lack of ideological coherence regarding the wars and insufficient financial resources to support veterans undermined Chechen war veterans as a model of masculinity in post-Soviet Russia.

Conclusion
Masculinity, Soldiering, and War in Post-Soviet Russia

A S BIOLOGICAL EXPLANATIONS for men's militarism and women's peacefulness persist,[1] feminist scholarship to document both the constructed and fluctuating nature of gender identities remains as relevant as ever. Men are not naturally militaristic, they become militarized. Gendered policies such as compulsory military service for men alert us to the significant role states and militaries play in militarizing men's identities. States and militaries put much effort into coercing and persuading men to serve and get anxious when men resist their militarization. Changing political, social, and economic conditions lead to changes in state-society relations that affect the link between masculinity and the military and society's support for men's militarization. But the waging of war and the militarization of men ultimately depend on the decisions of individual citizens. Whether women and men accept the idea that military service is key to masculine identity and/or men's citizenship has direct consequences for state policies of war and militarization. If men are not willing to serve and their mothers or female partners do not want them to join the military, the state is less able to wage war or legitimate its rule on the basis of militarized patriotism.

The Global Politics of Gendered Militarization

Masculinity plays a central role in states' (re)production of military violence. The world's armed forces are overwhelmingly made up of men, and states primarily rely on men to fight wars. Only a handful of countries, such as Peru, Malaysia, Taiwan, North Korea, Israel, Libya, and Eritrea, conscript women into their armed forces.[2] Yet it is important to note that the conscription of women does not necessarily change the primary association of masculinity with the military in a society, as Uta Klein has shown in the case of Israel.[3] Women are barred from military service in many countries. Other countries such as Brazil (1995), Argentina (1996), Austria (1998), and Italy (2000) relatively recently amended their policy to permit women to serve in active duty forces.[4] Non-conscription countries with the highest percentage of women serving include Slovenia (40.6 percent), South Africa (21 percent), Latvia (17.4 percent), Hungary (17 percent), New Zealand (16.5 percent), Australia (15.7 percent), Canada (14.5 percent), and the United States (14.3 percent).[5] These are exceptions, as the number of women in most national militaries is minuscule.

Russian women make up around 10 percent of the country's armed forces service personnel compared with approximately 1 to 2 percent female volunteers in the Soviet armed forces during the 1980s.[6] This increase is not a result of advances in gender equality policies but rather of "manpower" shortages, women's economic needs, and a smaller force size. Russian state and military leaders have not reconsidered the equation of male citizenship with military service despite the challenges to men's militarization and the greater reliance on female volunteers in the post-Soviet period.

The point here is not simply to decry women's near exclusion from militaries across the globe or suggest that women's better representation in militaries would make for a more peaceful world or greater gender equality. Rather I wish to underline the very gendered basis on which states organize for violence. Scholars of International Relations usually do not problematize the gendered assumptions about protection that inform theories and policy-making on war and security. Militarized masculinity is part of the foundation of the contemporary international system. Therefore an analysis of militarized masculinity enhances our understanding of how states and the international state system operate, and the potential for their transformation.

While militaries are still male-dominated institutions, there is a weakening of the link between male citizenship and military service both in Russia and more widely. The relationship between masculinity and militarization is in flux globally. Over the last decades, an increasing number of countries have abolished conscription and moved to all-volunteer forces, and states such as the U.S., UK, and others are more heavily relying on private military and security companies to wage war. These developments indicate a remaking of militarized masculinity rather than its demise. Some authors have theorized a new form of "tough but tender" militarized masculinity represented by U.S. soldiers in the Persian Gulf War.[7] A "tough" version of militarized masculinity today is primarily embodied by particular militarized men such as special forces soldiers or private military and security contractors. In the end, how the link between masculinity and the military will be reconfigured depends on state-societal struggles over military recruitment and deployment and on political and societal debates about how we as citizens want to define security and organize our military and security forces. The incorporation of women's and feminist voices into these struggles and debates is important, as redefining masculinity in ways that challenge rather than support war-making will require a broader transformation of gender hierarchies.

Militarized Masculinity in Russia

Too often, men's militarism is assumed to be a given. Equally problematic, the militaristic nature of Russia and its people is frequently taken for granted. On numerous occasions I have listened as presenters at conferences or workshops assert that Russia is essentially or culturally militaristic. Such an approach places Russia's waging of war in Chechnya in the context of a long tradition of militarism. There are serious problems with such assumptions, as they naturalize militarism (and militarized gender roles) and fail to recognize the complex process of militarization. Instead, an approach that historically situates militarism and militarization within state-society relations allows us to more closely study how countries become militarized and what potential for demilitarization they have. I have therefore examined militarism and militarization in Russia as elements in the (re)organization of social relations and political power, including the gender order.

Gender is integral to policies and processes of militarization. Policies such as conscription and the waging of war intimately rely on militarized masculinity and motherhood. Militarized masculinity is socially and politically constructed, and thus inherently contradictory and fragile. Whether Russian men perform their militarized gender roles depends on a myriad of factors: personal (self-identification, life goals), familial (family role models, mother's support, class background), societal (economic conditions, hegemonic notions of masculinity, soldiers' mothers movement), the military (service conditions, place in society), the state (ideological and material capabilities), and a context of peace or war (possibility of being sent into combat).

Hopes for a demilitarization of Russian society have waxed and waned, as militarized masculinity has been both challenged *and* reinforced in post-Soviet Russia. The tension between militarization and demilitarization can be found at all levels: the state, military, society, and the individual. Russia's continued policy of conscription is in tension with new notions of masculinity defined by class and the weakend link between patriotism and military service. Combat and hazing, often considered important to the initiation into militarized manhood, further undermined men's willingness to serve in post-Soviet Russia. The wars in Chechnya did not lead to a successful mobilization of young men for war, but instead exposed cracks in the facade of the tough and herroic warrior. Soldiers' mothers groups in Moscow and St. Petersburg have been at the forefront of the societal struggle against conscription. However, other mothers groups have reproduced militarized masculinity by calling on young men to serve and on their mothers to support their sons during military service. The draft is not popular, and most men do not see volunteer service as an attractive job.

Over the last decade and a half Russia's political leadership has repeatedly professed its intent to modernize the armed forces and move to a fully professionalized military. The transition to an all-volunteer force has strong societal support, but there is little likelihood of it materializing in the foreseeable future. The fact that the military is among the most trusted institutions in post-Soviet Russia has allowed the political leadership to tap into militarism as a source of legitimation and mobilization. The Russian state has encouraged its citizens to think of themselves as patriots and has supported civil society groups that promote militarized patriotism. Under Putin's presidency the government introduced a state patriotic education program aimed to revive militarized patriotism and increase young men's compliance with the draft. Thus, while support for conscription fell sharply and draft dodging was widely condoned in post-Soviet Russia, there was a parallel trend toward the remilitarization of men's and women's identities both from above and below.

The Postcommunist Transformation of Militarized Masculinity

Whether the Russian state will be successful in re-establishing a strong link between masculinity, military service, and patriotism will depend on ideological and economic factors. The serious challenges to the citizen-soldier model are a specific outcome of the postcommunist crisis and transformation. Universal male conscription was a key feature of Soviet militarization. Soviet notions of militarized masculinity relied not only on the idea of men's citizenship duty but also on notions of heroism and patriotism, and a gender ideology that defined military service as key to the transition from boyhood to manhood. The linkage of masculinity and military service established by conscription has undergone significant change between the Soviet and post-Soviet periods. In part, challenges to the draft were connected to the crisis of the Russian military and the systemic violence to which it has exposed young men. But the problems with draft compliance are also fundamentally related to the economic and political transformation. The opening up of the authoritarian Soviet political system and the prospects of a transition to democracy allowed conscription to become an issue of state-societal contestation. The economic transition on the other hand led to a breakdown of the social contract on which men's soldiering rested.

The Soviet state pursued economic and social policies aimed at redistribution and equity. Its social contract was based on an array of welfare benefits that were not especially generous, but provided a minimum of social and economic security for Soviet citizens. The postcommunist transition promised improved social and economic conditions, but the reality was a collapsed welfare regime, economic instability, and a sharp increase in inequality. Military service brings the tensions in state-society relations that have arisen from the economic and social crisis into view, as the breakdown of the social contract has undermined young men's willingness to serve.

My interviews demonstrate the important link between social citizenship and militarized citizenship. The post-Soviet state has for the most part failed to back up men's militarization with tangible rewards, whether for ideological or economic reasons.[8] Interviewees emphasized the fundamental shift in the relationship between citizens and the state since Soviet times. One draft evader argued that his unwillingness to serve in the military was partly a result of the state's lack of social guarantees. A former officer explained that the Soviet provision of housing and education were central to attracting men to the military as professional soldiers. Veterans of the Chechen wars have more often than not been socially and economically marginalized and were not legally recognized as veterans and thus not entitled to state benefits until 2002. Veterans' and soldiers' mothers groups on the other hand have highlighted militarized citizenship as a basis for social citizenship. They have emphasized men's fulfillment of their militarized duty to the motherland when trying to claim existing benefits or petition for improved benefits on behalf of soldiers.

The transition to capitalism has had ambivalent effects on militarized masculinity in post-Soviet Russia. It exacerbated the conscription crisis that began to emerge in the late 1980s and undermined Soviet notions of militarized, patriotic masculinity. The tensions between militarized masculinity and capitalist masculinity reflect the challenges to conscription in a market economy. Many young men see military service as incompatible with a fast-paced market economy and competitive labor market. The development of a black market that serves those who want to (and have resources to) buy their way out of service greatly increased the inequality of the draft. On the other hand, the crisis-prone and chaotic transition economy generated demand for more militarized men in the private sector. The mushrooming of private security companies, which often employ former soldiers, came to fill the void in security provision left by the weakened post-Soviet state.

Between Antimilitarism and Remilitarization

The Chechen wars further undermined Russia's citizen-soldier model. The wars resulted in a spike in draft evasion and solidified popular support for a transition to an all-volunteer force. For many of the conscripts and officers who served in the war, their participation was itself ambiguous. The analysis revealed a wide range of masculinities: men who were not prepared to kill or who were morally opposed to the war, and men who condoned the use of excessive force. Veterans often faced difficult psychological, economic, and social repercussions for their participation in the wars. Thus Russia's societal crisis of militarized masculinity is evident not only in widespread draft evasion but also in the experiences of veterans.

A majority of Russians today do not consider the wars to have been just, even though the second war had much support early on. In a poll conducted in early 2010, Russians were asked which of the last century's wars they considered just. World War Two retains its special status in Russian history as the only war a majority of respondents (75 percent) perceive as just.[9] Most Russians define a just war as one fought "defending their home, their nearest and dearest, and their country from attack."[10] Among average Russians the Chechen wars are often depicted as being fought for political and economic interests, and not as necessary for the protection of the country and its people.

A significant gap exists between the state's use of militarism and militarized patriotism, and much of the population's skepticism toward recent wars waged by the Russian state. However, the populace's war-critical stance rarely translates into political activism, except in the case of some soldiers' mothers groups. Nor has there been much critical public debate on the excessive violence of militarized men such as Colonel Budanov. Veterans who felt that the war was morally wrong did not organize politically in opposition to the war (unlike, for example, some Vietnam and Iraq veterans in the United States).[11] Such a depoliticized, private, and passive position against war is likely not sufficient to counter the concerted efforts by the state and military leadership to revive militarized patriotism in post-Soviet Russia. Even if Russians embrace militarized patriotism, whether they will be willing to sacrifice themselves or their close relatives in future wars remains at issue considering the many challenges to men's militarization in post-Soviet Russia.

Reference Matter

Notes

Introduction

1. Cynthia Enloe, "Military," *Routledge International Encyclopedia of Women: Global Women's Issues and Knowledge* (New York: Routledge, 2000), pp. 1373–1374.

2. Interview with Vadim, Samara, June 2006.

3. Pavel Fel'gengauer, "A sluzhit' vnov' pridetsia dva-tri goda: Prizyvnaia armiia pobedila kontraktnuiu," *Novaia gazeta*, March 1, 2010.

4. My definition draws on Cynthia Enloe, *Maneuvers: The International Politics of Militarizing Women's Lives* (Berkeley: University of California Press, 2000), ch. 1.

5. Joan W. Scott, "Gender: A Useful Category of Historical Analysis," *American Historical Review* 91, no. 5 (1986): 1067.

6. J. Ann Tickner, *Gender in International Relations: Feminist Perspectives on Achieving Global Security* (New York: Columbia University Press, 1992); Jacqui True, "Feminism," in Scott Burchill and Andrew Linklater (eds.), *Theories of International Relations* (New York: Macmillan, 1996), pp. 225–236.

7. For example, Charlotte Hooper, *Manly States, International Relations, and Gender Politics* (New York: Columbia University Press, 2001); Simona Sharoni, "De-Militarizing Masculinities in the Age of Empire," *Austrian Political Science Journal* 37, no. 2 (2008): 147–164; Sandra Whitworth, *Men, Militarism and UN Peacekeeping: A Gendered Analysis* (Boulder, CO: Lynne Rienner Publishers, 2004); Marysia Zalewski and Jane Parpart (eds.), *The "Man" Question in International Relations* (Boulder, CO: Westview Press, 1998); Jane Parpart and Marysia Zalewski (eds.), *Rethinking the Man Question: Sex, Gender and Violence in International Relations* (London: Zed Books, 2008).

8. R. W. Connell, *Gender and Power: Society, the Person and Sexual Politics* (Stanford: Stanford University Press, 1987). Connell adopts the concept of gender order from Jill J. Matthews, *Good and Mad Women: The Historical Construction of Femininity in*

Twentieth-Century Australia (Sydney: George Allen and Unwin, 1984). Matthews (p. 13) explains: "This ordering according to gender is one of the main ideological and material grids within which social meaning is created, an ordering which encompasses the entire society."

9. Yasmeen Abu-Laban (ed.), *Gendering the Nation-State: Canadian and Comparative Perspectives* (Vancouver: University of British Columbia Press, 2008); Susan Gal and Gail Kligman, *Reproducing Gender: Politics, Public, and Everyday Life after Socialism* (Princeton: Princeton University Press, 1997); Sarah Ashwin (ed.), *Gender, State and Society in Soviet and Post-Soviet Russia* (London: Routledge, 2000).

10. J. Ann Tickner, *Gendering World Politics: Issues and Approaches in the Post-Cold War Era* (New York: Columbia University Press, 2001), ch. 2; Spike V. Peterson, "Security and Sovereign States: What Is at Stake in Taking Feminism Seriously?" in Peterson (ed.), *Gendered States: Feminist (Re)Visions of International Relations Theory* (Boulder, CO: Lynne Rienner Publishers, 1992), pp. 31–64; Judith Stiehm, "The Protected, the Protector, the Defender," *Women's Studies International Forum* 5, nos. 3–4 (1982): 367–376; Iris Marion Young, "The Logic of Masculinist Protection: Reflections on the Current Security State," *Signs: Journal of Women in Culture and Society* 29, no. 1 (2003): 1–25.

11. The importance of such an approach is also stressed by feminist scholars such as Enloe and Cockburn. Cynthia Enloe, *The Morning After: Sexual Politics at the End of the Cold War* (Berkeley: University of California Press, 1993), p. 37; Cynthia Cockburn, "The Continuum of Violence: A Gender Perspective on War and Peace," in Wenona Giles and Jennifer Hyndman (eds.), *Sites of Violence: Gender and Conflict Zones* (Berkeley: California University Press, 2004), pp. 24–25.

12. On this point, see Hooper's discussion of Connell's work. Hooper, *Manly States*, pp. 32, 41.

13. Connell, *Gender and Power;* R. W. Connell, *The Men and the Boys* (Berkeley: University of California Press, 2000).

14. For feminist analyses of militarized masculinity, see Cynthia Enloe, *The Curious Feminist: Searching for Women in a New Age of Empire* (Berkeley: University of California, 2004); Whitworth, *Men, Militarism and UN Peacekeeping.*

15. For feminist analyses of the significance of conscription in shaping notions of masculinity and men's identities, see Ayşe Gül Altinay, *The Myth of the Military Nation: Militarism, Gender, and Education in Turkey* (New York: Palgrave Macmillan, 2004); Lesley Gill, "Creating Citizens, Making Men: The Military and Masculinity in Bolivia," *Cultural Anthropology* 12, no. 4 (1997): 527–550; Insook Kwon, "A Feminist Exploration of Military Conscription: The Gendering of the Connections between Nationalism, Militarism and Citizenship in South Korea," *International Feminist Journal of Politics* 3, no. 1 (April 2000): 26–54; Seungsook Moon, "Trouble with Conscription, Entertaining Soldiers: Popular Culture and the Politics of Militarized Masculinity in South Korea," *Men and Masculinities* 8, no. 1 (July 2005): 64–92; Orna Sasson-Levy, "Military, Masculinity, and Citizenship: Tensions and Contradictions in the Experience of Blue-Collar Soldiers," *Identities: Global Studies in Culture and Power* 10 (2003): 319–345.

16. For a discussion of the various approaches to the study of postcommunist transformations, see Andreas Pickel, Frank Bönker, and Klaus Müller (eds.), *Postcommunist Transformation and the Social Sciences: Cross-Disciplinary Approaches* (Boulder, CO: Rowman and Littlefield, 2002).

17. Michael Burawoy and Katherine Verdery, "Introduction," in Burawoy and Verdery (eds.), *Uncertain Transitions: Ethnographies of Change in the Postsocialist World* (Lanham, MD: Rowman and Littlefield, 1999), p. 14.

18. Rudra Sil and Cheng Chen, "State Legitimacy and the (In)significance of Democracy in Post-Communist Russia," *Europe-Asia Studies* 56, no. 3 (2004): 349.

19. Marlène Laruelle, "Introduction," in Laruelle (ed.), *Russian Nationalism and the National Reassertion of Russia* (New York: Routledge, 2009), pp. 1–10.

20. In addition to the Russian-Chechen wars, Russia experienced military violence during the siege of the White House in 1993.

21. Ben Fowkes (ed.), *Russia and Chechnia: The Permanent Crisis* (London: Macmillan Press, 1998).

22. Gail W. Lapidus, "Contested Sovereignty: The Tragedy of Chechnya," *International Security* 23, no. 1 (1998): 9.

23. Ibid.

24. Valery Tishkov, *Chechnya: Life in a War-Torn Society* (Berkeley: University of California Press, 2004), pp. 41, 45.

25. Matthew Evangelista, *The Chechen Wars: Will Russia Go the Way of the Soviet Union?* (Washington, DC: Brookings Institution Press, 2002), p. 3; Omar Ashour, "Security, Oil, and Internal Politics: The Causes of the Russo-Chechen Conflicts," *Studies in Conflict and Terrorism* 27 (2004): 127–143.

26. Tracey C. German and Markus Soldner are examples of authors who analyze the first Chechen war within the context of Russia's postcommunist transformation. The former focuses on how weak institutions contributed to the outbreak of military violence, while the latter places emphasis on shifting elite politics. Tracey C. German, *Russia's Chechen War* (New York: RoutledgeCurzon, 2003); Markus Soldner, *Rußlands Čečnja-Politik seit 1993: Der Weg in den Krieg vor dem Hintergrund innenpolitischer Machtverschiebungen* (Hamburg: LIT, 1999).

27. Valerie Sperling, "The Last Refuge of a Scoundrel: Patriotism, Militarism and the National Idea," *Nations and Nationalism* 9, no. 2 (2003): 240.

28. In this respect I follow Serguei Oushakine and Lisa Sundstrom, who have furthered our knowledge of soldiers' mothers groups in Russia's regions. Serguei Alex. Oushakine, *The Patriotism of Despair: Nation, War, and Loss in Russia* (Ithaca, NY: Cornell University Press, 2009), ch. 4; Lisa McIntosh Sundstrom, *Funding Civil Society: Foreign Assistance and NGO Development in Russia* (Stanford: Stanford University Press, 2006).

29. Another reason for choosing Samara for my fieldwork was more practical. My attention had been caught by a reference to one of the soldiers' mothers groups in Samara in a publication on women's activism in Samara region authored by feminist scholar Liudmila Popkova, the director of the Gender Studies Center at

Samara State University: Liudmila Popkova, "Women's Political Activism in Russia: The Case of Samara," in Kathleen Kuehnast and Carol Nechemias (eds.), *Post-Soviet Women Encountering Transition: Nation Building, Economic Survival, and Civic Activism* (Washington, DC: Woodrow Wilson Center Press; Baltimore, MD: Johns Hopkins University Press, 2004), pp. 172–194. I consulted with Serguei Oushakine, an anthropologist and scholar of gender studies and Russia, who confirmed that conducting fieldwork in Samara would make sense and agreed to put me in touch with the local Gender Studies Center, which sponsored my visa. I spent approximately eleven weeks in Samara from late May to mid-August 2006, during which time I was affiliated with the Gender Studies Center.

30. The organizations were located through a publication of the Samara Regional Parliament on regional and municipal nongovernmental organizations. A few interviewees were referred to me by the members of the Gender Studies Center, others were found through the snowball technique whereby interviewees help identify and establish contact with further interviewees. The interviews were, with one exception, all recorded and transcribed. I conducted the interviews by myself, in Russian, except for the first two interviews, where I was accompanied by a member of the Samara Gender Studies Center. I followed ethics guidelines and acquired oral consent from all interviewees. The names of the interviewees have been changed to ensure their anonymity. Fourteen men and ten women participated in the interviews. The great majority of interviewees either had received some form of higher education, at the university and college level, or had pursued a skilled trade. The occupations of the interviewees included student, government employee, engineer, emergency-services technician, architect, singer, and retired military personnel. The interviewees were made up of five veterans of the Chechen wars (four male, one female), four draft evaders, one male antidraft activist, four soldiers' mothers who were activists (not including the chairs of two committees), a former conscript, a male Afghan war veteran active in the local veterans' movement, a mother of a teenage son nearing draft age, and a young woman who wanted to serve in the military. In addition, I interviewed the chairs of six organizations: the Samara *Oblast'* Committee of Parents of Servicemen *Sodeistvie* ("Assistance"), the Regional Voluntary Organization of Parents of Servicemen *Synov'ia* ("Sons"), the Samara Regional Committee *Chechnya*, the Regional *Oblast'* Organization of Participants of Combat Operations in Chechnya and Dagestan *Pamiat'* ("Memory"), the Samara Regional Public Fund Offering Social Support to Retired Military Personnel, Invalids, Veterans of Local Wars, and Liquidators of the Chernobyl' Accident, and the Samara Regional Chechen National-Cultural Organization *Vainakh*. With one exception, the interviewees were all ethnic Russians. I directly quote from twenty-one of these interviews in Chapters 3, 4, and 5.

31. "Interview with Tanya Lokshina, President of the Demos Center, Conducted by Olga Filippova, Moscow, 11 May 2007," *Journal of Power Institutions in Post-Soviet Societies* no. 6/7 (2007): paragraph 3, available at http://www.pipss.org/index772.html (accessed January 11, 2008).

32. I came across one person who was happy that someone from the West was interested in Russia and another who felt that sharing the sensitive information he did

with me in the interview might lead to some good. I also had the impression that my younger age, student status, and gender were of advantage, as interviewees saw me as less threatening than they might have someone more established, older, and male.

33. See Cynthia Enloe, *Bananas, Beaches and Bases: Making Feminist Sense of International Politics* (Berkeley: University of California Press, 1989).

Chapter 1

1. Nina Tumarkin, "The Great Patriotic War as Myth and Memory," *European Review* 11, no. 4 (2003): 598–599.
2. Cited ibid., p. 599.
3. Alexander M. Golts and Tonya L. Putnam, "State Militarism and Its Legacies: Why Military Reform Has Failed in Russia," *International Security* 29, no. 2 (Fall 2004): 123–124. Golts and Putnam trace this legacy to the reign of Peter the Great and argue that it continues to impede military reform in the post-Soviet period.
4. David J. Betz and Sergei Plekhanov, "Civil-Military Relations in Post-Soviet Russia: Rebuilding the 'Battle Order'?" in Natalie L. Mychajlyszyn and Harald von Riekhoff (eds.), *The Evolution of Civil-Military Relations in East-Central Europe and the Former Soviet Union* (Westport, CT: Praeger), pp. 161–162; the quotation is from p. 162.
5. Manfred Sapper, "Diffuse Militanz in Rußland: Ein Erbe des militarisierten Sozialismus?" *Berliner Debatte Initial* 8, no. 6 (1997): 94. See also Sanborn's study, which argues that the road to the mass violence of World War I and the Civil War was paved by the introduction of universal conscription in 1874, and the emergence of an ideology of the nation and the new political subjectivity of the citizen-soldier. Joshua A. Sanborn, *Drafting the Russian Nation: Military Conscription, Total War, and Mass Politics, 1905–1925* (DeKalb: Northern Illinois University Press, 2003).
6. Sapper, "Diffuse Militanz in Rußland," pp. 94–95.
7. David Holloway, "War, Militarism, and the Soviet State," in Erik P. Hoffmann and Robbin F. Laird (eds.), *The Soviet Polity in the Modern Era* (New York: Aldine Publishing Company, 1984), p. 365.
8. Quoted in Golts and Putnam, "State Militarism and Its Legacies," p. 145.
9. Roger D. Markwick, "Stalinism at War," *Kritika: Explorations in Russian and Eurasian History* 3, no. 3 (Summer 2002): 515. Markwick writes: "The 1930s had witnessed a retreat from class-struggle internationalism to Soviet patriotism, though the doctrine of Marxism-Leninism remained. Official skepticism about its efficacy as a mobilizer led to the rapid abandonment of class in favor of the 'Russification of Soviet patriotism,' in which Stalin became the embodiment of nationhood" (ibid.).
10. Fredric S. Zuckerman, "To Justify a Nation: Inter-War Soviet Nationalism," *History of European Ideas* 15, nos. 1–3 (1992): 386.
11. Markwick, "Stalinism at War," p. 509 and passim.
12. Sapper, "Diffuse Militanz in Rußland," p. 95. See also Golts and Putnam, "State Militarism and Its Legacies," p. 146.

13. Lev Gudkov, "The Army as an Institutional Model," in Stephen L. Webber and Jennifer G. Mathers (eds.), *Military and Society in Post-Soviet Russia* (Manchester: Manchester University Press, 2006), p. 42.

14. In its official version, memory of the war focused on a resurrection of Russia as a great power, the heroism of the Soviet people, and a minimization of Nazism as a form of capitalism, and excluded alternative memories and interpretations. Maria Ferretti, "Neprimirimaia pamiat': Rossiia i voina," *Neprikosnovennyi zapas: Debaty o politike i kul'ture* nos. 40–41 (2005): 78–79. To this day, the Great Patriotic War is commemorated as the most important event shaping Russians' collective memory and identity. In a 2003 poll 87 percent of people responded that the Great Patriotic War was the event they were most proud of in their history. This number was up from 44 percent in 1996. Lev Gudkov, "Die Fesseln des Sieges: Rußlands Identität aus der Erinnerung an den Krieg," *Osteuropa* 55, nos. 4–6 (April–June 2005): 56–73; the polling data is cited on p. 61.

15. Roger R. Reese, *The Soviet Military Experience: A History of the Soviet Army, 1917–1991* (London: Routledge, 2000), p. 4.

16. Tumarkin, "The Great Patriotic War," pp. 597–598. See also Tumarkin, *The Living and the Dead: The Rise and Fall of the Cult of World War II in Russia* (New York: Basic Books, 1994).

17. Tumarkin, "The Great Patriotic War," pp. 600–601; Natalia Danilova, "The Development of an Exclusive Veterans' Policy: The Case of Russia," *Armed Forces and Society* 20, no. 10 (2010): 12–13; M. Steven Fish, "Reform and Demilitarization in Soviet Society from Brezhnev to Gorbachev," *Peace and Change* 15, no. 2 (April 1990): 153–159. See also Mark Edele, *Soviet Veterans of the Second World War: A Popular Movement in an Authoritarian Society 1941–1991* (Oxford: Oxford University Press, 2008). Edele's research shows that the struggle by a popular veterans' movement was crucial to attaining this privileged status in the Soviet welfare system.

18. Sapper, "Diffuse Militanz in Rußland," pp. 94–95.

19. The term "militarized socialism" was coined by Michael Mann in the article "The Roots and Contradictions of Modern Militarism," *New Left Review* no. I/162 (March–April 1987): 35–50. Mann argues that repression was the main political tool during the height of the Stalinist terror in 1937–1938, but that it was eventually replaced by a "subtle authoritarianism" to which militarism was central (p. 46).

20. Holloway, "War, Militarism, and the Soviet State," pp. 366–367.

21. Ellen Jones, *Red Army and Society: A Sociology of the Soviet Military* (Boston: Allen and Unwin, 1985), pp. 33–34; the quotation is from p. 34. On the effects of universal military conscription on politics, society, and personal identity in imperial and revolutionary Russia, see Sanborn, *Drafting the Russian Nation*.

22. Jones, *Red Army and Society*, pp. 35–36.

23. Ibid., p. 36.

24. Ibid., p. 37.

25. Linda Racioppi and Katherine O'Sullivan See, *Women's Activism in Contemporary Russia* (Philadelphia: Temple University Press, 1997), p. 73.

26. Ol'ga Nikonova, "Zhenshchiny, voina i 'figury umolchaniia,'" *Neprikosnovennyi*

zapas: Debaty o politike i kul'ture nos. 40–41 (2005): 284; Joshua S. Goldstein, *War and Gender* (Cambridge: Cambridge University Press, 2001), pp. 64–70.

27. Anna Krylova, "Women Fighters in 1930s Stalinist Russia," *Gender and History* 16, no. 3 (November 2004): 626–653. Krylova discusses the changes in prewar notions of militarized femininity and how the idea of women in combat, initially propagated by individual women, eventually gained wider acceptance. She emphasizes the role of Soviet gender equality discourse in this process.

28. Nikonova, "Zhenshchiny, voina i 'figury umolchaniia,'" p. 284; Goldstein, *War and Gender*, pp. 64–70.

29. Lisa A. Kirschenbaum, "'Our City, Our Hearths, Our Families': Local Loyalties and Private Life in Soviet World War II Propaganda," *Slavic Review* 59, no. 4 (Winter 2000): 825–847.

30. Kazimiera J. Cottam, "Hero of the Soviet Union, Women Recipients," in Reina Pennington (ed.), *Amazons to Fighter Pilots: A Biographical Dictionary of Military Women* (Westport, CT: Greenwood Press), pp. 197–200. See also Henry Sakaida and Christa Hook, *Heroines of the Soviet Union, 1941–45* (Oxford: Osprey Publishing, 2003), for a complete list of the women who received this distinction.

31. Reina Pennington, "'Do Not Speak of the Services You Rendered': Women Veterans of Aviation in the Soviet Union," *Journal of Slavic Military Studies* 9, no. 1 (March 1996): 120–151; the quotation is from p. 141.

32. Racioppi and O'Sullivan See, *Women's Activism in Contemporary Russia*, pp. 73–79.

33. Quoted in Jones, *Red Army and Society*, p. 52.

34. Colton and Mann emphasize the importance of soldiering to Soviet understandings of citizenship, but fail to explicitly consider its gendered basis. Timothy J. Colton, "The Impact of the Military on Soviet Society," in Erik P. Hoffmann and Robbin F. Laird (eds.), *The Soviet Polity in the Modern Era* (New York: Aldine Publishing Company, 1984), pp. 397–398; Mann, "The Roots and Contradictions of Modern Militarism," p. 46. Jones comes closest to problematizing the links between military service and masculinity in the Soviet Union. Jones, *Red Army and Society*. For feminist analyses of the role of conscription in gendering citizenship in different national contexts, including the contradictions inherent in this process, see Introduction, note 15.

35. Mary O'Brien and Chris Jefferies, "Women and the Soviet Military," *Air University Review* 33, no. 2 (January–February 1982): 77.

36. Ibid., passim. Jones, *Red Army and Society*, pp. 98–103. Writing in the early 1980s, Jones estimated the number of servicewomen at 10,000 (ibid., p. 101).

37. Jones, *Red Army and Society*, pp. 42–44.

38. Ibid., ch. 6; Colton, "The Impact of the Military on Soviet Society," p. 398.

39. Colton, "The Impact of the Military on Soviet Society," pp. 399–400.

40. This section draws on Maya Eichler, "Gender and Nation in the Soviet/Russian Transformation," in Yasmeen Abu-Laban (ed.), *Gendering the Nation-State: Canadian and Comparative Perspectives* (Vancouver: University of British Columbia Press, 2008), pp. 46–59.

41. Bickford makes a similar point in regard to the analysis of socialist gender orders more generally in "Male Identity, the Military, and the Family in the Former German Democratic Republic," *Anthropology of East Europe Review* 19, no. 1 (Spring 2001): 1, available at http://condor.depaul.edu/~rrotenbe/aeer/v19n1/Bickford.pdf (accessed July 6, 2006).

42. See, for example, Dorothy Atkinson, Alexander Dallin, and Gail Warshofsky Lapidus (eds.), *Women in Russia* (Stanford: Stanford University Press, 1977); Gail W. Lapidus, *Women in Soviet Society: Equality, Development, and Social Change* (Berkeley: University of California Press, 1978).

43. Karen Petrone, "Masculinity and Heroism in Imperial and Soviet Military-Patriotic Cultures," in Barbara Evans Clements, Rebecca Friedman, and Dan Healey (eds.), *Russian Masculinities in History and Culture* (Houndsmills: Palgrave), p. 190.

44. Bickford's gender analysis of militarization in the German Democratic Republic reveals close ties between masculinity, family relations, and the state. He aims to show that "the development of militarized gender roles is an explicit project on the part of the state" ("Male Identity, the Military, and the Family," p. 1). Bickford argues that obligatory male military service and military education in schools reinforced traditional gender roles despite the official policy of gender equality. Furthermore, he asserts that "[m]ilitarization also served to counter the 'demasculinization' of East German society brought about by the political program of equality (*Gleichberechtigung*) designed to win women's support for the Socialist Unity Party after World War II" (ibid., p. 7).

45. Olga Issoupova, "From Duty to Pleasure? Motherhood in Soviet and Post-Soviet Russia," in Sarah Ashwin (ed.), *Gender, State and Society in Soviet and Post-Soviet Russia* (London: Routledge, 2000), p. 31.

46. This was evident, for example, in state policies that challenged traditional notions of Muslim femininity in an attempt to undermine pre-Soviet cultural and kinship structures. Sarah Ashwin, "Introduction: Gender, State and Society in Soviet and Post-Soviet Russia," in Sarah Ashwin (ed.), *Gender, State and Society in Soviet and Post-Soviet Russia* (London: Routledge, 2000), pp. 3–4.

47. Lapidus, *Women in Soviet Society*, p. 166. Lapidus, "Gender and Restructuring: The Impact of Perestroika and Its Aftermath on Soviet Women," in Valentine M. Moghadam (ed.), *Democratic Reform and the Position of Women in Transitional Economies* (Oxford: Clarendon Press, 1993), p. 140.

48. Lapidus, "Gender and Restructuring," p. 140.

49. Valerie Sperling, *Organizing Women in Contemporary Russia: Engendering Transition* (Cambridge: Cambridge University Press, 1999), p. 17.

50. Lapidus, "Gender and Restructuring," p. 143.

51. Lapidus, *Women in Soviet Society*, pp. 166–167.

52. Suvi Salmenniemi, *Democratization and Gender in Contemporary Russia* (London: Routledge, 2008), p. 56. See also Lapidus, *Women in Soviet Society*, ch. 6.

53. Tatiana Zhurzhenko, *Sotsial'noe vosproisvodstvo i gendernaia politika v Ukraine* (Kharkov: Folio, 2001), p. 87.

54. Ibid., p. 85.

55. Michelle Rivkin-Fish, "Anthropology, Demography, and the Search for a Criti-

cal Analysis of Fertility: Insights from Russia," *American Anthropologist* 105, no. 2 (2003): 291–292.

56. For a discussion of the discourse of demographic decline in post-Soviet Russia, see Serguei Alex. Oushakine, *The Patriotism of Despair: Nation, War, and Loss in Russia* (Ithaca, NY: Cornell University Press, 2009), ch. 2.

57. Nira Yuval-Davis, *Gender and Nation* (London: Sage Publications, 1997), pp. 26–38.

58. Quoted in Lapidus, *Women in Soviet Society*, p. 295.

59. Ibid., p. 296.

60. Although "Muslim" is a religious descriptive and not an ethnic or national one, this is the term that was used in the Soviet Union and in studies on the Soviet Union to refer to the nationalities of the five Central Asian republics (Kazakhstan, Kirghizia, Tajikistan, Turkmenistan, and Uzbekistan) as well as Azerbaijan, where a majority of the population were followers of Islam. I reproduce this rather inadequate use of the term "Muslim" to capture the debates that were taking place on the ethnic balance between the Soviet nationalities.

61. Yuval-Davis, *Gender and Nation*, p. 30.

62. Robert Service, *A History of Twentieth-Century Russia* (Cambridge: Harvard University Press, 1997), p. 423.

63. Sergei Kukhterin, "Fathers and Patriarchs in Communist and Post-Communist Russia," in Sarah Ashwin (ed.), *Gender, State and Society in Soviet and Post-Soviet Russia* (London: Routledge, 2000), pp. 71–89.

64. Ibid., p. 74.

65. Zhurzhenko, *Sotsial'noe vosproisvodstvo i gendernaia politika v Ukraine*, p. 86.

66. Jones, *Red Army and Society*, p. 148.

67. Teresa Rakowska-Harmstone, "Nationalities and the Soviet Military," in Lubomyr Hajda and Mark Beissinger (eds.), *The Nationalities Factor in Soviet Politics and Society* (Boulder, CO: Westview Press, 1990), p. 72.

68. Lynne Attwood, "The New Soviet Man and Woman—Soviet Views on Psychological Sex Differences," in Barbara Holland (ed.), *Soviet Sisterhood: British Feminists on Women in the USSR* (London: Fourth Estate, 1985), pp. 54–77. There was a liberal variant of this debate that posited a crisis of masculinity as a result of the lack of private property and economic opportunities for men, although this was not explicitly stated in the pre-*perestroika* period. See Anna D. Tëmkina and Elena Zdravomyslova, "Die Krise der Männlichkeit im Alltagsdiskurs: Wandel der Geschlechterordnung in Rußland," *Berliner Debatte Initial* 12, no. 4 (2001): 78–90. Gapova points out that "the Soviet gender order made it difficult to confirm masculinity as constructed through access to 'money' (broadly understood)." Elena Gapova, "Conceptualizing Gender, Nation, and Class in Post-Soviet Belarus," in Kathleen Kuehnast and Carol Nechemias (eds.), *Post-Soviet Women Encountering Transition: Nation Building, Economic Survival, and Civic Activism* (Baltimore, MD: Johns Hopkins University Press, 2004), p. 93. The liberal critique of Soviet masculinity reproduced the dominant notion of men as breadwinners, but argued that it could not be adequately realized under Soviet conditions.

69. Jones, *Red Army and Society*, p. 153.

70. Ibid., p. 103.

71. Joris Van Bladel, "The All-Volunteer Force in the Russian Mirror: Transformation without Change," Ph.D. diss. (Proefschrift), Rijksuniversiteit Groningen, June 2004, pp. 163–164.

72. Jones, *Red Army and Society*, p. 154.

73. See also Ellen Jones, "Social Change and Civil-Military Relations," in Timothy J. Colton and Thane Gustafson (eds.), *Soldiers and the Soviet State: Civil-Military Relations from Brezhnev to Gorbachev* (Princeton: Princeton University Press, 1990), pp. 239–284.

74. Tumarkin, "The Great Patriotic War," pp. 600–601.

75. Rakowska-Harmstone, "Nationalities and the Soviet Military," p. 88. To put this discussion into broader context, Slavs made up 72.78 percent of the total population of the USSR according to the 1979 census (ibid.).

76. Anatol Lieven, *Chechnya: Tombstone of Russian Power* (New Haven: Yale University Press, 1991), pp. 191–192.

77. Rakowska-Harmstone, "Nationalities and the Soviet Military," p. 80.

78. Scholars have suggested a variety of factors to explain the Soviet invasion of Afghanistan. Among them are the history of Russian/Soviet or alternatively communist internationalist expansionism, the Brezhnev doctrine, the Cold War, and Soviet security interests. The invasion has also been seen as a response to Islamic fundamentalism or simply as a misjudgment by Soviet leaders. Manfred Sapper, *Auswirkungen des Afghanistan-Krieges auf die Sowjetgesellschaft: Eine Studie zum Legitimitätsverlust des Militärischen in der Perestroijka* (Münster: LIT, 1994), pp. 51–55. See also Mark Galeotti, *Afghanistan: The Soviet Union's Last War* (London: Frank Cass, 1995), pp. 11–12.

79. Reese, *The Soviet Military Experience*, p. 164.

80. Sapper, *Auswirkungen des Afghanistan-Krieges*, pp. 102, 138.

81. Quoted in Reese, *The Soviet Military Experience*, p. 168. Reese points out that the lack of a clear understanding of the war's purpose stood in stark contrast to popular perceptions of World War Two (p. 167). Galeotti also stresses the differences between the two wars, especially in terms of size and significance. Galeotti, *Afghanistan*.

82. Jones, "Social Change and Civil-Military Relations," p. 247.

83. Galeotti, *Afghanistan*, pp. 141–142.

84. Quoted ibid., p. 143.

85. Ibid., p. 18

86. Sarah E. Mendelson, *Changing Course: Ideas, Politics, and the Soviet Withdrawal from Afghanistan* (Princeton: Princeton University Press, 1998), pp. 112–114.

87. Oleg L. Sarin and Lev Dvoretsky, *The Afghan Syndrome: The Soviet Union's Vietnam* (Novato, CA: Presidio, 1993), pp. 179–180.

88. Rafael Reuveny and Aseem Prakash, "The Afghanistan War and the Breakdown of the Soviet Union," *Review of International Studies* 25, no. 4 (1999): 693–708.

89. See also Sarin and Dvoretsky, who make the point that other Soviet military interventions such as in Hungary and Czechoslovakia were considered "mistakes" after the war in Afghanistan: "[T]here could be no moral or political justification for our attempts to reshape the destiny of other nations." *The Afghan Syndrome*, p. xii.

90. Interestingly, Reuveney and Prakash fail to mention the activism of soldiers' mothers in this context, which would be an obvious example illustrating their point. Their focus is instead on the civil society organizing of Afghan war veterans.

91. Reuveny and Prakash, "The Afghanistan War and the Breakdown of the Soviet Union."

92. Galeotti, *Afghanistan*, pp. 224–245; Sapper, *Auswirkungen des Afghanistan-Krieges*, p. 355.

93. Sapper, *Auswirkungen des Afghanistan-Krieges*, p. 141.

94. See, for example, Sarin and Dvoretsky, *The Afghan Syndrome*.

95. Sapper, *Auswirkungen des Afghanistan-Krieges*, pp. 21–22.

96. For an example of the conservative position, see Sapper, who quotes from a typical letter that appeared in the military press in 1990: "He who tries to slander our soldiers and our army, slanders his country" (my translation, ibid., p. 341; see also p. 342).

97. These gendered similarities are overlooked in comparisons of the Vietnam and Afghanistan wars. For an analysis of the gendered effects of the Vietnam war, see Steve Niva, "Tough and Tender: New World Order Masculinity and the Gulf War," in Marysia Zalewski and Jane Parpart (eds.), *The "Man" Question in International Relations* (Boulder, CO: Westview Press, 1998), pp. 114–117. See also Susan Jeffords, *The Remasculinization of America: Gender and the Vietnam War* (Bloomington: Indiana University Press, 1989).

98. Galeotti, *Afghanistan*, p. 33. I discuss the gendered nature of *dedovshchina* in relation to militarized masculinity in Chapter 3.

99. Sapper, *Auswirkungen des Afghanistan-Krieges*, pp. 133–137. In the context of war, *dedovshchina* established hierarchies not only between newer and longer-serving conscripts but also between those who had combat experience and those new to the fighting.

100. Ibid., p. 137.

101. Jones, "Social Change and Civil-Military Relations," pp. 255–256.

102. Reuveny and Prakash, "The Afghanistan War and the Breakdown of the Soviet Union," pp. 702–704. See also Galeotti, *Afghanistan*, passim; and Natalia Danilova, "Veterans' Policy in Russia: A Puzzle of Creation," *Journal of Power Institutions in Post-Soviet Societies* no. 6/7 (2007): paragraphs 12–16, available at http://www.pipss.org/index873.html (accessed September 10, 2008). The lot of female veterans (*afganki*) was often worse than that of their fellow servicemen. As Kathryn Pinnick explains, their motivations for participating in the war were publicly questioned, and they were excluded from benefits upon their return. Kathryn Pinnick, "When the Fighting Is Over: The Soldiers' Mothers and the Afghan Madonnas," in Mary Buckley (ed.), *Post-Soviet Women: From the Baltic to Central Asia* (Cambridge: Cambridge University Press, 1997), pp. 150–153.

103. Galeotti, *Afghanistan*, p. 36; Sapper, *Auswirkungen des Afghanistan-Krieges*, p. 131.

104. Galeotti, *Afghanistan*, pp. 27–28.

105. Reuveny and Prakash, "The Afghanistan War and the Breakdown of the Soviet Union," pp. 704–705, see also p. 700.

106. Julie Elkner, "*Dedovshchina* and the Committee of Soldiers' Mothers under Gorbachev," *Journal of Power Institutions in Post-Soviet Societies* no. 1 (2004): paragraphs 36–42, available at www.pipss.org/document243.html (accessed September 17, 2006).

107. Pinnick, "When the Fighting Is Over," p. 145; Elkner, "*Dedovshchina* and the Committee of Soldiers' Mothers," paragraphs 5, 54.

108. Elkner, "*Dedovshchina* and the Committee of Soldiers' Mothers," paragraphs 2–3; Galina Eremitcheva and Elena Zdravomyslova, "Die Bewegung der Soldatenmütter—Eine zivilgesellschaftliche Initiative: Der Fall St. Petersburg," in Martina Ritter (ed.), *Zivilgesellschaft und Gender-Politik in Rußland* (Frankfurt: Campus Verlag, 2001), p. 226.

109. Elkner, "*Dedovshchina* and the Committee of Soldiers' Mothers," paragraphs 3, 6.

110. Ibid., paragraphs 31–35.

111. Cynthia Enloe, *The Morning After: Sexual Politics at the End of the Cold War* (Berkeley: University of California Press, 1993), p. 12.

112. Elkner characterizes the special status of motherhood in Soviet culture as a "cult of motherhood." "*Dedovshchina* and the Committee of Soldiers' Mothers," paragraph 24.

113. Issoupova, "From Duty to Pleasure?"

114. See, for example, the following book published on the occasion of the United Nations Decade for Women: Government of the USSR, *Women in the USSR* (Moscow: Progress Publishers, 1985). The authors of the publication make sure to point out that the Soviet Union's advocacy of peace is not due to weakness but rather to its strength and sense of responsibility (p. 145). The construction of peaceful Soviet motherhood can be seen as a maneuver that allowed the Soviet leadership to promote disarmament while avoiding its own feminization.

115. Elkner, "*Dedovshchina* and the Committee of Soldiers' Mothers," paragraph 12.

116. Eremitcheva and Zdravomyslova, "Die Bewegung der Soldatenmütter," pp. 228–229.

117. Elkner, "*Dedovshchina* and the Committee of Soldiers' Mothers," paragraphs 18–23.

118. Ibid., paragraph 29.

119. Ibid.

120. Ibid., paragraph 45.

121. Enloe, *The Morning After*, p. 13.

122. Elkner, "*Dedovshchina* and the Committee of Soldiers' Mothers," paragraph 58.

123. Ibid., paragraph 66.

124. Rosalind Marsh, "Women in Contemporary Russia and the Former Soviet Union," in Rick Wilford and Robert L. Miller (eds.), *Women, Ethnicity and Nationalism: The Politics of Transition* (London: Routledge, 1998), p. 90.

125. True has made this argument in respect to the postcommunist transformation in the Czech Republic. Jacqui True, *Gender, Globalization, and Postsocialism: The Czech Republic after Communism* (New York: Columbia University Press, 2003). For a discussion of the post-Soviet Russian gender order, see Eichler, "Gender and Nation in the Soviet/Russian Transformation," pp. 53–57.

Chapter 2

1. Boris N. Yeltsin, *Midnight Diaries* (London: Phoenix, 2000), p. 70.
2. Vladimir Putin was the fifth prime minister in less than a year and a half. Yeltsin and his entourage rejected the previous four as potential successor.
3. Shevtsova makes this point in regard to Sergei Stepashin, who was appointed to the post of prime minister before Putin. Stepashin had served as director of the Federal Counterintelligence Service, minister of justice, and minister of interior affairs. Lilia Shevtsova, *Putin's Russia* (Washington, DC: Carnegie Endowment for International Peace, 2003), pp. 28–29.
4. While Putin has a background in the secret service, where he attained the rank of lieutenant colonel, he worked in a number of civilian posts after leaving the KGB in 1991. Putin insisted on his civilian status when Yeltsin appointed him director of the Federal Security Service in 1998. Bettina Renz, "Putin's Militocracy? An Alternative Interpretation of *Siloviki* in Contemporary Russian Politics," *Europe-Asia Studies* 58, no. 6 (2006): 920.
5. Eva Kreisky, "Diskreter Maskulinismus: Über geschlechtsneutralen Schein politischer Idole, politischer Ideale und politischer Institutionen," in Eva Kreisky and Birgit Sauer (eds.), *Das geheime Glossar der Politikwissenschaft: Geschlechtskritische Inspektion der Kategorien einer Disziplin* (Frankfurt am Main: Campus, 1997), pp. 185–186.
6. Cynthia Enloe, "Masculinity as Foreign Policy Issue," *Foreign Policy in Focus* 5, no. 36 (October 1, 2000), available at http://www.fpif.org/pdf/vol5/36ifmasculinity.pdf (accessed January 20, 2004).
7. Joane Nagel, "Masculinities and Nations," in Michael S. Kimmel, Jeff Hearn, and R. W. Connell (eds.), *Handbook of Studies on Men and Masculinities* (Thousand Oaks, CA: Sage Publications, 2004), p. 402.
8. Enloe, "Masculinity as Foreign Policy Issue." Enloe is posing this question in regard to U.S. foreign policy and U.S. leaders' desire to appear manly to political allies and competitors. However, the question is just as relevant to domestic politics and leaders' desire to appear manly in the eyes of the public.
9. It should be noted that this analysis focuses only on the federal state leadership and not on that of the Chechen separatists.
10. David J. Betz and Sergei Plekhanov, "Civil-Military Relations in Post-Soviet Russia: Rebuilding the 'Battle Order'?" in Natalie L. Mychajlyszyn and Harald von Riekhoff (eds.), *The Evolution of Civil-Military Relations in East-Central Europe and the Former Soviet Union* (Westport, CT: Praeger), p. 165.

11. Ibid., pp. 185–186.

12. This section is intended to offer the reader some background on the major events surrounding the wars, but cannot do justice to the complex course of both Chechen wars. For more detailed accounts, see: Claudia Wagner, *Rußlands Kriege in Tschetschenien: Politische Transformation und militärische Gewalt* (Münster: LIT, 2000); Tanja Wagensohn, "Krieg in Tschetschenien," *Aktuelle Analysen* no. 18 (München: Hans-Seidel-Stiftung, 2000); Markus Soldner, *Rußlands Čečnja-Politik seit 1993: Der Weg in den Krieg vor dem Hintergrund innenpolitischer Machtverschiebungen* (Hamburg: LIT, 1999); Matthew Evangelista, *The Chechen Wars: Will Russia Go the Way of the Soviet Union?* (Washington, DC: Brookings Institution Press, 2002); Robert Seely, *Russo-Chechen Conflict, 1888–2000: A Deadly Embrace* (London: Frank Cass, 2001); John B. Dunlop, *Russia Confronts Chechnya: Roots of a Separatist Conflict* (Cambridge: Cambridge University Press, 1998); Tracey C. German, *Russia's Chechen War* (London: RoutledgeCurzon, 2003); Carlotta Gall and Tom de Waal, *Chechnya: A Small Victorious War* (London: Pan, 1997); Anatol Lieven, *Chechnya: Tombstone of Russian Power* (New Haven: Yale University Press, 1999); Anna Politkovskaya, *A Dirty War: A Russian Reporter in Chechnya* (London: Harvill Press, 2001); Dmitri V. Trenin and Aleksei Malashenko with Anatol Lieven, *Russia's Restless Frontier: The Chechnya Factor in Post-Soviet Russia* (Washington, DC: Carnegie Endowment, 2004); John Russell, *Chechnya—Russia's "War on Terror"* (London: Routledge, 2007); Dmitrii E. Furman (ed.), *Chechnia i Rossiia: Obshchestvo i gosudarstvo* (Moscow: Polinform, 1999).

13. See, for example, Seely, *Russo-Chechen Conflict*, ch. 6.

14. Wagner, *Rußlands Kriege in Tschetschenien*, p. 42.

15. *Ukas* (decree) 2166 and *ukas* 1360, issued on December 9, 1994, formed the legal basis for the military intervention. See the following collection of documents pertaining to the first Chechen war: I. N. Eremenko, *Rossiia i Chechnia (1990–1997 gody): Dokumenty svidetsel'stvuiut* (Moscow: RAU-Universitet, 1997).

16. Wagensohn, "Krieg in Tschetschenien," pp. 18–36.

17. Gail W. Lapidus, "Putin's War on Terrorism: Lessons from Chechnya," *Post-Soviet Affairs* 18, no. 1 (2002): 43; Wagner, *Rußlands Kriege in Tschetschenien*, p. 162. See also Yuri Felshtinsky, Alexander Litvinenko, and Geoffrey Andrews, *Blowing Up Russia: Terror from Within* (London: Gibson Square Books, 2007).

18. Wagensohn, "Krieg in Tschetschenien," p. 40.

19. Pavel K. Baev, "The Targets of Terrorism and the Aims of Counter-Terrorism in Moscow, Chechnya and the North Caucasus," paper presented at the International Studies Association Annual Convention, Chicago, March 3, 2007; John B. Dunlop, *The 2002 Dubrovka and 2004 Beslan Hostage Crises: A Critique of Russian Counter-Terrorism* (Stuttgart: Ibidem-Verlag, 2006).

20. For an analysis of Russia's war on terror and a comparison with the U.S. war on terror, see Margot Light, "Russia and the War on Terror," in Christopher Ankersen with Michael O'Leary (eds.), *Understanding Global Terror* (Cambridge: Polity Press, 2007), pp. 95–110.

21. Serguei Alex. Oushakine, *The Patriotism of Despair: Nation, War, and Loss in Russia* (Ithaca, NY: Cornell University Press, 2009), p. 154.

22. John B. Dunlop, "Do Ethnic Russians Support Putin's War in Chechnya?" Jamestown Foundation's *Chechnya Weekly* 6, no. 4 (January 26, 2005): 6, available at www.jamestown.org (accessed August 10, 2008).

23. Pavel Felgenhauer, "The Russian Army in Chechnya," *Crimes of War Project: The Magazine* (April 2003): 6–9, available at http://www.crimesofwar.org/chechnya-mag/ChechnyaMagazine.pdf (accessed May 2, 2004). Felgenhauer's figures refer to both the first war (1994–1996) and the period of 1999 to early 2003 of the second war. Zürcher estimates that during 1994–1996 and 1999–2002, 7,000 Chechen fighters, 53,000 civilians, and 12,000 Russian soldiers (7,500 during the first war and 4,500 during the second war) were killed. Christoph Zürcher, *The Post-Soviet Wars: Rebellion, Ethnic Conflict, and Nationhood in the Caucasus* (New York: New York University Press, 2007), p. 100. Unfortunately, there are no reliable up-to-date figures on Russian military casualties during the second war.

24. Dunlop, "Do Ethnic Russians Support Putin's War in Chechnya?" p. 7.

25. For a detailed discussion of human rights violations perpetrated by federal forces during the Chechen wars, see Human Rights Watch, *"Welcome to Hell": Arbitrary Detention, Torture, and Extortion in Chechnya* (New York: Human Rights Watch, 2000); Politkovskaya, *A Dirty War*; Emma Gilligan, *Terror in Chechnya: Russia and the Tragedy of Civilians in War* (Princeton: Princeton University Press, 2010). For human rights violations committed by the *kadyrovtsy*, see Human Rights Watch, "Widespread Torture in the Chechen Republic: Human Rights Watch Briefing Paper for the 37th UN Committee against Torture," New York: Human Rights Watch, November 2006, available at http://www.hrw.org/backgrounder/eca/chechnya1106/ (accessed July 15, 2008).

26. Some sentences from this and the following section have previously appeared in Maya Eichler, "Russia's Post-Communist Transformation: A Gendered Analysis of the Chechen Wars," *International Feminist Journal of Politics* 8, no. 4 (2006): 486–511.

27. George Breslauer, *Gorbachev and Yeltsin as Leaders* (Cambridge: Cambridge University Press, 2002), pp. 196, 203.

28. Ibid., p. 196, emphasis added.

29. The term "Near Abroad" is commonly used to refer to the countries of the former Soviet Union.

30. Peter Lentini, "Hegemonic Masculinities in Russia," in Vladimir Tikhomirov (ed.), *In Search of Identity: Five Years since the Fall of the Soviet Union* (Melbourne: University of Melbourne Centre for Russian and Euro-Asian Studies, 1996), p. 166.

31. Between January and October 1994 the percentage of respondents who absolutely did not trust President Yeltsin more than doubled, growing from 14 to 31 percent. Fond "Obshchestvennoe mnenie," "S ianvaria po oktiabr' dolia doveriaiushchikh prezidentu Rossii snizilis' na 12 punktov," December 11, 1994, available at http://bd.fom.ru (accessed July 15, 2008).

32. Quoted in Gall and de Waal, *Chechnya*, p. 161. Apparently, Lobov cited the positive effect of the U.S. intervention in Haiti on President Bill Clinton's popularity. The Chechen war, it was hoped, would have a similar effect on Yeltsin's approval rating (ibid.).

33. Soldner, *Rußlands Čečnja-Politik seit 1993*, pp. 162–163.

34. Boris El'tsin, "Obrashchenie k grazhdanam Rossii," *Rossiiskaia gazeta*, December 14, 1994, p. 1.

35. Soldner first drew my attention to this shift in the official justification of the war. Soldner, *Rußlands Čečnja-Politik seit 1993*, pp. 150–157.

36. Viktor Chernomyrdin, "Za Rossiiu my stoiali i stoiat' budem," *Rossiiskaia gazeta*, December 14, 1994, pp. 1, 3. Chernomyrdin's speech was delivered at the national conference "Women and Development, Law, Reality, and Perspectives." Russian feminist Marina Liborakina criticized that Chernomyrdin used the conference to justify the use of military force. Apparently, he told women they needed to correctly understand the government's policy toward Chechnya. Marina Liborakina, "Women Fight to Be Heard in Chechen Dialogue," undated manuscript, available at http://www.isar.org/pubs/ST/Chechwomen44.html (accessed October 23, 2003).

37. Boris El'tsin, "Obrashchenie Borisa El'tsina v sviazi s situatsiei v Chechne," *Rossiiskaia gazeta*, December 28, 1994, p. 1.

38. Chernomyrdin, "Za Rossiiu my stoiali i stoiat' budem," p. 1.

39. Ibid.; El'tsin, "Obrashchenie Borisa El'tsina." In my view, their line of argumentation does not avoid the stereotyping of Chechens, but rather shows an attempt to deflect possible accusations of scapegoating Chechens or Muslims more generally.

40. During the tumultuous transition of the early 1990s, the state's role as protector and provider of order had been badly tarnished. The lack of order was a common theme in political and social discourse. Ipsa-Landa remarks that the image of a criminal and lawless Russia that dominated Western representations of Russia during the early 1990s was similar to Russia's discourse regarding the criminal and lawless nature of Chechnya. She argues, "It may be that Russia deflects negative self-images onto its own nemesis, Chechnya: whether or not that is true, this volley of insults demonstrates the extent to which Russia's search for a positive 'national idea' or identity has been inextricable linked to the wars in Chechnya." Simone Ipsa-Landa, "Russian Preferred Self-Image and the Two Chechen Wars," *Demokratizatsiya* 11, no. 1 (Winter 2003): 305–319; the quotation is from p. 308.

41. Meredith L. Roman, "Making Caucasians Black: Moscow since the Fall of Communism and the Racialization of Non-Russians," *Journal of Communist Studies and Transition Politics* 18, no. 2 (2002): 10.

42. The construction of criminal Chechens drew on older Russian stereotypes of Chechens as aggressive bandits, which coexist with the romanticized notion of the wild and noble mountain warrior. John Russell, "Mujahedeen, Mafia, Madmen: Russian Perceptions of Chechens during the War in Chechnya, 1994–96 and 1999–2001," *Journal of Communist Studies and Transition Politics* 18, no. 1 (2002): 78.

43. B. Z. Doktorov, A. A. Oslon, and E. S. Petrenko, *Epokha El'tsina: Mneniia rossiian. Sotsiologicheskie ocherki* (Moscow: Institut Fonda "Obshchestvennoe mnenie," 2002), pp. 137–138.

44. Ibid., p. 132. Before the start of the war, public opinion also did not support military intervention, as Alexseev writes: "In September 1994, only 7 per cent of Russian respondents in an authoritative VTsIOM poll supported Russia's use of military force in

Chechnia, while 42 per cent said Russia should not get involved at all and 31 per cent favoured Russia's involvement only as a mediator between the warring factions in Chechnia." Mikhail A. Alexseev, "Back to Hell: Civilian-Military 'Audience Costs' and Russia's Wars in Chechnia," in Stephen L. Webber and Jennifer G. Mathers (eds.), *Military and Society in Post-Soviet Russia* (Manchester: Manchester University Press, 2006), p. 100.

45. This refers to one of the explanations circulated by the press, in which the war was seen as "part of a cover-up of an unprecedented financial fraud involving the sale of petroleum from Grozny." Lilia Shevtsova, *Yeltsin's Russia: Myths and Reality* (Washington, DC: Carnegie Endowment for International Peace, 1999), p. 115.

46. Doktorov, Oslon, and Petrenko, *Epokha El'tsina*, p. 133.

47. Fond "Obshchestvennoe mnenie," "Esli god nazad na odnogo doveriaiushchego presidentu prikhodilos' dva nedoveriaiushchikh, to seichas—desiat,'" March 10, 1995, available at http://bd.fom.ru (accessed July 15, 2008). See also "In Brief: President's Rating Falls," *Nezavisimaia gazeta*, December 28, 1994, p. 1, *Current Digest of the Post-Soviet Press* 46, no. 52 (January 25, 1995): 16.

48. Doktorov, Oslon, and Petrenko, *Epokha El'tsina*, p. 133.

49. Wagner, *Rußlands Kriege in Tschetschenien*, p. 124.

50. "The State and the President Need Devoted Officers," *Rossiiskie vesti*, January 13, 1995, p. 2, *Current Digest of the Post-Soviet Press* 47, no. 2 (February 2, 1995): 5.

51. Wagner, *Rußlands Kriege in Tschetschenien*, p. 129.

52. Quoted in Robert V. Barylski, *The Soldier in Russian Politics: Duty, Dictatorship, and Democracy under Gorbachev and Yeltsin* (New Brunswick, NJ: Transaction Publishers, 1998), p. 314.

53. Today Gromov is chair of the country's leading veterans' organization, *Boevoe Bratstvo* (Military Brotherhood).

54. Wagner, *Rußlands Kriege in Tschetschenien*, p. 129

55. Lyle J. Goldstein, "Russian Civil-Military Relations in the Chechen War, December 1994–February 1995," *Journal of Slavic Military Studies* 10, no. 1 (March 1997): 114.

56. Barylski, *The Soldier in Russian Politics*, p. 314.

57. Wagner, *Rußlands Kriege in Tschetschenien*, p. 50.

58. Goldstein, "Russian Civil-Military Relations in the Chechen War," p. 110.

59. Lieven, *Chechnya*, pp. 104–105.

60. Olivier Roget, "Eyewitness: Grozny under Siege. The Unheated City Is Short of Food and Medical Supplies," *Segodnia*, December 24, 1995, p. 3, *Current Digest of the Post-Soviet Press* 46, no. 51 (January 18, 1995): 9.

61. The troops under Babichev's command did eventually continue their advance and participated in the storming of Grozny. Goldstein, "Russian Civil-Military Relations in the Chechen War," p. 111.

62. Natal'ia Baturina, "Okopnaia pravda. Komkor Rokhlin: 'Afganskaia voina byla progulkoi...,'" *Argumenty i fakty*, February 1, 1995, p. 2.

63. Barylski, *The Soldier in Russian Politics*, p. 319.

64. Quoted ibid., p. 315.

65. Boris El'tsin, "O deistvennosti gosudarstvennoi vlasti v Rossii: Poslanie Presidenta RF Sobraniiu Rossiiskoi Federatsii," 1995, available at http://public-service.narod.ru/appearance.html (accessed July 15, 2008).

66. Boris El'tsin, "Rossiia, za kotoruiu my v otvete: Poslanie Presidenta RF Sobraniiu Rossiiskoi Federatsii," 1996, available at http://public-service.narod.ru/appearance.html (accessed July 15, 2008).

67. Barylski, *The Soldier in Russian Politics*, p. 368

68. El'tsin, "Rossiia, za kotoruiu my v otvete."

69. Doktorov, Oslon, and Petrenko, *Epokha El'tsina*, p. 137.

70. Wagner, *Rußlands Kriege in Tschetschenien*, p. 116.

71. Alexseev, "Back to Hell," p. 99.

72. Yitzhak M. Brudny, "In Pursuit of the Russian Presidency: Why Yeltsin Won the 1996 Russian Presidential Election," *Communist and Post-Communist Studies* 30, no. 3 (September 1997): 262–263.

73. Barylski, *The Soldier in Russian Politics*, p. 373.

74. Barany says about Yeltsin's promise to abolish conscription: "It is hard to imagine another pledge that would have been more popular." Zoltan Barany, *Democratic Breakdown and the Decline of the Russian Military* (Princeton: Princeton University Press, 2007), p. 147.

75. Doktorov, Oslon, and Petrenko, *Epokha El'tsina*, p. 140.

76. The top five candidates were Boris Yeltsin, Gennadii Ziuganov, Aleksandr Lebed, Grigorii Iavlinksii, and Vladimir Zhirinovskii. See, for example, Richard Sakwa, *Russian Politics and Society*, 4th ed. (London: Routledge, 2008), pp. 174–175.

77. Lebed had made a name for himself as commander of Russia's 14th Army in Transdniestr (Moldova). For a detailed account of Lebed's background and political ideas, see Benjamin S. Lambeth, *The Warrior Who Would Rule Russia: A Profile of Aleksandr Lebed* (Santa Monica, CA: RAND, 1996). Lebed served as governor of Krasnoiarsk Krai from 1998 to 2002, when he was killed in a helicopter crash.

78. Quoted in Barylski, *The Soldier in Russian Politics*, p. 402.

79. The following report on Putin's selection as most popular politician of 1999 also includes previous results for the "Man of the Year." Fond "Obshchestvennoe mnenie," "V. Putin samyi populiarnyi rossiiskii politik 1999 goda," January 13, 2000, available at http://bd.fom.ru (accessed July 15, 2008).

80. Wagner, *Rußlands Kriege in Tschetschenien*, pp. 116–117.

81. Wagensohn, "Krieg in Tschetschenien," p. 16.

82. Doktorov, Oslon, and Petrenko, *Epokha El'tsina*, p. 146.

83. Ibid., p. 149.

84. Wagensohn, "Krieg in Tschetschenien," pp. 38–39. See also Robert Bruce Ware, "Revisiting Russia's Apartment Block Blasts," *Journal of Slavic Military Studies* 18, no. 4 (2005): 599–606.

85. Doktorov, Oslon, and Petrenko, *Epokha El'tsina*, p. 150.

86. Emil Pain, "The Chechen War in the Context of Contemporary Russian Politics," in Richard Sakwa (ed.), *Chechnya: From Past to Future* (London: Anthem Press, 2005), p. 69.

87. Alexseev, "Back to Hell," p. 108.
88. Fond "Obshchestvennoe mnenie," "V. Putin samiy populiarnyi rossiiskii politik 1999 goda."
89. Ziuganov, leader of the Communist Party, came in second with almost 30 percent of the vote. Shevtsova, *Putin's Russia*, pp. 74–75.
90. Boris Kagarlitsky, "Ethnic Problems and National Issues in Contemporary Russian Society," in Judyth L. Twigg and Kate Schecter (eds.), *Social Capital and Social Cohesion in Post-Soviet Russia* (Armonk, NY: M. E. Sharpe, 2003), p. 70.
91. Richard Sakwa, *Putin: Russia's Choice* (New York: Routledge, 2004), pp. 171–173.
92. Government of the Russian Federation, "Zaiavlenie Pravitel'stva RF o situatsii v Chechenskoi respublike i merakh po ee uregulirovaniiu," *Krasnaia zvezda*, October 23, 1999. Despite the official policy of distinguishing between Chechen terrorists and civilians, Simonsen writes that Chechens nonetheless quickly "became synonymous with 'terrorists,' 'bandits' and Islamic 'fundamentalists.'" Sven Gunnar Simonsen, "Putin's Leadership Style: Ethnocentric Patriotism," *Security Dialogue* 31, no. 3 (2000): 377.
93. Quoted in Russell, *Chechnya—Russia's "War on Terror,"* p. 69.
94. Vladimir Putin with Nataliya Gevorkyan, Natalya Timakova, and Andrei Kolesnikov, *First Person: An Astonishingly Frank Self-Portrait by Russia's President Vladimir Putin* (London: Hutchinson, 2000), p. 168.
95. Vladimir Putin, interview with Mayak radio station, March 18, 2000, available at www.kremlin.ru (accessed January 19, 2008).
96. Chechen suicide bombings became part of the conflict after mid-2000, and most of the bombers were women. See Irina Bazarya, "The Phenomenon of Chechen 'Black Widows': Becoming a Suicide Terrorist," paper presented at the Midwest Political Science Association Conference, Chicago, April 20–23, 2006; Anne Nivat, "The Black Widows: Chechen Women Join the Fight for Independence—and Allah," *Studies in Conflict and Terrorism* 28, no. 5 (2005): 413–419. For a gender analysis of this phenomenon in the context of the Russian-Chechen wars, see Laura Sjoberg and Caron Gentry, *Mothers, Monsters, Whores: Women's Violence in Global Politics* (London: Zed Books, 2007), ch. 4.
97. Quoted in Alexseev, "Back to Hell," p. 101.
98. Doktorov, Oslon, and Petrenko, *Epokha El'tsina*, p. 149.
99. Shevtsova, *Putin's Russia*, p. 36.
100. Yeltsin, *Midnight Diaries*, p. 338.
101. Ibid.
102. Shevtsova, *Putin's Russia*, p. 43.
103. Andrei P. Tsygankov, "Double Standard, Lots of Blame: Russia, Chechnya and the West," *Los Angeles Times*, January 28, 2000, p. B13.
104. Pain, "The Chechen War in the Context of Contemporary Russian Politics," p. 70.
105. Tatiana Sivaeva, "Women NGOs and the War in Chechnya," paper prepared for the Global Network for Women's Advocacy and Civil Society, 2000, p. 9, available at http://www.ciaonet.org/wps/sito3/sito3.pdf (accessed April 29, 2004).
106. Shevtsova, *Putin's Russia*, p. 145.

107. Putin, *First Person*, pp. 139–140.
108. Quoted in Shevtsova, *Putin's Russia*, p. 37.
109. See Appendix of Putin, *First Person*.
110. "Russians Believe Putin Will Restore Military and Economic Might," *Izvestiia*, February 19, 2000, p. 3, *Current Digest of the Post-Soviet Press* 52, no. 9 (March 29, 2000): 14.
111. Ibid.
112. Quoted in Rudra Sil and Cheng Chen, "State Legitimacy and the (In)significance of Democracy in Post-Communist Russia," *Europe-Asia Studies* 56, no. 3 (2004): 361. Sil and Chen argue that Putin is appealing here to ethnic Russians.
113. Enloe argues that "nationalism typically has sprung from masculinized memory, masculinized humiliation and masculinized hope." Cynthia Enloe, *Bananas, Beaches and Bases: Making Feminist Sense of International Politics* (Berkeley: University of California Press, 1989), p. 44.
114. Yeltsin, *Midnight Diaries*, p. 335.
115. Putin, *First Person*, p. 171.
116. See Genadii Troshev, *Moia Voina: Chechenskii dnevnik okopnogo generala* (Moscow: Vagrius, 2001).
117. Quoted in Barylski, *The Soldier in Russian Politics*, p. 387.
118. Pavel K. Baev, "The Russian Armed Forces: Failed Reform Attempts and Creeping Regionalization," *Journal of Communist Studies and Transition Politics* 17, no. 1 (2001): 23.
119. Putin, *First Person*, p. 139.
120. Thomas Gomart, *Russian Civil-Military Relations: Putin's Legacy* (Washington, DC: Carnegie Endowment for International Peace, 2008), p. 24.
121. Yeltsin, *Midnight Diaries*, p. 342.
122. Vladimir V. Putin, "Kakuiu Rossiiu my stroem: Poslanie Presidenta RF Sobraniiu Rossiiskoi Federatsii," 2000, available at http://public-service.narod.ru/appearance.html (accessed July 15, 2008).
123. Vladimir V. Putin, "Ne budet ni revolutsii, ni kontrrevoliutsii: Poslanie Presidenta RF Sobraniiu Rossiiskoi Federatsii," 2001, available at http://public-service.narod.ru/appearance.html (accessed July 15, 2008).
124. Dale R. Herspring, *The Kremlin and the High Command: Presidential Impact on the Russian Military from Gorbachev to Putin* (Lawrence: University Press of Kansas, 2006), p. 146.
125. Pavel K. Baev, "Putin's War in Chechnya: Who Steers the Course?" *PONARS Policy Memo* 345 (November 2004), available at http://www.csis.org/ruseura/ponars/pm/ (accessed July 30, 2008), p. 2.
126. "Ia – Shamanov," Interview conducted by Anna Politkovskaia, *Novaia gazeta*, June 19–25, 2000.
127. Andrei Smirnov, "From Military Butcher to Political Loser: A Portrait of General Shamanov," *North Caucasus Analysis* 8, no. 14 (April 5, 2007), available at http://www.jamestown.org/single/?no_cache=1&tx_ttnews[tt_news]=4065 (accessed August 5, 2008).

128. Chris Stephen, "Chechen War Veteran Flexes Political Muscles, Sending Shiver Down the Spine of the Kremlin," *Irish Times*, January 14, 2003, *Johnson's Russia List* no. 7018 (January 15, 2003), available at http://www.cdi.org/russia/johnson/7018-17.cfm (accessed August 15, 2008).

129. Quoted in Russell, *Chechnya—Russia's "War on Terror,"* p. 78.

130. Quoted in Pain, "The Chechen War in the Context of Contemporary Russian Politics," p. 75.

131. Quoted ibid., p. 76.

132. Russell, *Chechnya—Russia's "War on Terror,"* pp. 82–86.

133. Michaela Pohl, "Anna Politkovskaya and Ramzan Kadyrov," *Problems of Post-Communism* 54, no. 5 (September/October 2007): 32.

134. Lawrence A. Uzzell, "Hero of Russia . . . ," The Jamestown Foundation's *Chechnya Weekly* 6, no. 1 (January 5, 2005): 1, available at www.jamestown.org (accessed August 10, 2008).

135. Quoted in Pohl, "Anna Politkovskaya and Ramzan Kadyrov," p. 36.

136. Tanya Lokshina, "Chechnya: Choked by Headscarves," *openDemocracy Russia*, September 27, 2010, available at http://www.opendemocracy.net/tanya-lokshina/chechnya-choked-by-headscarves (accessed October 15, 2010).

137. See polling results of the Levada Center: www.levada.ru/chechnya.html (accessed August 15, 2008).

138. Ibid. Support for negotiations has been consistently higher among women. Thirty-one percent of women and 14 percent of men in March 2000, and 73 percent of female respondents and 47 percent of male respondents in May 2002, were in favor of negotiations. A. G. Levinson, "The Role of Gender in Russians' Attitudes toward the Second Chechen Campaign," *Sociological Research* 43, no. 2 (2004): 88–89.

139. Fond "Obshchestvennoe mnenie," "Glavnaia neudacha V. Putina—'ne utikhla Chechnia,'" March 21, 2002, available at http://bd.fom.ru (accessed July 15, 2008).

140. Fond "Obshchestvennoe mnenie," "Politik goda"—snova V. Putin," December 16, 2004, available at http://bd.fom.ru (accessed July 15, 2008).

141. Alexander Golts, "Putin and the Chechen War: Together Forever," *Moscow Times*, February 14, 2004, available at http://www.countercurrents.org/golts140204.htm (accessed January 23, 2007).

142. Iris Marion Young, "The Logic of Masculinist Protection: Reflections on the Current Security State," *Signs: Journal of Women in Culture and Society* 29, no. 1 (2003): 2.

143. Marlène Laruelle, *In the Name of the Nation: Nationalism and Politics in Contemporary Russia* (New York: Palgrave Macmillan, 2009), pp. 194–195. Sakwa, *Russian Politics and Society*, p. 224.

144. Yeltsin left negotiations to his prime minister, Chernomyrdin. After a number of failed attempts to storm the hospital and numerous casualties, Chernomyrdin and Basaev agreed on conditions to end the hostage taking. The incident led to a nonconfidence vote against the government in the Duma. Wagner, *Rußlands Kriege in Tschetschenien*, pp. 47–50.

145. Yeltsin, *Midnight Diaries,* p. 60.

146. Eliot Borenstein, *Overkill: Sex and Violence in Contemporary Russian Popular Culture* (Ithaca, NY: Cornell University Press, 2008), p. 226.

147. Ibid., p. 227.

148. Opinion polls conducted in 2002 showed that Putin was considered Russia's new sex symbol. Tat'iana Riabova and Oleg Riabov, "'U nas seksa net': Gender, Identity and Anti-Communist Discourses in Russia," undated manuscript, p. 6, available at nations.gender-ehu.org/text/Riabovy_u%20nas%20seksa%20net.doc (accessed July 29, 2008).

149. Quoted ibid.

150. Sarah Rainsford, "Putin Is Russia's New Pop Idol," BBC online, August 23, 2002, available at http://news.bbc.co.uk/2/hi/europe/2212885.stm (accessed October 15, 2010).

151. Gomart prefers the term "FSB-ization" to militarization, as it acknowledges the leading role of the security services and especially of the Federal Security Service. Furthermore, he emphasizes the many divisions within and between the military and other security services. While it is not my intention to brush over these important differences, my point here is to underscore the overall effect of these developments on the gender balance in Russian politics. Gomart, *Russian Civil-Military Relations,* ch. 3.

152. Ol'ga Kryshtanovskaya and Stephen White, "The Sovietization of Russian Politics," *Post-Soviet Affairs* 25, no. 4 (2009): 295.

153. Valerie Sperling, "The Gender Gap in Russian Politics and Elections," *PONARS Policy Memo* no. 259 (October 2002), p. 3, available at http://www.csis.org/files/media/csis/pubs/pm_0259.pdf (accessed 30 July 2008).

154. Kryshtanovskaya and White, "The Sovietization of Russian Politics," p. 300. Nadezhda Shvedova, "Gender Politics in Russia," in Linda Racioppi and Katherine O'Sullivan See (eds.), *Gender Politics in Post-Communist Eurasia* (East Lansing: Michigan State University Press, 2009), pp. 155–156.

Chapter 3

1. Ellen Jones, *Red Army and Society: A Sociology of the Soviet Military* (Boston: Allen and Unwin, 1985), pp. 56–57.

2. Aleksandr Oliinik, "A uklonistov stanovitsia bol'she," *Krasnaia zvezda,* May 28, 1997; Stephen L. Webber and Alina Zilberman, "The Citizenship Dimension of the Society-Military Interface," in Stephen L. Webber and Jennifer G. Mathers (eds.), *Military and Society in Post-Soviet Russia* (Manchester: Manchester University Press, 2006), pp. 174, 177; Fred Weir, "In Russia, an Army of Desertion," *Christian Science Monitor,* September 30, 2002.

3. Government of the Russian Federation, *Konstitutsiia Rossiiskoi Federatsii,* Moscow, December 12, 1993, statute 59.1, available at http://public-service.narod.ru/law.html (accessed July 15, 2008).

4. The Law on Military Obligation and Service passed in 1993 was replaced by a new

law in 1998. See Government of the Russian Federation, *Federal'nyi zakon o "Voinskoi obiazannosti i voennoi sluzhbe,"* no. 53-F3, March 28, 1998, Moscow.

5. The length of service was extended from eighteen to twenty-four months in 1995.

6. Irina Isakova, "The Russian Defense Reform," *China and Eurasia Forum Quarterly* 5, no. 1 (2007): 78.

7. Since 2008, conscripts are no longer recruited into the Border Guard Service. International Institute for Strategic Studies, *The Military Balance 2008* (London: Institute for Strategic Studies, 2008), p. 208.

8. Jones, *Red Army and Society*, pp. 53–57.

9. Isakova, "The Russian Defense Reform," p. 78.

10. Government of the Russian Federation, *Konstitutsiia*, Statute 59.3.

11. Government of the Russian Federation, *Federal'nyi zakon "Ob al'ternativnoi grazhdanskoi sluzhbe,"* Moscow, 2003.

12. Igor Fedyukhin, "No Alternatives: Experts Say the Law on Alternative Civilian Service Will Not Be Popular," *CDI Russia Weekly* no. 266 (July 25, 2003), available at www.cdi.org/Russia/266–9.cfm (accessed November 16, 2004); Aleksandr Golts, "The Social and Political Condition of the Russian Military," in Steven E. Miller and Dmitri Trenin (eds.), *The Russian Military: Power and Policy* (Cambridge: MIT Press, 2004), p. 74.

13. This figure is based on a 2009 report by Andrey Kalikh and Lev Levinson, "Implementation of the Right to Conscientious Objection in Russian Federation 2004 ¨C [sic] 2009," published on the website of the European Bureau of Conscientious Objection, available at http://www.ebco-beoc.eu/ (accessed June 15, 2010). See also the very informative website of the All-Russian Coalition of NGOs "For Democratic Alternative Service" (*Vserossiiskaia koalitsiia obshchestvennykh organizatsii "Za demokraticheskuiu al'ternativnuiu grazhdanskuiu sluzhbu"*): http://ags.demokratia.ru.

14. These figures are based on the annual reports of the International Institute for Strategic Studies, *The Military Balance*, published in London, in particular the 1991, 1996–2002, as well as the 2005–2009 issues; and Pavel Felgenhauer, "Medvedev Acknowledges Problems in the 'New Look' Armed Forces," *Eurasia Daily Monitor*, March 11, 2010, available at http://www.jamestown.org/single/?no_cache=1&tx_ttnews[tt_news]=36145 (accessed June 1, 2010).

15. Human Rights Watch, "Conscription through Detention in Russia's Armed Forces," New York: Human Rights Watch, November 2002, p. 8, available at http://www.hrw.org/en/reports/2002/11/21/conscription-through-detention-russias-armed-forces (accessed October 15, 2008).

16. Vasilii Smirnov, "Iz pervykh ruk: Problemy osennogo prizyva," *Voenno-promyshlennyi kur'er*, December 1, 2004.

17. "'Rossiiskaia Gazeta' otmenila alternativnuiu sluzhbu," *Regnum*, March 31, 2004, available at http://www.regnum.ru/news/240003.html (accessed June 15, 2010).

18. "Genshtab podschital uklonistov," *Krasnyi voin*, April 5, 2008; Aleksandra Beluza and Dmitrii Litovkin, "Novobrantsam ne do smekha," *Izvestiia*, April 1, 2009.

19. Viktor Litovkin, "Opiat' prizyv, opiat' problemy," *Nezavisimoe voennoe obozrenie*, April 9, 2010.

20. On the shadow economy of draft exemptions, see Igor' Kliamkin and Lev Timofeev, *Tenevaia Rossiia: Ekonomiko-sotsiologicheskoe issledovaniie* (Moscow: Rossiiskii gosudarstevennii gumanitarnii universitet, 2000), pp. 114–121.

21. Harley Balzer, "The Implications of Demographic Change for Russian Politics and Security," paper presented at the Health and Demography in the States of the Former Soviet Union Conference, Weatherhead Center for International Affairs, Harvard University, Cambridge, MA, April 29–30, 2005.

22. Pavel Felgenhauer, "Personnel Problems Impact on Russian Military Reform," *Eurasia Daily Monitor*, April 29, 2010, available at http://www.jamestown.org/single/?no_cache=1&tx_ttnews[tt_news]=36329 (accessed June 1, 2010).

23. In 2003 the state took control of the All-Russian Center for the Study of Public Opinion (VTsIOM). The center's researchers left in protest and formed a new organization called VTsIOM-A, which was renamed Analytical Center of Iurii Levada ("Levada Center") in 2004.

24. The cited polling results can be found on the website of the Levada Center under www.levada.ru/army (October 15, 2010).

25. Levada-Tsentr, "Rossiiskaia armiia," February 17, 2010, available at http://www.levada.ru/press/2010021701.html (accessed June 12, 2010).

26. Some sentences from this and the following two sections have previously appeared in Maya Eichler, "Russia's Post-Communist Transformation: A Gendered Analysis of the Chechen Wars," *International Feminist Journal of Politics* 8, no. 4 (2006): 486–511.

27. Interview with Iurii, Samara, July 2006.

28. See Natalie Gross, "Youth and the Army in the USSR in the 1980s," *Soviet Studies* 42, no. 3 (July 1990): 481–483.

29. It is hard to determine the exact figure of military spending in Russia, although it is certain that military spending fell steadily in the post-Soviet period. According to one estimate cited by Deriglazova, military spending declined from 15 percent of GDP in the late 1980s to 2.4 percent in 1998, but started to increase again during Putin's first presidency. Larisa Deriglazova, "To Fear or to Respect?: Two Approaches to Military Reform in Russia," *Journal of Power Institutions in Post-Soviet Societies* no. 3 (2005): paragraph 21, available at http://www.pipss.org/document415.html (accessed September 17, 2006.). For an analysis of the development of the military budget during Putin's presidencies, see Julian Cooper, "The Security Economy," in Mark Galeotti (ed.), *The Politics of Security in Modern Russia* (Surrey: Ashgate Publishing Limited, 2010), pp. 145–170. The author shows that there was a steady increase in military spending from 2000 to 2008, but that as a share of GDP it remained constant at approximately 2.6 percent (p. 147).

30. See Human Rights Watch, "To Serve without Health? Inadequate Nutrition and Health Care in the Russian Armed Forces," New York: Human Rights Watch, November 2003, available at http://www.hrw.org/en/reports/2003/11/13/serve-without-health-0 (accessed October 15, 2008).

31. Estimates for noncombat-related deaths range from 1,000 to 5,000 per year. There are no reliable figures on suicides, as the label "death due to illness" is often used to cover up suicides among service personnel. Golts, "The Social and Political Condition of the Russian Military," pp. 75–76; Weir, "In Russia, an Army of Desertion"; Webber and Zilberman, "The Citizenship Dimension of the Society-Military Interface," p. 174.

32. Human Rights Watch, "The Wrongs of Passage: Inhuman and Degrading Treatment of New Recruits in the Russian Armed Forces," New York: Human Rights Watch, October 2004, p. 2, available at http://www.hrw.org/en/node/11940/section/1 (accessed October 15, 2008).

33. Interview with Iurii, Samara, July 2006.

34. Interview with Valerii, Samara, July 2006.

35. Interview with Sergei, Samara, June 2006; Interview with Iurii, Samara, July 2006.

36. Soldiers' Mothers of St. Petersburg (SMSP), "The Facade Is Crumbling," 1996, available at http://www.openweb.ru/smo/english/english.htm (accessed June 15, 2001).

37. Human Rights Watch, "The Wrongs of Passage."

38. As one of my interviewees who had served as a conscript in the special forces (GRU) pointed out, *dedovshchina* is less violent in the special forces than in the regular armed forces. Nonetheless, his stories of conscript life consisted almost exclusively of recollections of abuse he had suffered or witnessed. Interview with Anatolii, Samara, July 2006.

39. Françoise Daucé and Elisabeth Sieca-Kozlowski, "Introduction," in Françoise Daucé and Elisabeth Sieca-Kozlowski (eds.), *Dedovshchina in the Post-Soviet Military: Hazing of Russian Army Conscripts in a Comparative Perspective* (Stuttgart: Ibidem-Verlag, 2007), p. 22.

40. Joris Van Bladel, "Russian Soldiers in the Barracks: A Portrait of a Subculture," in Anne Aldis and Roger N. McDermott (eds.), *Russian Military Reform, 1992–2002* (Portland, OR: Frank Cass, 2003), pp. 60–72; the quotation is from p. 64.

41. Ibid., p. 63.

42. Ibid., p. 69.

43. Human Rights Watch, "The Wrongs of Passage," pp. 31–42. See also Van Bladel, "Russian Soldiers in the Barracks," pp. 66–67.

44. Recent attempts to introduce a corps of professional noncommissioned officers into the Russian military have not been successful. International Institute for Strategic Studies, *The Military Balance 2010* (London: Institute for Strategic Studies, 2010), p. 215.

45. This point is emphasized in Dale R. Herspring, "Dedovshchina in the Russian Army: The Problem That Won't Go Away," *Journal of Slavic Military Studies* 18, no. 4 (2005): 609–610; and Bladel, "Russian Soldiers in the Barracks," p. 71.

46. For an exception, see I. S. Kon, "Dedovshchina v svete issledovanii zakrytykh muzhskikh soobshchestv," in *Muzhchina v ekstremal'noi situatsii* (St. Petersburg: Indrik, 2007), pp. 84–88. See also van Bladel's Ph.D. dissertation, in which he acknowledges that same-sex rape is "used symbolically to strip a soldier

of his masculine dignity." Joris Van Bladel, "The All-Volunteer Force in the Russian Mirror: Transformation without Change," Ph.D. diss. (Proefschrift), Rijksuniversiteit Groningen, June 2004, p. 179.

47. For analyses of hazing in other militaries, see Lesley Gill, "Creating Citizens, Making Men: The Military and Masculinity in Bolivia" *Cultural Anthropology* 12, no. 4 (1997): 527–550; Sandra Whitworth, *Men, Militarism and UN Peacekeeping*, ch. 6; and Paul R. Higate (ed.), *Military Masculinities: Identity and the State* (Westport, CT: Praeger, 2003).

48. Interview with Anatolii, Samara, July 2006.

49. Human Rights Watch, "The Wrongs of Passage," pp. 50–52.

50. On hegemonic and subordinate masculinities, see R. W. Connell, *Gender and Power: Society, the Person and Sexual Politics* (Stanford: Stanford University Press, 1987); and Charlotte Hooper, "Masculinist Practices and Gender Politics: The Operation of Multiple Masculinities in International Relations," in Marysia Zalewski and Jane Parpart (eds.), *The "Man" Question in International Relations* (Boulder, CO: Westview Press, 1998), pp. 28–53.

51. Van Bladel, "Russian Soldiers in the Barracks," p. 67.

52. Human Rights Watch, "The Wrongs of Passage," p. 23.

53. Interview with Anatolii, Samara, July 2006.

54. Interview with Iurii, Samara, July 2006.

55. Interview with Igor', Samara, July 2006.

56. Quoted in Judith Matloff, "Russia's Army Faces Battle within Its Ranks," *Christian Science Monitor*, February 1, 1999.

57. Sarah Brown, "Modern Tales of the Russian Army," *World Policy Journal* 14, no. 1 (1997): 62.

58. Fond "Obshchestvennoe mnenie," "Kak vy schitaete, prizyvniki dolzhny obiazatel'no prokhodit' sluzhbu v armii ili luchshe predostavit' im vozmozhnost' al'ternativnoi sluzhby v grazhdanskoi sfere (rabota na predpriiatiiakh, v bol'nitsakh i t.d.)?" May 6, 1998, available at http://bd.fom.ru (accessed October 15, 2010).

59. Rebecca Kay, *Men in Contemporary Russia: The Fallen Heroes of Post-Soviet Change* (Aldershot: Ashgate, 2006), pp. 67–68.

60. Interview with Valerii, Samara, July 2006.

61. Interview with Igor', Samara, July 2006.

62. Interview with Nikolai, Samara, June 2006, emphasis added.

63. Other events potentially leading to a downward trajectory in men's employment are alcohol abuse, divorce, and their own or a family member's ill health. Marina Ilyina, "Critical Life Events and Downward Trajectories," in Sarah Ashwin (ed.), *Adapting to Russia's New Labour Market: Gender and Employment Behaviour* (New York: Routledge, 2006), pp. 193–212.

64. Webber and Zilberman, "The Citizenship Dimension of the Society-Military Interface," p. 167.

65. Interview with Valerii, Samara, July 2006.

66. Interview with Igor', Samara, July 2006.

67. Interview with Ol'ga T., chair of *Sodeistvie*, Samara, June 2006.
68. Interview with Igor', Samara, July 2006.
69. Interview with Valerii, Samara, July 2006.
70. Interview with Nikolai, Samara, June 2006.
71 Theodore P. Gerber and Sarah E. Mendelson, "Strong Public Support for Military Reform in Russia," *PONARS Policy Memo* 288 (May 2003), available at http://www.gwu.edu/~ieresgwu/assets/docs/ponars/pm_0288.pdf (accessed October 15, 2010), p. 8. The survey also found that sympathy for draft evaders and support for an all-volunteer force is significantly higher than the average among women aged thirty to forty-nine and respondents with a college degree.
72. Elena Gapova, "Conceptualizing Gender, Nation, and Class in Post-Soviet Belarus," in Kathleen Kuehnast and Carol Nechemias (eds.), *Post-Soviet Women Encountering Transition: Nation Building, Economic Survival, and Civic Activism* (Baltimore, MD: Johns Hopkins University Press, 2004), pp. 92–94. This development has been accelerated by Russia's capitalist transformation, but it is not an entirely new phenomenon. Processes of urbanization and modernization began to affect the identities and values of young men during the last two decades of the Soviet Union. Also, alternative notions of masculinity, in particular those tied to the criminal world, existed at the margins of society throughout the Soviet period. On the latter point, see Stephen Handelman, *Comrade Criminal: Russia's New Mafiya* (New Haven: Yale University Press, 1995).
73. Anatol Lieven, *Chechnya: Tombstone of Russian Power* (New Haven: Yale University Press, 1999), p. 204. Lieven's quotation acknowledges that for men, class privilege comes with the promise of power over women and access to women's bodies.
74. Elena Meshcherkina, "New Russian Men: Masculinity Regained?" in Sarah Ashwin (ed.), *Gender, State and Society in Soviet and Post-Soviet Russia* (London: Routledge, 2000), p. 105.
75. Ibid., p. 109.
76. Gapova, "Conceptualizing Gender, Nation, and Class in Post-Soviet Belarus"; Alexei Yurchak, "Muzhskaia ekonomia: Ne do glupostei kogda kar'eru kuësh'," in Sergei Ushakin (ed.), *O Muzhe(n)stvennosti* (Moscow: Novoe literaturnoe obozrenie, 2001), pp. 245–267.
77. Human Rights Watch, "The Wrongs of Passage," p. 7.
78. Michael Lokshin and Ruslan Yemtsov, "Who Bears the Cost of Russia's Military Draft?" *Economics of Transition* 16, no. 3 (2008): 382. These economists have attempted to capture the social cost of the draft using an econometric analysis. Their conclusion is that "[t]he narrowly defined static opportunity cost (expressed as lost wages) of the military draft amounts, on average, to 15 percent of household consumption, but could be as high as 30 percent of *per capita* consumption of poor households" (ibid.).
79. Konstantin L. Bannikov, "Regimented Communities in a Civil Society," *Journal of Power Institutions in Post-Soviet Societies* no. 1 (July 2004): paragraph 51, available at http://www.pipss.org/document40.html (accessed August 13, 2004).
80. Interview with Sergei, Samara, June 2006.
81. Interview with Iurii, Samara, July 2006.

82. Fond "Obshchestvennoe mnenie," "'Poteriannye gody' v 'shkole zhizni,'" November 23, 2000, available at http://bd.fom.ru (accessed October 15, 2010).

83. Herspring, "Dedovshchina in the Russian Army," p. 622.

84. Interviews with Igor' and Valerii, Samara, July 2006.

85. Interview with Valerii, Samara, July 2006.

86. In 2003, the Russian military published new medical guidelines that prohibited gays, alcoholics, and drug users from conscription, except in times of war. Such a measure constructs the abuse and violence among conscripts as linked to particular (deviant) men and denies its structural nature. "Russia Bans Gays, Alcohol and Drug Users from Army," *Agence France-Press,* March 13, 2003, reprinted in *CDI Russia Weekly* no. 248 (March 14, 2003), available at http://www.cdi.org/russia/248-11-pr.cfm (accessed April 1, 2009). The medicalization of homosexuals, by lumping them together with alcoholics and drug users, was especially troubling. The military's medical service restated its position in late 2003, announcing that gays are not banned from the military, though it acknowledged the difficulties and violence openly gay men are likely to encounter while serving. "Gays Are Not Willingly Accepted in the Russian Army," *Pravda,* December 1, 2003, available at http://english.pravda.ru/business/finance/01-12-2003/4207-gayarmy-0/ (accessed June 1, 2010).

87. Vadim Volkov, *Violent Entrepreneurs: The Use of Force in the Making of Russian Capitalism* (Ithaca, NY: Cornell University Press, 2002), pp. 137–138.

88. SMSP, "The Glorious Facade of the Russian Army," 1996, available at http://www.openweb.ru/smo/english/english.htm (accessed June 15, 2001). On movie representations of militarized masculinity (often in the context of the Chechen wars), see Kathrin Hartmann, "Die Konstruktion von Männerbildern in Russland—Kontinuität und Wandel von Männerbildern in den 90er Jahren am Beispiel sowjetischer und postsowjetischer Filme," *Working Paper* no. 39 (Berlin: Osteuropa-Institut der Freien Universität Berlin, 2002); Galina Zvereva, "'Rabota dlia muzhchin?' Chechenskaia voina v massovom kino Rossii," *Neprikosnovennyi zapas: Debaty o politike i kul'ture* no. 26 (2002): 102–109; Ol'ga Sarkisova, "Skazhi mne, kto tvoi vrag ... chechenskaia voina v rossiiskom kino," *Neprikosnovennyi zapas: Debaty o politike i kul'ture* no. 26 (2002): 94–101; Christine Engel, "Kulturelles Gedächtnis, neue Diskurse: Zwei russische Filme über die Kriege in Tschetschenien," *Osteuropa* 53, no. 5 (2003): 604–617; and David Gillespie, "Confronting Imperialism: The Ambivalence of War in Post-Soviet Film," in Stephen L. Webber and Jennifer G. Mathers (eds.), *Military and Society in Post-Soviet Russia* (Manchester: Manchester University Press, 2006), pp. 80–93.

89. Government of the Russian Federation, *Federal'nyi zakon o "Voinskoi obiazannosti i voennoi sluzhbe."*

90. Alexander M. Golts and Tonya L. Putnam, "State Militarism and Its Legacies: Why Military Reform Has Failed in Russia," *International Security* 29, no. 2 (Fall 2004): 134. As the authors point out, there is some doubt as to whether maintaining a conscription army is really less expensive.

91. Ibid., 126.

92. Andrew Spivak and William Alex Pridemore, "Conscription and Reform in the Russian Army," *Problems of Post-Communism* 51, no. 6 (2004): 41.

93. International Institute for Strategic Studies, *The Military Balance 2005–2006* (London: Institute for Strategic Studies, 2005), p. 151.

94. Valerie Sperling, *Organizing Women in Contemporary Russia: Engendering Transition* (Cambridge: Cambridge University Press, 1999), pp. 146–158.

95. Jennifer G. Mathers, "Women in the Russian Armed Forces: A Marriage of Convenience?" *Minerva: Quarterly Report on Women and the Military* 18, nos. 3–4 (2000): 135.

96. Christine Eifler, "'Weil man nun mit ihnen rechnen muss . . .': Frauen in den Streitkräften Russlands," in Ruth Seifert and Christine Eifler (eds.), *Gender und Militär: Internationale Erfahrungen mit Männern und Frauen in den Streitkräften* (Königstein: Ulrike Helmer, 2004), p. 106.

97. Cynthia Enloe, *Maneuvers: The International Politics of Militarizing Women's Lives* (Berkeley: University of California Press, 2000), pp. 259–260; Mathers, "Women in the Russian Armed Forces," pp. 129–130; A. I. Smirnov, "Zhenshchiny na sluzhbe v rossiiskoi armii," *Sotsiologicheskie issledovaniia* no. 11 (2000): 128; Eifler, "'Weil man nun mit ihnen rechnen muss,'" pp. 103–105. See also Jennifer G. Mathers, "Women, Society and the Military: Women Soldiers in Post-Soviet Russia," in Stephen L. Webber and Jennifer G. Mathers (eds.), *Military and Society in Post-Soviet Russia* (Manchester: Manchester University Press, 2006), pp. 207–227.

98. Christine Eifler, "The Armed Forces as a Place of Social Construction of Gender: Women in the Russian Military," in Gabriele Jähnert et al. (eds.), *Gender in Transition: Eastern and Central Europe Proceedings* (Berlin: Trafo Verlag, 2001), p. 277.

99. Ibid., p. 275.

100. Mathers, "Women in the Russian Armed Forces," p. 131.

101. An excerpt of the report written by M. Kolosnityna was published in "Ledi v dospekhakh," *Interfaks Vremia*, August 23, 2006, available at http://www.ifvremya.ru/cgi-bin/res.pl?FIL=work/arc/2006/0823/3_20060823.txt (accessed September 30, 2006).

102. Enloe, *Maneuvers*, pp. 237–238.

103. Militaries in other countries have also increasingly come to rely on women volunteers (for example, New Zealand, Australia, the United States, and Canada). In contrast with the Russian discourse, Western states often deal with the ambivalence about their greater reliance on women through the language of progress and democracy.

104. Svetlana Pleshakova, "Mamania-Kombat: Zhena-komandir—podarok dlia liubogo mushchiny," *Moskovskii komsomolets*, February 22, 2007, p. 4.

105. Interviews, Samara, June–August 2006.

106. Quoted in Golts and Putnam, "State Militarism and Its Legacies," p. 135.

107. Dmitri V. Trenin and Aleksei Malashenko with Anatol Lieven, *Russia's Restless Frontier: The Chechnya Factor in Post-Soviet Russia* (Washington, DC: Carnegie Endowment, 2004), p. 109

108. Dale R. Herspring, "Undermining Combat Readiness in the Russian Military, 1992–2005," *Armed Forces and Society* 32, no. 4 (2006): 519.

109. Interview with Nikolai, Samara, June 2006.

110. Interview with Larissa, Samara, July 2006. Larissa also told me that she

planned to marry a U.S. citizen and immigrate to the United States, and that this plan was strongly linked to her desire to help her son evade the draft. She was able to follow through with this plan, as I later found out. Anecdotal evidence suggests that in families with boys the draft is an important "push-factor" in Russians' decision to emigrate.

111. The war caused a massive wave of refugees, with approximately 250,000 internally displaced persons in 1995. Christoph Zürcher, *The Post-Soviet Wars: Rebellion, Ethnic Conflict, and Nationhood in the Caucasus* (New York: New York University Press, 2007), p. 101.

112. Pavel Felgenhauer, "Russia's Forces Unreconstructed," Institute for the Study of Conflict, Ideology, and Policy's *Perspective* 10, no. 4 (March–April 2000), available at www.bu.edu/iscip/vol10/Felgenhauer.html (accessed September 16, 2008).

113. Dale R. Herspring, *The Kremlin and the High Command: Presidential Impact on the Russian Military from Gorbachev to Putin* (Lawrence: University Press of Kansas, 2006), p. 151.

114. The war resulted in large numbers of refugees, and their displacement lasted longer than during the first war. Zürcher cites numbers of between 56,000 and 239,000 displaced persons during the period from September 1999 to August 2001. Zürcher, *The Post-Soviet Wars*, pp. 99–102.

115. Felgenhauer, "Russia's Forces Unreconstructed."

116. Claudia Wagner, *Rußlands Kriege in Tschetschenien: Politische Transformation und militärische Gewalt* (Münster: LIT, 2000), p. 163.

117. Trenin and Malashenko with Lieven, *Russia's Restless Frontier*, p. 106; Tatiana Sivaeva, "Women NGOs and the War in Chechnya," paper prepared for the Global Network for Women's Advocacy and Civil Society, 2000, pp. 8–9, available at http://www.ciaonet.org/wps/sit03/sit03.pdf (accessed April 29, 2004).

118. "Analysis: Media Swings against Military," BBC News online, January 11, 2000, available at http://news.bbc.co.uk/2/hi/europe/599516.stm (accessed September 16, 2008).

119. "Analysis: Russia's Suffering Conscripts," BBC News online, January 18, 2000, available at http://news.bbc.co.uk/2/hi/europe/607642.stm (accessed September 16, 2008).

120. Arkady Babchenko, *One Soldier's War in Chechnya* (London: Portobello Books, 2007).

121. Trenin and Malashenko with Lieven, *Russia's Restless Frontier*, p. 141.

122. Babchenko, *One Soldier's War in Chechnya*.

123. Ibid., p. 83.

124. Herspring, "Dedovshchina in the Russian Army," p. 621.

125. Viktor Litovkin, "Draftees Name the War in Chechnya, Hazing and Bad Food as Their Reasons for Refusing to Serve," *Izvestia*, April 5, 1996, pp. 1-2, *Current Digest of Post-Soviet Press* 48, no. 15 (May 8, 1996): 5.

126. "Russia Launches Spring Military Draft Campaign," *Jamestown Foundation Monitor* 6, no. 68 (April 5, 2000), reprinted in *CDI Russia Weekly* no. 96 (April 7, 2000),

available at http://www.cdi.org/russia/apr0700.html#10 (accessed September 16, 2008). Babchenko expresses resentment toward the men who were able to and chose to evade the draft, underscoring the class makeup of troops in the war zone. As he writes:

> You won't find any smart, handsome boys in these tents. They were got out of the war by their rich daddies, leaving it to us ordinary folk to die in Grozny, the ones who didn't have the money to pay our way out. Heaped in these tents are the sons of labourers, teachers, peasants and blue-collar workers, basically all those who were made penniless by the government's thieving reforms and then left to waste away. These tents contain the ones who didn't know how to give a bribe to the right person, or who thought that army service was the duty of every man.

In this quotation Babchenko not only portrays the inequality of military service in contemporary Russia but also addresses the fact that so many young men no longer consider military service a duty of every man and therefore choose not to serve. Both class and notions of masculinity influence who serves in the military and who ends up fighting wars on behalf of the state. Babchenko, *One Soldier's War in Chechnya*, p. 115.

127. See the results for 1997 to 2007 available at www.levada.ru/army (accessed October 15, 2010).

128. Fond "Obshchestvennoe mnenie," "Bol'shinstvo rossiian polagaiut, shto sozdanie professional'noi armii—nailuchshii sposob usileniia ee boesposobnosti," February 24, 1995, available at http://bd.fom.ru (accessed September 16, 2008). The poll also illustrated the generational differences in attitudes, as 76 percent of sixteen- to twenty-four-year-olds and only 55 percent of over fifty-five-year-olds held that opinion.

129. Fond "Obshchestvennoe mnenie," "Srochnaia sluzhba v armii," October 3, 2002, available at http://bd.fom.ru (accessed June 1, 2010). Similar results regarding support for an all-volunteer force and sympathy for draft evaders were found in a poll conducted in 2003, the results of which are published in Gerber and Mendelson, "Strong Public Support for Military Reform in Russia."

130. Elena Zdravomyslova, "Soldiers' Mothers Fighting the Military Patriarchy: Re-invention of Responsible Activist Motherhood for Human Rights' [sic] Struggle," in Ilse Lenz, Charlotte Ullrich, and Barbara Fersch (eds.), *Gender Orders Unbound: Globalisation, Restructuring and Reciprocity* (Opladen: Barbara Budrich, 2007), p. 213.

131. Amy Caiazza, *Mothers and Soldiers: Gender, Citizenship, and Civil Society in Contemporary Russia* (New York: Routledge, 2002), pp. 139–141. I discuss the role of soldiers' mothers in relation to men's obligatory military service in more detail in Chapter 4.

132. Viktor Sokirko, "U rodiny—nastoichivyi prizyv," *Moskovskii komsomolets*, January 4, 2000.

133. Sergei Tkachuk, "Voiui ne spesha," *Novye izvestiia*, July 8, 2005, p. 2.

134. Vladimir Isachenkov "State TV Runs Chechnya Ads," *Moscow Times*, January 26, 2005, available at http://www.themoscowtimes.com/stories/2005/01/26/017.html (accessed January 30, 2005).

135. "Nesmotria na obeshchaniia Ivanova, soldat-srochnikov otpravliaiut Chechniu,"

Novyi region, February 28, 2006, available at www.nr2.ru/society/57672.html (accessed September 16, 2008).

136. Interview with Nikolai, Samara, June 2006.

137. Spivak and Pridemore, "Conscription and Reform in the Russian Army," pp. 37–38.

138. Human Rights Watch, "Conscription through Detention in Russia's Armed Forces."

139. "Russia Launches Spring Military Draft Campaign."

140. Gerber and Mendelson, "Strong Public Support for Military Reform in Russia," p. 5.

141. Robert V. Barylski, *The Soldier in Russian Politics: Duty, Dictatorship, and Democracy under Gorbachev and Yeltsin* (New Brunswick, NJ: Transaction Publishers, 1998), pp. 322–323.

142. Viktor Litovkin, "The Army Is Shooting at Its Own Men: The Main Reason for Today's Tragedies Is Unbearable Living and Service Conditions," *Izvestiia*, June 6, 1997, pp. 1, 5, *Current Digest of Post-Soviet Press* 49, no. 24 (July 16, 1997): 2.

143. Pavel Felgenhauer, "The Russian Army in Chechnya," *Crimes of War Project: The Magazine* (April 2003): 6–9, available at http://www.crimesofwar.org/chechnya-mag/ChechnyaMagazine.pdf (accessed May 2, 2004), p. 7; Golts and Putnam, "State Militarism and Its Legacies," p. 136.

144. Trenin and Malashenko with Lieven, *Russia's Restless Frontier*, p. 139. Contract soldiers engaged in combat operations were promised almost $1,000 a month but eventually received only one-third that amount. Golts and Putnam, "State Militarism and Its Legacies," p. 136.

145. Stephen Shenfield, "Chechnya at a Turning Point," *Brown Journal of World Affairs* 8, no. 1 (Winter–Spring 2001): 65.

146. Felgenhauer, "The Russian Army in Chechnya," p. 7. See also Anna Politkovskaya, *A Dirty War: A Russian Reporter in Chechnya* (London: Harvill Press, 2001).

147. Nikolai Poroskov, "Call to Arms Barely Heard: Young Men in Russia Are Now Trying to Even Evade Alternative Service," *Vremia novostei*, October 1, 2004, p. 4, *Current Digest of Post-Soviet Press* 56, no. 40 (November 3, 2004): 16.

148. Litovkin, "The Army Is Shooting at Its Own Men," p. 2.

149. Webber and Zilberman, "The Citizenship Dimension of the Society-Military Interface," p. 200, note 30.

150. Vladimir Shlapentokh, "Trust in Public Institutions in Russia: The Lowest in the World," *Johnson's Russia List* no. 9186 (June 27, 2005), available at http://www.cdi.org/russia/johnson/9186-29.cfm (accessed May 15, 2009). Shlapentokh cites a poll conducted by the Levada Center in 2005, which found that 47 percent of Russians trust Putin, 41 percent the Church, and 31 percent the army. These numbers for Russia's most trusted institutions indicate how low overall levels of trust in public institutions are (ibid.).

151. Martin Shaw, *Post-Military Society: Militarism, Demilitarization and War at the End of the Twentieth Century* (Cambridge: Polity Press, 1991).

152. Webber and Zilberman, "The Citizenship Dimension of the Society-Military Interface," p. 160.

153. Ibid., p. 163.

154. Gross, "Youth and the Army in the USSR in the 1980s," pp. 484–485. See also Lieven, *Chechnya*, pp. 213–215.

155. Interview with Igor', Samara, July 2006.

156. Interview with Valerii, Samara, July 2006.

157. Ibid.

158. See Chapter 1, note 14.

159. Interview with Iurii, Samara, July 2006.

160. Government of the Russian Federation, "Gossudarstvennaia Programma 'Patrioticheskoe Vospitanie Grazhdan Rossiiskoi Federatsii 2001–2005 Gody," February 16, 2001, available at http://www.rg.ru/oficial/doc/postan_rf/122_1.shtm (accessed June 12, 2010).

161. Government of the Russian Federation, "Gossudarstvennaia Programma 'Patrioticheskoe Vospitanie Grazhdan Rossiiskoi Federatsii 2006–2010 Gody," July 11, 2005, available at http://www.llr.ru/razdel3.php?id_r2=55 (accessed June 12, 2010). See also Valerie Sperling, "Making the Public Patriotic: Militarism and Anti-Militarism in Russia," in Marlène Laruelle (ed.), *Russian Nationalism and the National Reassertion of Russia* (New York: Routledge, 2009), pp. 228–245; Marlène Laruelle, *In the Name of the Nation: Nationalism and Politics in Contemporary Russia* (New York: Palgrave Macmillan, 2009), pp. 175–180.

162. Levada-Tsentr, "Rossiiskaia armiia."

163. Fond "Obshchestvennoe mnenie," "O sluzhbe v armii," July 8, 2004, available at http://bd.fom.ru (accessed October 15, 2010).

164. Ibid.

165. Cited in Douglas W. Blum, "Official Patriotism in Russia: Its Essence and Implications," *PONARS Policy Memo* no. 420 (December 2006), p. 2, available at http://csis.org/files/media/csis/pubs/pm_0420.pdf (accessed June 15, 2010).

166. Pavel Felgenhauer, "Russian Military Personnel Crisis: Medvedev and the General Staff Join the Fray," *Eurasia Daily Monitor*, May 6, 2010, available at http://www.jamestown.org/single/?no_cache=1&tx_ttnews[tt_news]=36350 (accessed June 1, 2010).

Chapter 4

1. Liudmila Vakhnina, "Zashchitit' synovei: Ob organizatsii soldatskikh materei," *Informatsionnyi biulleten' pravleniia obshchestva "Memorial"* no. 25 (May 2002), available at http://www.memo.ru/about/bull/b25/6.htm (accessed November 16, 2004).

2. Rosamund Shreeves, "Mothers against the Draft: Women's Activism in the USSR," *RFE/RL Report on the USSR* 2, no. 38 (1990): 6.

3. Julie Elkner, "*Dedovshchina* and the Committee of Soldiers' Mothers under Gorbachev," *Journal of Power Institutions in Post-Soviet Societies* no. 1 (2004): paragraph 45, available at www.pipss.org/document243.html (accessed September 17, 2006).

4. Eva Bertrand, "Les militaires ne savent plus comment travailler sans les Comités de mères de soldats," Interview with Valentina Melnikova, Union of Soldiers' Mothers Committees in Russia, Moscow, April 30, 2008 (in French/Russian version in Annex), *Journal of Power Institutions in Post-Soviet Societies* no. 9 (2009), available at http://pipss.revues.org/index1971.html (accessed June 15, 2010), fn 18 of Russian version.

5. Lisa McIntosh Sundstrom, *Funding Civil Society: Foreign Assistance and NGO Development in Russia* (Stanford: Stanford University Press, 2006), pp. 64–65.

6. My interest in the differences within the soldiers' mothers movement was sparked by the following publications that include analysis of soldiers' mothers groups outside of Moscow and St. Petersburg: Natal'ia Danilova, "Pravo materi soldata: Instinkt zaboty ili grazhdanskii dolg?" in Sergei Ushakin (ed.), *Semeinye uzy: Modeli dlia sborki*, vol. 2 (Moscow: Novoe literaturnoe obozrenie, 2004), pp. 188–210; Serguei Alex. Oushakine, *The Patriotism of Despair: Nation, War, and Loss in Russia* (Ithaca, NY: Cornell University Press, 2009), ch. 4; Liudmila Popkova, "'Missiia nevypolnima': Zhenskie strategii politicheskogo uchastiia," in L. N. Popkova and I. N. Tartakovskii (eds.), *Gendernye otnosheniia v sovremennoi Rossii: issledovaniia 1990-kh godov* (Samara: Isdatel'stvo "Samarskii universitet," 2003), pp. 221–241; and Sundstrom, *Funding Civil Society*.

7. Cynthia Enloe, *Maneuvers: The International Politics of Militarizing Women's Lives* (Berkeley: University of California Press, 2000).

8. Cynthia Enloe, *The Curious Feminist: Searching for Women in a New Age of Empire* (Berkeley: University of California, 2004), p. 151.

9. Enloe, *Maneuvers*.

10. Jean Bethke Elshtain, *Women and War* (Chicago: University of Chicago Press, 1995); Joshua Goldstein, *War and Gender: How Gender Shapes the War System and Vice Versa* (Cambridge: Cambridge University Press, 2001), pp. 301–331.

11. Jean Bethke Elshtain, "War," in Cheris Kramarae and Dale Spender (eds.), *Routledge International Encyclopedia of Women: Global Women's Issues and Knowledge* (New York: Routledge, 2000), p. 2028.

12. See, for example, Michael S. Foley, *Confronting the War Machine: Draft Resistance during the Vietnam War* (Chapel Hill: University of North Carolina Press, 2003); Cynthia Cockburn, *From Where We Stand: War, Women's Activism and Feminist Analysis* (London: Zed Books, 2007); Enloe, *Maneuvers*, pp. 244–260.

13. Parts of this section have been previously published in Maya Eichler, "Russia's Post-Communist Transformation: A Gendered Analysis of the Chechen Wars," *International Feminist Journal of Politics* 8, no. 4 (2006): 486–511.

14. While there are differences between the groups, this chapter focuses on their commonalities. For an analysis of the differences between the two groups as well as in relation to other soldiers' rights groups, see Sundstrom, *Funding Civil Society*, pp. 66–70.

15. The committee claims to be linked to more than 300 regional and local groups. However, based on conversations with soldiers' mothers activists during my fieldwork, I believe that to be an exaggeration.

16. Union of the Committees of Soldiers' Mothers of Russia (CSMR), "To the History of the UCSMR," 2003, available at http://www.ucsmr.ru/english/ucsmr/history.htm (accessed January 7, 2005).

17. Soldiers' Mothers of St. Petersburg (SMSP), "Obshchestvennaia pravozashchitnaia organizatsiia 'Soldatskie Materi Sankt-Peterburga,'" 2002, available at http://www.soldiersmothers.spb.org/rus/AboutUs/AboutUs_rus.htm (accessed November 16, 2004). See also Elena Zdravomyslova, "Ot sotsial'noi problemy k kollektivnomu deistviiu: Pravozashchitnaia organizatsiia 'Soldatskie materi,'" in V. V. Kostiushev (ed.), *Obshchestvennye dvizheniia v sovremennoi Rossii: Ot sotsial'noi problemy k kollektivnomu deistviiu* (Moscow: Rossiiskaia akademiia nauk, 1999), pp. 51–64.

18. The CSMR has received financial support from donors in Norway, Switzerland, and Germany, as well as from international NGOs. Valerie Zawilski, "Saving Russia's Sons: The Soldiers' Mothers and the Russian-Chechen War," in Stephen L. Webber and Jennifer G. Mathers (eds.), *Military and Society in Post-Soviet Russia* (Manchester: Manchester University Press, 2006), p. 237, note 5.

19. For details, see Human Rights Watch, "Conscription through Detention in Russia's Armed Forces," New York: Human Rights Watch, November 2002, available at http://www.hrw.org/en/reports/2002/11/21/conscription-through-detention-russias-armed-forces (accessed October 15, 2008).

20. CSMR, "To the History of the UCSMR"; SMSP, "Obshchestvennaia pravozashchitnaia organizatsiia."

21. Jennifer Matloff, "Russia's Powerhouses of Dissent: Mothers. The Soldiers' Mothers Committee Takes on the Military in Ways Others Can't," *Christian Science Monitor*, February 24, 2000.

22. Amy Caiazza, *Mothers and Soldiers: Gender, Citizenship, and Civil Society in Contemporary Russia* (New York: Routledge, 2002); Larisa Deriglazova, "To Fear or to Respect?: Two Approaches to Military Reform in Russia," *Journal of Power Institutions in Post-Soviet Societies* no. 3 (2005), available at http://www.pipss.org/document415.html (accessed September 17, 2006); Eva Maria Hinterhuber, "Between Neotraditionalism and New Resistance—Soldiers' Mothers of St. Petersburg," *Anthropology of East Europe Review* 19, no. 1 (Spring 2001): 1–13, available at http://condor.depaul.edu/~rrotenbe/aeer/v19n1/Hinterhuber.pdf (accessed November 16, 2004); Brenda Vallance, "Russia's Mothers: Voices of Change," *Minerva: Quarterly Report on Women and the Military* 18, nos. 3–4 (2000): 109–128; Hendrik Vanderheeren, "Methods of 'The Soldiers' Mothers of St. Petersburg' in Conflict Resolution," August 2002–January 2003, pp. 26–32, available at www.soldiersmothers.ru/pages/english/books.htm (accessed January 20, 2009).

23. As Zawilski notes: "At the time of the Chechen war in 1994, the SMO [Soldiers' Mothers Organization] of St. Petersburg, along with the CSMR of Moscow, took a leading role against Russian military aggression in the region." Zawilski, "Saving Russia's Sons," p. 239, note 20.

24. CSMR, "To the History of the UCSMR."

25. Elena Zdravomyslova, "Soldiers' Mothers Fighting the Military Patriarchy: Reinvention of Responsible Activist Motherhood for Human Rights' [*sic*] Struggle," in Ilse Lenz, Charlotte Ullrich, and Barbara Fersch (eds.), *Gender Orders Unbound: Globalisation, Restructuring and Reciprocity* (Opladen: Barbara Budrich, 2007), p. 212; see also Galina Eremitcheva and Elena Zdravomyslova, "Die Bewegung der Soldatenmütter—Eine zivilge-

sellschaftliche Initiative: Der Fall St. Petersburg," in Martina Ritter (ed.), *Zivilgesellschaft und Gender-Politik in Rußland* (Frankfurt: Campus Verlag, 2001), p. 232.

26. Kathryn Pinnick, "When the Fighting Is Over: The Soldiers' Mothers and the Afghan Madonnas," in Mary Buckley (ed.), *Post-Soviet Women: From the Baltic to Central Asia* (Cambridge: Cambridge University Press, 1997), pp. 144–145; Vakhnina, "Zashchitit' synovei."

27. Deriglazova, "To Fear or to Respect?" paragraph 39.

28. Zdravomyslova, "Soldiers' Mothers Fighting the Military Patriarchy," p. 213.

29. Hinterhuber, "Between Neotraditionalism and New Resistance," p. 6.

30. SMSP, "Political Mentality in Russia," 1996, available at http://www.openweb.ru/smo/english/english.htm (accessed June 15, 2001). For the position of the CSMR, see Ida Kuklina, "Acceptance Speech," Right Livelihood Award, December 9, 1996, available at www.rightlivelihood.org/csmr_speech.html (accessed January 15, 2009).

31. Vallance, "Russia's Mothers," p. 111.

32. "'Goriachaia Linia' Soldatskikh materei," *Izvestiia*, October 17, 1995.

33. Zawilski, "Saving Russia's Sons," p. 229.

34. Quoted in Vakhnina, "Zashchitit' synovei."

35. Caiazza, *Mothers and Soldiers*, p. 140.

36. Quoted in Zdravomyslova, "Soldiers' Mothers Fighting the Military Patriarchy," p. 214.

37. Caiazza, *Mothers and Soldiers*, pp. 133–135.

38. Ibid., pp. 135–137; for more detail, see Lisa McIntoch Sundstrom, "Soldiers' Rights Groups in Russia: Civil Society through Russian and Western Eyes," in Alfred B. Evans, Jr., Laura A. Henry, and Lisa McIntosh Sundstrom (eds.), *Russian Civil Society: A Critical Assessment* (London: M. E. Sharpe, 2006), p. 180.

39. Caiazza, *Mothers and Soldiers*, p. 127.

40. On the potential for cross-ethnic and cross-national alliances of women in conflict zones, see Cynthia Cockburn, *The Space between Us: Negotiating Gender and National Identities in Conflict* (London: Zed Books); and Nira Yuval-Davis, *Gender and Nation* (London: Sage Publications, 1997), ch. 6.

41. On the discourse of the "hero's mother," see Marina Liborakina, "Women Fight to Be Heard in Chechen Dialogue," undated manuscript, available at http://www.isar.org/pubs/ST/Chechwomen44.html (accessed October 23, 2003).

42. Kuklina, "Acceptance Speech."

43. "Mothers' March to Grozny," *WRI Women* no. 19 (June 1995), available at www.wri-irg.org/node/3778 (accessed January 15, 2009); Elena Zdravomyslova, "Peaceful Initiatives: Soldiers' Mothers Movement in Russia," in Ingeborg Breines, Dorota Gierycz, and Betty Reardon (eds.), *Towards a Women's Agenda for a Culture of Peace* (Geneva: UNESCO Publishing, 1999), pp. 165–180. See also Zawilski, "Saving Russia's Sons," pp. 234–235.

44. Zdravomyslova, "Peaceful Initiatives."

45. Elena Zdravomyslova points out that the soldiers' mothers were an important force in the mobilization of the initially weak antiwar movement. Zdravomyslova, "Soldiers' Mothers Fighting the Military Patriarchy," p. 213. In addition to domestic attention,

the CSMR received international recognition for its work during the first Chechen War. It was awarded the Sean MacBride Peace Prize in 1995, the Rafto Prize in 1995, and the Right Livelihood Award ("Alternative Nobel Prize") in 1996.

46. Fond "Obshchestvennoe mnenie," "Bol'shinstvo rossiian odobriaiut soldatskikh materei, pytaiushchikhsia zabrat' svoikh detei iz chastei, voiuiushchikh v Chechne," February 3, 1995, available at http://bd.fom.ru (accessed June 1, 2010).

47. Caiazza, *Mothers and Soldiers*, p. 137; Valerie Sperling, "The Last Refuge of a Scoundrel: Patriotism, Militarism and the National Idea," *Nations and Nationalism* 9, no. 2 (2003): 247; Pinnick, "When the Fighting Is Over," p. 145; "Interview with Natal'ia Zhukova," conducted by Anna Maria Tramonti, *The Current*, CBC Radio, November 23, 2004. Political and military leaders also argued that the activist mothers were pursuing individualist goals or were being exploited by political groups. Caiazza, *Mothers and Soldiers*, p. 137.

48. CSMR, "Annual Report 2002," 2002, available at http://www.ucsmr.ru/english/ucsmr/report/report2002.htm (accessed January 7, 2005).

49. Quoted in Vakhnina, "Zashchitit' synovei."

50. This position was articulated at the conference "Chechen Deadlock: Where to Search a Road to Peace?" which was organized by the CSMR in 2002. CSMR, "Annual Report 2002."

51. Sperling, "The Last Refuge of a Scoundrel."

52. Vanderheeren, "Methods of 'The Soldiers' Mothers of St. Petersburg' in Conflict Resolution," p. 35.

53. While the SMSP and the CSMR received less domestic support during the second war, they again were awarded with international peace prizes. The CSMR received the Friedrich Ebert Foundation Award in 2000. The SMSP was given the Aachener-Friedenspreis in 2004.

54. Arzu Abdullayeva, Sophia Dobinskaya, Ida Kuklina, Liubov Vinogradova, and Fatima Yandieva, "Civil Society and Peace-Building in the North and South Caucasus" (transcript), Cambridge, MA: Caspian Studies Program, Harvard University, November 16, 2000, available at http://belfercenter.ksg.harvard.edu/publication/12773 (accessed January 17, 2005).

55. Ibid.

56. Zawilski, "Saving Russia's Sons," p. 236; Caiazza, *Mothers and Soldiers*, p. 141; Tatiana Sivaeva, "Women NGOs and the War in Chechnya," paper prepared for the Global Network for Women's Advocacy and Civil Society, 2000, available at http://www.ciaonet.org/wps/sito3/sito3.pdf (accessed April 29, 2004).

57. Sivaeva, "Women NGOs and the War in Chechnya," pp. 8–12.

58. CSMR, "Press-reliz 'Edinaia Narodnaia Partiia Soldatskikh Materei,'" 2003, available at http://www.ucsmr.ru/party/pressrelease.htm (accessed January 7, 2005); Julie Glasser, "United People's Party of Soldiers' Mothers: An Analysis of a Grassroots Movement," *Жe: Stanford's Student Journal of Russian, East European, and Eurasian Studies* 1 (Spring 2005), available at http://zhe.stanford.edu/spring05/soldiers%20mothers2.pdf (accessed June 16, 2008).

59. Anna Politkovskaia, "Soldatskie materi uekhali dumat' nad predlozheniiami chechenskoi storony: Ostanovit li eto terakti?" *Novaia gazeta*, February 28, 2005, p. 2.

60. Nationalist Duma Deputy Viktor Alksnis described the founding of the soldiers' mothers party as aimed at undermining the defense capabilities of the country. Deriglazova, "To Fear or to Respect?" paragraphs 45–46.

61. Sundstrom, "Soldiers' Rights Groups in Russia," p. 180.

62. Ministry of Defense of the Russian Federation, "Ob obrazovanii Obshchestvennogo Soveta pri Ministerstve Oborny Rossiiskoi Federatsii," decree no. 490, November 16, 2006, available at http://sovet.mil.ru/Documents.html (accessed June 15, 2010).

63. See Chapter 2, note 96.

64. Caiazza, *Mothers and Soldiers*, p. 125; "Interview with Natal'ia Zhukova"; Danilova, "Pravo materi soldata," p. 192.

65. Quoted in Caiazza, *Mothers and Soldiers*, p. 125.

66. Quoted in Zdravomyslova, "Soldiers' Mothers Fighting the Military Patriarchy," p. 219.

67. Ibid.

68. Caiazza, *Mothers and Soldiers*, p. 123.

69. Hinterhuber, "Between Neotraditionalism and New Resistance," p. 6.

70. Rebecca Kay, *Russian Women and Their Organizations: Gender, Discrimination, and Grassroots Women's Organizations, 1991–96* (New York: St. Martin's Press, 1999), pp. 18–24.

71. Quoted in Lynne Attwood, *The New Soviet Man and Woman: Sex-Role Socialization in the USSR* (Bloomington: Indiana University Press, 1990), p. 140.

72. Mary Buckley, *Women and Ideology in the Soviet Union* (Ann Arbor: University of Michigan Press, 1989); Anastasia Posadskaya (ed.), *Women in Russia: A New Era in Russian Feminism* (London: Verso, 1994); Sue Bridger, Rebecca Kay, and Kathryn Pinnick, *No More Heroines? Russia, Women and the Market* (London: Routledge, 1996).

73. Zdravomyslova, "Soldiers' Mothers Fighting the Military Patriarchy," p. 219.

74. Caiazza, *Mothers and Soldiers*, p. 46.

75. Anne White, "New Mothers' Campaigning Organizations in Russia," in Anna Cento Bull, Hanna Diamond, and Rosalind J. Marsh (eds.), *Feminisms and Women's Movements in Contemporary Europe* (New York: St. Martin's Press, 2000), pp. 211–227.

76. Suvi Salmenniemi, *Democratization and Gender in Contemporary Russia* (London: Routledge, 2008), p. 56.

77. Hinterhuber, "Between Neotraditionalism and New Resistance," p. 9.

78. As Kuklina points out, the CSMR was "the very first women's NGO in the former USSR which began to act on the traditionally masculine field—in the military sphere." Kuklina, "Acceptance Speech."

79. Sperling, "The Last Refuge of a Scoundrel," p. 246. Zawilski, "Saving Russia's Sons," pp. 231–233; Zdravomyslova, "Soldiers' Mothers Fighting the Military Patriarchy," p. 225.

80. Valerie Sperling, *Organizing Women in Contemporary Russia: Engendering Transition* (Cambridge: Cambridge University Press, 1999), pp. 64–73.

81. Caiazza, *Mothers and Soldiers*, pp. 128–129.

82. Quoted in Sperling, *Organizing Women in Contemporary Russia*, p. 72.
83. CSMR, "Istoriia Soiusa Komitetov Soldatskikh Materei Rossii," 2003, available at http://www.ucsmr.ru/ucsmr/history.htm (accessed January 7, 2005).
84. Sundstrom, "Soldiers' Rights Groups in Russia," p. 185.
85. Caiazza, *Mothers and Soldiers*, p. 156.
86. Although the Russian word *voennosluzhaiushchie* is gender neutral, I translate it with the English word "servicemen" since the Russian context implies a male subject.
87. "Kratkaia spravka o nashei rabote," organizational material obtained during visit to the office of *Sodeistvie*, Samara, June 2006.
88. Interview with Maria, member of *Sodeistvie*, Samara, June 2006.
89. These actions are mentioned in this order in the write-up about the group in the directory of NGOs in the Samara region. *Duma i obshchestvennost': Informatsionnyi sbornik* (Samara: Samarskaia Gubernskaia Duma, 2005), p. 122. See also "Kratkaia spravka o nashei rabote."
90. Interview with Tat'iana N., chair of *Synov'ia*, Samara, July 2006.
91. Ibid.
92. "Anketa," organizational material obtained during visit to the office of *Synov'ia*, Samara, July 2006.
93. Interview with Ol'ga T., chair of *Sodeistvie*, Samara, June 2006.
94. Ibid.
95. Ibid.
96. Interview with Natal'ia, member of *Sodeistvie*, Samara, June 2006.
97. Interview with Liudmila, member of *Sodeistvie*, Samara, June 2006.
98. Interview with Maria, member of *Sodeistvie*, Samara, June 2006.
99. Ibid.
100. Ibid.
101. See Ellen Jones, *Red Army and Society: A Sociology of the Soviet Military* (Boston: Allen and Unwin, 1985), p. 153.
102. Interview with Tat'iana N., chair of *Synov'ia*, Samara, June 2006.
103. Interview with Iulia, member of *Synov'ia*, Samara, June 2006.
104. Interview with Irina, member of *Synov'ia*, Samara, June 2006.
105. Interview with Ol'ga T., chair of *Sodeistvie*, Samara, June 2006.
106. Ibid.
107. Interview with Tat'iana N., chair of *Synov'ia*, Samara, July 2006.
108. Ibid.
109. Ibid.
110. Interview with Ol'ga T., chair of *Sodeistvie*, Samara, June 2006.
111. Interview with Tat'iana N., chair of *Synov'ia*, Samara, July 2006.
112. Interview with Irina, member of *Synov'ia*, Samara, June 2006.
113. Letter obtained during visit to the office of *Sodeistvie*, July 2006.
114. Interview with Irina, member of *Synov'ia*, Samara, July 2006.
115. Interview with Ol'ga T., chair of *Sodeistvie*, Samara, June 2006.
116. Oushakine, *The Patriotism of Despair*, ch. 4.

117. Interview with Ol'ga T., chair of *Sodeistvie*, Samara, June 2006.

118. See John Russell, *Chechnya—Russia's "War on Terror"* (London: Routledge, 2007), ch. 4.

119. Interview with Tat'iana N., chair of *Synov'ia*, Samara, July 2006.

120. Interview with Ol'ga T., chair of *Sodeistvie*, Samara, June 2006.

121. See Sundstrom, "Soldiers' Rights Groups in Russia," p. 182.

122. Interview with Ol'ga T., chair of *Sodeistvie*, Samara, June 2006.

123. Interview with Tat'iana N., chair of *Synov'ia*, Samara, June 2006.

124. Interestingly, Anna Colin Lebedev found a similar gendered and patriotic discourse in her analysis of letters sent to the Moscow CSMR by soldiers' families from across the country. Anna Colin Lebedev, "The Test of Reality: Understanding Families' Tolerance regarding Mistreatment of Conscripts in the Russian Army," in Françoise Daucé and Elisabeth Sieca-Kozlowski (eds.), *Dedovshchina in the Post-Soviet Military: Hazing of Russian Army Conscripts in a Comparative Perspective* (Stuttgart: Ibidem-Verlag, 2007), pp. 47–74.

125. According to the chair of the Council of Servicemen's Parents, this preparation for military service must begin from the boy's day of birth. Natal'ia Chernova, "Materinskii zakaz," *Novaia gazeta*, October 6, 2003, pp. 12–13.

126. Quoted in Vadim Udmantsev, "'Reforma po Serdiukovu' glazami materi soldata," *Segodnia*, March 17, 2009.

Chapter 5

1. A shorter version of this chapter appeared under the title "Russian Veterans of the Chechen Wars: A Feminist Analysis of Militarized Masculinities," in J. Ann Tickner and Laura Sjoberg (eds.), *Feminist International Relations: Conversations about the Past, Present and Future* (London: Routledge, 2011).

2. Anna Politkovskaya, *Putin's Russia* (London: Harvill Press, 2004), p. 46.

3. See Introduction, note 10.

4. David H. J. Morgan, "Theater of War: Combat, the Military, and Masculinities," in Harry Brod and Michael Kaufman (eds.), *Theorizing Masculinities* (London: Sage, 1994), p. 165.

5. Sandra Whitworth, *Men, Militarism and UN Peacekeeping: A Gendered Analysis* (Boulder, CO: Lynne Rienner Publishers, 2004), pp. 166–171.

6. Yuri Zarakhovich, "Chechnya's Walking Wounded," *Time Europe*, September 28, 2003, available at http://www.time.com/time/europe/html/031006/syndrome.html (accessed June 10, 2009).

7. See Introduction, note 30, for more information on the interviewees.

8. For example, see interview with Aleksei S., Samara, June 2006.

9. Interviews with Vadim and Anton, Samara, June 2006.

10. Interview with Aleksei S., Samara, June 2006.

11. Interview with Anton, Samara, June 2006.

12. Interview with Roman, Samara, July 2006.

13. Interview with Vadim, Samara, June 2006.

14. Except for Anatolii, my interviewees did not openly talk about their own experiences of hazing but only about hazing as a more general problem of military service. Interview with Anatolii, Samara, June 2006. I discuss some of the negative combat-related experiences below in the section "Fragile Warriors."

15. Interview with Dmitrii, Samara, June 2006.

16. Interview with Anton, Samara, June 2006.

17. "Interview with Tanya Lokshina, President of the Demos Center, Conducted by Olga Filippova, Moscow, 11 May 2007," *Journal of Power Institutions in Post-Soviet Societies* nos. 6/7 (2007): paragraph 61, available at http://www.pipss.org/index772.html (accessed January 11, 2009).

18. Interview with Anton, Samara, June 2006.

19. Morgan, "Theater of War," p. 166.

20. Interview with Anatolii, Samara, July 2006. The speaker did not seem aware of the irony of his statement. In part, I think my status as a foreign researcher overshadowed my gender, placing me outside of the Russian gender order. On the other hand, my interest in the military may have disassociated me from femininity.

21. Pavel Felgenhauer, "Call-up: No Professional Army Yet in Sight in Russia," *Segodnia*, May 4, 1995, p. 2, *Current Digest of Post-Soviet Press* 47, no. 18 (May 31, 1995): 16–17.

22. Whitworth, *Men, Militarism and UN Peacekeeping*, pp. 151–152.

23. Joshua Goldstein, *War and Gender: How Gender Shapes the War System and Vice Versa* (Cambridge: Cambridge University Press, 2001), pp. 266–267.

24. A smaller number actively resisted service. As discussed in Chapter 2, more than 500 officers, as well as a few prominent generals, resigned over their opposition to the war.

25. An estimated 1,000 Russian federal troops died in the New Year's Eve storming of Grozny. Galina Koval'skaia, "Shturm i glupost," *Ezhenedel'nyi zhurnal*, April 1, 2003, p. 17.

26. Interview with Mikhail R., Samara, July 2006.

27. Dmitri V. Trenin and Aleksei Malashenko with Anatol Lieven, *Russia's Restless Frontier: The Chechnya Factor in Post-Soviet Russia* (Washington, DC: Carnegie Endowment, 2004), p. 109. See also Reserve Col. Yury Deryugin, "Incompetents in the Science of Winning Victory Are Creating a Slaughterhouse," *Rossiiskie vesti*, January 10, 1995, p. 2, *Current Digest of Post-Soviet Press* 47, no. 2 (February 2, 1995): 2–4.

28. Babchenko's memoir illustrates soldiers' lack of morale. Arkady Babchenko, *One Soldier's War in Chechnya* (London: Portobello Books, 2007), for example, p. 94.

29. Lt. Gen. Nikolai Tsymbal, "A Demoralized Army Cannot Be Combat-Ready," *Rossiiskie vesti*, January 10, 1995, p. 2, *Current Digest of Post-Soviet Press* 47, no. 2 (February 2, 1995): 4.

30. Anatol Lieven, *Chechnya: Tombstone of Russian Power* (New Haven: Yale University Press, 1999), p. 211.

31. Ibid., pp. 104–105; the quotation is from p. 105.

32. Pavel Felgenhauer, "Russia's Forces Unreconstructed," Institute for the Study of Conflict, Ideology, and Policy's *Perspective* 10, no. 4 (March–April 2000), available at www.bu.edu/iscip/vol10/Felgenhauer.html (accessed September 16, 2008).

33. Interview with Aleksei S., Samara, June 2006. On fear during combat, see Goldstein, *War and Gender*, pp. 253–257, 267–269.

34. Interview with Aleksei S., Samara, June 2006.

35. For an interesting comparison, see the following book: Lt. Col. Dave Grossman, *On Killing: The Psychological Cost of Learning to Kill in War and Society* (Boston: Little, Brown and Company, 1995). The author argues that a majority of U.S. soldiers (80 to 85 percent) failed to shoot at the enemy during World War Two, but that desensitization to violence has since greatly increased soldiers' willingness to fire at the enemy in war.

36. Interview with Aleksei S., Samara, June 2006.

37. Dmitrii Pisarenko, "Rany voiny: Chechenskii sindrom," *Argumenty i fakty*, August 21, 1996, p. 13.

38. See Chapter 2 for opinion polls on the wars.

39. Babchenko, *One Soldier's War in Chechnya*, p. 161.

40. Quoted ibid., p. 94.

41. "The Majority of Russia's People Are Against Putting Military Men Who Refuse to Serve [in Chechnya] on Trial," *Segodnia*, January 28, 1995, p. 3, *Current Digest of Post-Soviet Press* 47, no. 4 (February 22, 1995): 12.

42. Fond "Obshchestvennoe mnenie," "Srochnaia sluzhba v armii," October 3, 2002, available at http://bd.fom.ru (accessed June 1, 2010); Theodore P. Gerber and Sarah E. Mendelson, "Strong Public Support for Military Reform in Russia," *PONARS Policy Memo* 288 (May 2003), available at http://www.gwu.edu/~ieresgwu/assets/docs/ponars/pm_0288.pdf (accessed October 15, 2010).

43. See, for example, Human Rights Watch, *"Welcome to Hell": Arbitrary Detention, Torture, and Extortion in Chechnya* (New York: Human Rights Watch, 2000); Anna Politkovskaya, *A Dirty War: A Russian Reporter in Chechnya* (London: Harvill Press, 2001); Pavel Felgenhauer, "The Russian Army in Chechnya Is Being Systematically Stripped of What Remains of Its Human Face," *Ekho Moskvy*, February 13, 2000, *Current Digest of Post-Soviet Press* 52, no. 7 (March 15, 2000): 5. Emma Gilligan, *Terror in Chechnya: Russia and the Tragedy of Civilians in War* (Princeton: Princeton University Press, 2010).

44. Whitworth, *Men, Militarism and UN Peacekeeping*, p. 99.

45. Ibid., chs. 4, 6.

46. When soldiers start empathizing with the enemy, they lose their ability to commit physical violence. This process is evident in the stories of soldiers who become war resisters. See, for example, Joshua Key and Lawrence Hill, *The Deserter's Tale: The Story of an Ordinary Soldier Who Walked Away from the War in Iraq* (Toronto: House of Anasi, 2007).

47. Interview with Dmitrii, Samara, June 2006.

48. Interview with Anton, Samara, June 2006.

49. Ibid.

50. Anton is referring to the private network NTV's coverage of the first war which was highly critical of the official line on the war. See Ellen Mickiewicz, *Changing Chan-*

nels: Television and the Struggle for Power in Russia, 2nd ed. (Durham, NC: Duke University Press, 1999), ch. 11.

51. Interview with Anton, Samara, June 2006.

52. See Linda E. Boose, "Techno-Muscularity and the 'Boy Eternal': From the Quagmire to the Gulf," in Miriam Cooke and Angela Woollacott (eds.), *Gendering War Talk* (Princeton: Princeton University Press, 1993), pp. 67–106.

53. See Whitworth, *Men, Militarism and UN Peacekeeping,* pp. 107–108.

54. "Maybe Guilty, Maybe Sane: Supreme Court Reviews Yury Budanov Case," *Kommersant,* March 1, 2003, pp. 1, 3, *Current Digest of Post-Soviet Press* 55, no. 9 (April 2, 2003): 9.

55. Mikhail Sokolov, "Predely primeneniia doktriny prav cheloveka v sovremennoi rossiiskoi kul'ture: Sud nad polkovnikom Budanovym i ego protivniki," undated manuscript, p. 1, available at www.iie.ru/ifp/Alumni/Sokolov/Downloads/art2.doc (accessed April 10, 2009).

56. Amandine Regamey, "L'opinion public russe et l'affair Boudanov," *Journal of Power Institutions in Post-Soviet Societies* no. 8 (2008): paragraph 32, available at http://www.pipss.org/document1493.html (accessed April 1, 2009). Regamey's article helped me identify a number of the sources used in this section of the chapter.

57. Arkady Yuzhny, "Trial of Col. Budanov Postponed: Atmosphere Surrounding Trial Is Becoming More and More Tense," *Segodnia,* March 6, 2001, p. 2, *Current Digest of Post-Soviet Press* 53, no. 10 (April 4, 2001): 13.

58. Quoted in "'Sud dolzhen polnost'iu opravdat' polkovnika Budanova,'" *Na boevom postu,* March 7, 2001, p. 2.

59. Ibid.

60. Quoted in Sokolov, "Predely primeneniia doktriny prav cheloveka."

61. Regamey, "L'opinion public russe et l'affair Boudanov," paragraph 14.

62. Quoted in Oleg Getmanenko, "What War Can Do to a Man," *Novye izvestiia,* March 31, 2000, pp. 1–2, *Current Digest of Post-Soviet Press* 52, no. 13 (April 26, 2000): 9.

63. Quoted in "Vy soglasny c prigovorom Budanovu?" *Kommersant Vlast'* no. 30, August 4, 2003, available at www.kommersant.ru/doc.aspx?DocsID=401110 (accessed March 15, 2009).

64. Quoted in Aleksandr Andryukhin, "Officer's Last Word," *Izvestiia,* July 26, 2003, p. 8, *Current Digest of Post-Soviet Press* 55, no. 30 (August 27, 2003): 11.

65. The public too showed little concern about the human rights violations committed by federal troops. As one survey shows, less than 5 percent of the population expressed shame for such abuses during 2001–2004, in contrast to more than 60 percent who were alarmed at Russian troop casualties. Theodore P. Gerber and Sarah E. Mendelson, "Casualty Sensitivity in a Post-Soviet Context: Russian Views of the Second Chechen War, 2001–2004," *Political Science Quarterly* 123, no. 1 (2008): 49.

66. Usam Baysayev, "The Yuri Budanov Case," Prague Watchdog Kavkaz Center, January 9, 2009, available at http://www.kavkazcenter.com/eng/content/2009/01 (accessed July 5, 2006).

67. Regamey, "L'opinion public russe et l'affair Boudanov," paragraph 3.

68. Baysayev, "The Yuri Budanov Case."
69. Regamey, "L'opinion public russe et l'affair Boudanov."
70. Levada-Tsentr, "Delo polkovnika Budanova: Chechnia," July 31, 2002, available at www.levada.ru/press/2002073100.html (accessed March 15, 2009).
71. Ibid.
72. Sokolov, "Predely primeneniia doktriny prav cheloveka."
73. Levada-Tsentr, "Delo polkovnika Budanova."
74. Ibid.
75. Ibid.
76. Regamey, "L'opinion public russe et l'affair Boudanov," paragraph 26.
77. Sokolov, "Predely primeneniia doktriny prav cheloveka," p. 5.
78. Quoted in Regamey, "L'opinion public russe et l'affair Boudanov," paragraph 56.
79. Quoted in Politkovskaya, *Putin's Russia*, pp. 70–71.
80. Ibid, p. 101.
81. For example, see chapter 2 of the study by the United Nations Secretary-General, *Women, Peace and Security* (New York: United Nations, 2002), available at http://www.un.org/womenwatch/daw/public/eWPS.pdf (accessed October 15, 2010).
82. Goldstein, *War and Gender*, pp. 362–371.
83. Cynthia Enloe, *Does Khaki Become You? The Militarization of Women's Lives* (London: Pandora, 1983), pp. 35–36; the quotation is from p. 35. Enloe also distinguishes between different types of rape committed by militarized men: rape as "recreation," as "instrument of national security," and as weapon of war such as for the purposes of ethnic cleansing. Cynthia Enloe, *Maneuvers: The International Politics of Militarizing Women's Lives* (Berkeley: University of California Press, 2000), pp. 108–152.
84. W. Andy Knight and Tanya Narozhna, "Rape and Other War Crimes in Chechnya: Is There a Role for the International Criminal Court?" *spacesofidentity* 5, no. 1 (2005): 92–93, available at http://pi.library.yorku.ca/ojs/index.php/soi/article/view/8002/7152 (accessed March 16, 2009). See also Valentina Rousseva, "Rape and Sexual Assault in Chechnya," *Culture, Society and Praxis* 3, no. 1 (November 2004), available at http://culturesocietypraxis.org/index.php/csp/article/viewFile/46/43 (accessed March 15, 2009).
85. John Russell, *Chechnya—Russia's "War on Terror"* (London: Routledge, 2007), p. 12.
86. Whitworth, *Men, Militarism and UN Peacekeeping*, pp. 166–167.
87. Tracy Xavia Karner, "Engendering Violent Men: Oral Histories of Military Masculinity," in Lee H. Bowker (ed.), *Masculinities and Violence* (Thousand Oaks, CA: Sage Publications, 1998), p. 231.
88. Timothy L. Thomas and Charles P. O'Hara, "Combat Stress in Chechnya: 'The Equal Opportunity Disorder,'" *U.S. Army Medical Department Journal* (January–March 2000): 49.
89. A. B. Belinskii and M. V. Liamin, "Mediko-psikhologicheskaia reabilitatsiia uchastnikov boevykh deistvii v mnogoprofil'nom gospitale," *Voenno-meditsinskii zhurnal* 321, no. 1 (January 2000): 62–66. Some military psychologists report lower rates,

with only 18 percent of officers and 25 percent of conscripts of the first war affected by post-traumatic stress. Ivan Egorov, "Chechenskii sindrom," *Vremia Moskovskie novosti*, January 31, 2000. In addition, hundreds of thousands of veterans have incurred physical disabilities as a result of their participation in the Chechen wars. Larisa Deriglazova, "To Fear or to Respect?: Two Approaches to Military Reform in Russia," *Journal of Power Institutions in Post-Soviet Societies* no. 3 (2005): paragraph 34, available at http://www.pipss.org/document415.html (accessed September 17, 2006).

90. Zarakhovich, "Chechnya's Walking Wounded"; Igor' Mangazeev, "Chechenskii sindrom," *Veche Tveri*, September 6, 2007, available at www.tverinfo.ru/analitika/chechenskii_sindrom.html (accessed December 1, 2010); Marina Gagina, "Istoriia bolezni: Chechenskii sindrom," *Krasnyi sever*, February 25, 2003; Mikhail Lukanin, "Chechenskii sindrom," *Trud*, December 11, 2009; "Kak lechat 'chechenskii sindrom,'" *Svobodnyi kurs*, April 5, 2001; Andrei Miaken'kii, "Posle Boia: Vtoroi chechenskii sindrom?" *Moskovskaia pravda*, January 29, 2000.

91. D. D. Pozhidaev, "Ot boevykh deistvii—k grazhdanskoi zhizni," *Sotsiologicheskie issledovaniia* no. 1 (1999): 71.

92. Quoted in Irina Mastykina, "When I Return: Psychiatrists Know a Very Terrible Truth about the 'Chechen Conflict,'" *Komsomolskaia pravda*, April 25, 1995, p. 3, *Current Digest of Post-Soviet Press* 47, no. 17 (May 24, 1995): 10.

93. Babchenko, *One Soldier's War in Chechnya*, p. 103.

94. Ibid., p. 214.

95. Interview with Anton, Samara, June 2006.

96. Ibid.

97. Interview with Mikhail R., Samara, July 2006. This interview was not taped and the quotation is based on detailed notes taken during the interview.

98. Morgan, "Theater of War," p. 169; Babchenko, *One Soldier's War in Chechnya*, p. 405; Pozhidaev, "Ot boevykh deistvii," p. 71.

99. Ol'ga Shepeleva, "Sem'i veteranov: Do i posle konflikta," in *Militsiia mezhdu Rossiei i Chechnei: Veterany konflikta v rossiiskom obshchestve* (Moscow: Demos, 2007), pp. 109–111.

100. Ibid., p. 111.

101. Ibid., p. 115.

102. Ibid., p. 111. One mother of a veteran of the first war I interviewed made a similar observation. She argued that her son's army service had brought her son and her closer because of suffering through so much together. Interview with Iulia, member of *Synov'ia*, Samara, June 2006.

103. Shepeleva, "Sem'i veteranov," p. 116.

104. Nick Sturdee, "Chechen Syndrome," Aljazeera documentary, 2007, available at http://english.aljazeera.net/programmes/witness/2007/04/200852518464052803.html (accessed March 16, 2009). The quotation is from part two of this two-part documentary.

105. Interview with Mikhail R., Samara, July 2006. Mikhail R.'s point was borne out in a survey among Chechen and Afghan veterans which found that a quarter of them

had difficulty functioning in the work place and half of them had repeatedly switched jobs. The survey was conducted in 1996 among 3,144 veterans of the Chechen and Afghan wars living in Riazan *Oblast'*. Pozhidaev, "Ot boevykh deistvii," p. 71.

106. Interview with Ol'ga T., chair of *Sodeistvie*, Samara, June 2006; see also Rebecca Kay, *Men in Contemporary Russia: The Fallen Heroes of Post-Soviet Change* (Aldershot: Ashgate, 2006), p. 51.

107. Sturdee, "Chechen Syndrome." The quotation is taken from part one of the documentary.

108. Interview with Ol'ga T., chair of *Sodeistvie*, Samara, June 2006.

109. Interview with Maria, member of *Sodeistvie*, Samara, June 2006.

110. Serguei Alex. Oushakine, *The Patriotism of Despair: Nation, War, and Loss in Russia* (Ithaca, NY: Cornell University Press, 2009), p. 177.

111. Pozhidaev, "Ot boevykh deistvii," p. 72.

112. Ibid.

113. Babchenko, *One Soldier's War in Chechnya*, p. x.

114. Oushakine, *The Patriotism of Despair*, p. 179.

115. Quoted in "I'm Afraid That I Won't Be Able to Forget the War: Psychological Rehabilitation of Chechen War Veterans," *Kommersant*, May 25, 2000, p. 9, *Current Digest of Post-Soviet Press* 52, no. 21 (June 21, 2000): 19.

116. Whitworth, *Men, Militarism, and UN Peacekeeping*, p. 168.

117. Pisarenko, "Rany voiny."

118. Ibid.

119. Ibid.

120. Ibid.

121. Ibid.

122. Ibid.

123. Aleksandr A. Kucher, "Zhizn' posle voennoi sluzhby," *Nezavisimoe voennoe obozrenie* no. 43, November 21, 1997.

124. Ibid.

125. As the example of Colonel Budanov illustrated, societal opposition to the war did not translate into critical discussion of war crimes; however, following Kucher's prescription would certainly not have allowed for such discussion to take place.

126. Miaken'kii, "Posle boia." See also Egorov, "Chechenskii Sindrom."

127. Asmik Novikova, "Reabilitatsiia veteranov Chechni," in *Militsiia mezhdu Rossiei i Chechnei: Veterany konflikta v rossiiskom obshchestve* (Moscow: Demos, 2007), p. 76; Oleg Odnokolenko, "Forgotten for Political Reasons: Chechen War Soldiers Denied Veteran Status," *Segodnia*, February 4, 2000, p. 4, *Current Digest of the Post-Soviet Press* 52, no. 5 (March 1, 2000): 5–6.

128. In the Soviet Union, veterans of the Great Patriotic War held a special place within the welfare system. In the 1960s and 1970s these veterans' entitlements were greatly expanded to bolster their support for the regime. They enjoyed "the most diverse and developed" set of provisions and thus had an exclusive and privileged citizenship status. Natalia Danilova, "Veterans' Policy in Russia: A Puzzle of Creation," *Journal of Power Institutions in Post-Soviet Societies* nos. 6/7 (2007): paragraph 5, available at http://

www.pipss.org/index873.html (accessed September 10, 2008). See also Mark Edele, *Soviet Veterans of the Second World War: A Popular Movement in an Authoritarian Society 1941–1991* (Oxford: Oxford University Press, 2008). Soviet veterans of "local" wars (all wars other than the Great Patriotic War) never were able to gain the same recognition. Danilova, "Veterans' Policy in Russia," paragraphs 10–16. On the experiences of Afghan war veterans, see also the excellent study by Mark Galeotti, *Afghanistan: The Soviet Union's Last War* (London: Frank Cass, 1995). The differentiation between veterans of the Great Patriotic War and "lesser" veterans continued in post-Soviet Russia.

129. In-kind benefits (*l'goty*) offer particular groups in society a special advantage or privilege to access public services for free or at a reduced cost. *L'goty* were a key component of the Soviet welfare state and were carried forth into the post-Soviet period, although many were monetized during Putin's 2005 welfare state reform. Susanne Wengle and Michael Rasell, "The Monetisation of L'goty: Changing Patterns of Welfare Politics and Provision in Russia," *Europe-Asia Studies* 60, no. 5 (2008): 739–756.

130. "Chechnia—ne voina?" *Argumenty i fakty*, November 28, 2001.

131. "S otsrochkoi na god: L'goty voevavshim v Chechne," *Trud*, April 3, 2003, p. 30.

132. Members of both soldiers' mothers groups in Samara mentioned assistance to veterans in claiming benefits as an important part of their work. Interviews, Samara, June–July 2006.

133. Pozhidaev, "Ot boevykh deistvii," pp. 72–73.

134. Interview with Anton, Samara, July 2006.

135. Interview with Dmitrii, Samara, July 2006.

136. Compare Oushakine, *The Patriotism of Despair*, pp. 164–165.

137. Interview with Mikhail R., Samara, July 2006. As one Afghan war veteran told me in an interview, the Afghan veterans' movement in Samara is also fragmented. It started out as one organization but split into a number of groups. Interview with Roman, Samara, July 2006. In 2007 there was an attempt by the federal veterans' organization *Boevoe Bratstvo* under the leadership of Boris Gromov to unite the Chechen and Afghan war veterans in Samara, but I do not have any information on the outcome.

138. Interview with Pavel, Samara, July 2006.

139. Ibid.

140. Ibid.

141. Interview with Valentina, Samara, June 2006.

142. Ibid.

143. Elisabeth Sieca-Kozlowski, "Russian Military Patriotic Education: A Control Tool against the Arbitrariness of Veterans," *Nationalities Papers* 38, no. 1 (January 2010): 76.

144. Ibid., pp. 77–78.

145. Valerie Sperling, "Making the Public Patriotic: Militarism and Anti-Militarism in Russia," in Marlène Laruelle (ed.), *Russian Nationalism and the National Reassertion of Russia* (New York: Routledge, 2009), pp. 230–241; Oushakine, *The Patriotism of Despair*, p. 187–189.

146. On the latter point, see quotation by Svetlana Sidorenko in "Vspominaia po-

gibshikh," *Oblastnoi telekanal RIO*, December 12, 2008, available at http://www.rio-tv.ru/index.php?link=news&action=show&id=1232 (accessed March 15, 2009).

147. Sturdee, "Chechen Syndrome," part two.

148. Ellen Jones, *Red Army and Society: A Sociology of the Soviet Military* (Boston: Allen and Unwin, 1985), pp. 103, 153.

149. Compare Oushakine, *The Patriotism of Despair*, pp. 185–190.

150. Sieca-Kozlowksi, "Russian Military Patriotic Education," p. 76.

151. Iurii Strelets, "Vechnaia pamiat' pavshim," *Samarskie izvestiia*, December 13, 2008.

152. Quoted in Nataliia Krainova, "Vechnaia pamiat'," RIA "Samara," December 12, 2008, available at http://www.riasamara.ru/rus/news/region/society/article36605.shtml (accessed April 15, 2009).

153. Quoted ibid.

Conclusion

1. A recent example in this body of literature is Malcolm Potts and Thomas Hayden, *Sex and War: How Biology Explains Warfare and Terrorism and Offers a Path to a Safer World* (Dallas, TX: Benbella Books, 2008).

2. Joni Seager, *The Penguin Atlas of Women in the World*, 4th ed. (New York: Penguin Books, 2009), p. 102–103.

3. Uta Klein, "The Military and Masculinities in Israeli Society," in Paul R. Higate (ed.), *Military Masculinities: Identity and the State* (London: Praeger, 2003), pp. 191–200.

4. Seager, *The Penguin Atlas of Women in the World*, pp. 102–103.

5. The numbers for South Africa and Hungary are based on ibid. The other numbers are drawn from the publication by the Women's Research and Education Institute, *Women in the Military: Where They Stand*, 7th ed. (Arlington, Virginia: WREI, 2010).

6. Estimates of the percentage of women in the Soviet armed forces vary from a low of 0.5 percent to a high of 3.5 percent for the final years of the Soviet Union. The first number is from Christine Eifler, "'Weil man nun mit ihnen rechnen muss...': Frauen in den Streitkräften Russlands," in Ruth Seifert and Christine Eifler (eds.), *Gender und Militär: Internationale Erfahrungen mit Männern und Frauen in den Streitkräften* (Königstein: Ulrike Helmer, 2004), p. 105. The second figure is cited by A. I. Smirnov, "Zhenshchiny na sluzhbe v rossiiskoi armii," *Sotsiologicheskie issledovaniia* no. 11 (2000): 128. The military magazine *Nezavisimoe voennoe obozrenie* mentions that women made up 1.6 percent of the overall armed forces personnel in 1980 and 1.8 percent in 1985. "Rossiiskoi armii nuzhny zhenshchiny," *Nezavisimoe voennoe obozrenie* no. 22, June 23, 2000.

7. Steve Niva, "Tough and Tender: New World Order Masculinity and the Gulf War," in Marysia Zalewski and Jane Parpart (eds.), *The "Man" Question in International Relations* (Boulder, CO: Westview Press, 1998), pp. 109–125.

8. While there were small improvements in officers' salaries during Putin's presidencies, these measures did not go far enough in resolving the deep social problems

afflicting the military. Also, officers faced new social burdens such as having to pay for their own housing and utilities as well as no longer being exempted from taxation. Aleksandr Golts, "The Social and Political Condition of the Russian Military," in Steven E. Miller and Dmitri Trenin (eds.), *The Russian Military: Power and Policy* (Cambridge: MIT Press, 2004), pp. 78–79. The recent military reform launched in October 2008 foresees further improvements for armed forces personnel such as increases in salaries and pension and support for housing.

9. Alexei Levinson, "Russia's People: What Is a Just War?" *openDemocracy Russia*, April 13, 2010, available at http://www.opendemocracy.net/od-russia/alexei-levinson/russia%E2%80%99s-people-what-is-just-war (accessed June 15, 2010).

10. Quoted ibid.

11. Serguei Alex. Oushakine, *The Patriotism of Despair: Nation, War, and Loss in Russia* (Ithaca, NY: Cornell University Press, 2009), p. 132.

References

Abdullayeva, Arzu, Sophia Dobinskaya, Ida Kuklina, Liubov Vinogradova, and Fatima Yandieva. "Civil Society and Peace-Building in the North and South Caucasus [transcript]." Cambridge, MA: Caspian Studies Program, Harvard University, November 16, 2000. Available at http://belfercenter.ksg.harvard.edu/publication/12773 (accessed January 17, 2005).

Abu-Laban, Yasmeen (ed.). *Gendering the Nation-State: Canadian and Comparative Perspectives*. Vancouver: University of British Columbia Press, 2008.

Alexseev, Mikhail A. "Back to Hell: Civilian-Military 'Audience Costs' and Russia's Wars in Chechnia." In Stephen L. Webber and Jennifer G. Mathers (eds.), *Military and Society in Post-Soviet Russia*. Manchester: Manchester University Press, 2006, pp. 97–113.

Altinay, Ayşe Gül. *The Myth of the Military Nation: Militarism, Gender, and Education in Turkey*. New York: Palgrave Macmillan, 2004.

"Analysis: Media Swings against Military." BBC News online, January 11, 2000. Available at news.bbc.co.uk/2/hi/europe/599516.stm (accessed September 16, 2008).

"Analysis: Russia's Suffering Conscripts." BBC News online, January 18, 2000. Available at news.bbc.co.uk/2/hi/europe/607642.stm (accessed September 16, 2008).

Andryukhin, Aleksandr. "Officer's Last Word." *Izvestiia*, July 26, 2003, p. 8. *Current Digest of the Post-Soviet Press* 55, no. 30 (August 27, 2003): 10–11.

Ashour, Omar. "Security, Oil, and Internal Politics: The Causes of the Russo-Chechen Conflicts." *Studies in Conflict and Terrorism* 27 (2004): 127–143.

Ashwin, Sarah (ed.). *Gender, State and Society in Soviet and Post-Soviet Russia*. London: Routledge, 2000.

———. "Introduction: Gender, State and Society in Soviet and Post-Soviet Russia." In

Sarah Ashwin (ed.), *Gender, State and Society in Soviet and Post-Soviet Russia*. London: Routledge, 2000, pp. 1–29.

Atkinson, Dorothy, Alexander Dallin, and Gail Warshofsky Lapidus (eds.). *Women in Russia*. Stanford: Stanford University Press, 1977.

Atwood, Lynne. "The New Soviet Man and Woman—Soviet Views on Psychological Sex Differences." In Barbara Holland (ed.), *Soviet Sisterhood: British Feminists on Women in the USSR*. London: Fourth Estate, 1985, pp. 54–77.

———. *The New Soviet Man and Woman: Sex-Role Socialization in the USSR*. Bloomington: Indiana University Press, 1990.

Babchenko, Arkady. *One Soldier's War in Chechnya*. London: Portobello Books, 2007.

Baev, Pavel K. "The Russian Armed Forces: Failed Reform Attempts and Creeping Regionalization." *Journal of Communist Studies and Transition Politics* 17, no. 1 (March 2001): 23–42.

———. "Putin's War in Chechnya: Who Steers the Course?" *PONARS Policy Memo* 345 (November 2004). Available at http://www.csis.org/ruseura/ponars/pm/ (accessed July 30, 2008).

———. "The Targets of Terrorism and the Aims of Counter-Terrorism in Moscow, Chechnya and the North Caucasus." Paper presented at the International Studies Association Annual Convention, Chicago, February 28–March 3, 2007.

Balzer, Harley. "The Implications of Demographic Change for Russian Politics and Security." Paper presented at the Health and Demography in the States of the Former Soviet Union Conference, Weatherhead Center for International Affairs, Harvard University, Cambridge, MA, April 29–30, 2005.

Bannikov, Konstantin L. "Regimented Communities in a Civil Society." *Journal of Power Institutions in Post-Soviet Societies* no. 1 (July 2004). Available at http://www.pipss.org/document40.html (accessed August 13, 2004).

Barany, Zoltan. *Democratic Breakdown and the Decline of the Russian Military*. Princeton: Princeton University Press, 2007.

Barylski, Robert V. *The Soldier in Russian Politics: Duty, Dictatorship, and Democracy under Gorbachev and Yeltsin*. New Brunswick, NJ: Transaction Publishers, 1998.

Baturina, Natal'ia. "Okopnaia pravda. Komkor Rokhlin: 'Afganskaia voina byla progulkoi . . .'" *Argumenty i fakty*, February 1, 1995, p. 2.

Baysayev, Usam. "The Yuri Budanov Case." Prague Watchdog Kavkaz Center, January 9, 2009. Available at http://www.kavkazcenter.com/eng/content/2009/01 (accessed July 5, 2009).

Bazarya, Irina. "The Phenomenon of Chechen 'Black Widows': Becoming a Suicide Terrorist." Paper presented at the Midwest Political Science Association Annual Conference, Chicago, April 20–23, 2006.

Belinskii, A. B., and M. V. Liamin. "Mediko-psikhologicheskaia reabilitatsiia uchastnikov boevykh deistvii v mnogoprofil'nom gospitale." *Voenno-meditsinskii zhurnal* 321, no. 1 (January 2000): 62–66.

Beluza, Aleksandra, and Dmitrii Litovkin. "Novobrantsam ne do smekha." *Izvestiia*, April 1, 2009.

Bertrand, Eva. "Les militaires ne savent plus comment travailler sans les Comités de mères de soldats." Interview with Valentina Melnikova, Union of Soldiers' Mothers Committees in Russia, Moscow, April 30, 2008 (in French/Russian version in Annex). *Journal of Power Institutions in Post-Soviet Societies* 9 (2009). Available at http://pipss.revues.org/index1971.html (accessed June 15, 2010).

Betz, David J., and Sergei Plekhanov. "Civil-Military Relations in Post-Soviet Russia: Rebuilding the 'Battle Order'?" In Natalie L. Mychajlyszyn and Harald von Riekhoff (eds.), *The Evolution of Civil-Military Relations in East-Central Europe and the Former Soviet Union*. Westport, CT: Praeger, 2004, pp. 159–189.

Bickford, Andrew. "Male Identity, the Military, and the Family in the Former German Democratic Republic." *Anthropology of East Europe Review* 19, no. 1 (Spring 2001). Available at http://condor.depaul.edu/~rrotenbe/aeer/v19n1/Bickford.pdf (accessed July 6, 2006).

Blum, Douglas W. "Official Patriotism in Russia: Its Essence and Implications." *PONARS Policy Memo* no. 420 (December 2006). Available at http://csis.org/files/media/csis/pubs/pm_0420.pdf (accessed June 15, 2010).

Boose, Linda E. "Techno-Muscularity and the 'Boy Eternal': From the Quagmire to the Gulf." In Miriam Cooke and Angela Woollacott (eds.), *Gendering War Talk* (Princeton: Princeton University Press, 1993), pp. 67–106.

Borenstein, Eliot. *Overkill: Sex and Violence in Contemporary Russian Popular Culture*. Ithaca, NY: Cornell University Press, 2008.

Breslauer, George. *Gorbachev and Yeltsin as Leaders*. Cambridge: Cambridge University Press, 2002.

Bridger, Sue, Rebecca Kay, and Kathryn Pinnick. *No More Heroines? Russia, Women and the Market*. London: Routledge, 1996.

Brown, Sarah. "Modern Tales of the Russian Army." *World Policy Journal* 14, no. 1 (March 1997): 61–70.

Brudny, Yitzhak M. "In Pursuit of the Russian Presidency: Why Yeltsin Won the 1996 Russian Presidential Election." *Communist and Post-Communist Studies* 30, no. 3 (September 1997): 255–275.

Buckley, Mary. *Women and Ideology in the Soviet Union*. Ann Arbor: University of Michigan Press, 1989.

Burawoy, Michael, and Katherine Verdery. "Introduction." In Michael Burawoy and Katherine Verdery (eds.), *Uncertain Transitions: Ethnographies of Change in the Postsocialist World*. Lanham, MD: Rowman and Littlefield, 1999, pp. 1–17.

Caiazza, Amy. *Mothers and Soldiers: Gender, Citizenship, and Civil Society in Contemporary Russia*. New York: Routledge, 2002.

"Chechnia—ne voina?" *Argumenty i fakty*, November 28, 2001.

Chernomyrdin, Viktor. "Za Rossiiu my stoiali i stoiat' budem." *Rossiiskaia gazeta*, December 14, 1994, pp. 1, 3.

Chernova, Natal'ia. "Materinskii zakaz." *Novaia gazeta*, October 6, 2003, pp. 12–13.

Cockburn, Cynthia. *The Space between Us: Negotiating Gender and National Identities in Conflict*. London: Zed Books, 2003.

———. "The Continuum of Violence: A Gender Perspective on War and Peace." In Wenona Giles and Jennifer Hyndman (eds.), *Sites of Violence: Gender and Conflict Zones*. Berkeley: California University Press, 2004, pp. 24–44.

———. *From Where We Stand: War, Women's Activism and Feminist Analysis*. London: Zed Books, 2007.

Colton, Timothy J. "The Impact of the Military on Soviet Society." In Erik P. Hoffmann and Robbin F. Laird (eds.), *The Soviet Polity in the Modern Era*. New York: Aldine Publishing Company, 1984, pp. 393–412.

Connell, R. W. *Gender and Power: Society, the Person and Sexual Politics*. Stanford: Stanford University Press, 1987.

———. *The Men and the Boys*. Berkeley: University of California Press, 2000.

Cooper, Julian. "The Security Economy." In Mark Galeotti (ed.), *The Politics of Security in Modern Russia*. Surrey: Ashgate Publishing Limited, 2010, pp. 145–170.

Cottam, Kazimiera J. "Hero of the Soviet Union, Women Recipients." In Reina Pennington (ed.), *Amazons to Fighter Pilots: A Biographical Dictionary of Military Women*. Westport, CT: Greenwood Press, 2003, pp. 197–200.

Danilova, Natal'ia. "Pravo materi soldata: Instinkt zaboty ili grazhdanskii dolg?" In Sergei Ushakin (ed.), *Semeinye uzy: Modeli dlia sborki*. Vol. 2. Moscow: Novoe literaturnoe obozrenie, 2004, pp. 188–210.

Danilova, Natalia. "Veterans' Policy in Russia: A Puzzle of Creation." *Journal of Power Institutions in Post-Soviet Societies* no. 6/7 (2007). Available at http://www.pipss.org/index873.html (accessed September 10, 2008).

———. "The Development of an Exclusive Veterans' Policy: The Case of Russia." *Armed Forces and Society* 20, no. 10 (2010): 1–27.

Daucé, Françoise, and Elisabeth Sieca-Kozlowski. "Introduction." In Françoise Daucé and Elisabeth Sieca-Kozlowski (eds.), *Dedovshchina in the Post-Soviet Military: Hazing of Russian Army Conscripts in a Comparative Perspective*. Stuttgart: Ibidem-Verlag, 2007, pp. 17–27.

Deriglazova, Larisa. "To Fear or to Respect?: Two Approaches to Military Reform in Russia." *Journal of Power Institutions in Post-Soviet Societies* no. 3 (2005). Available at http://www.pipss.org/document415.html (accessed September 17, 2006).

Deryugin, Reserve Col. Yury. "Incompetents in the Science of Winning Victory Are Creating a Slaughterhouse." *Rossiiskie vesti*, January 10, 1995, p. 2. *Current Digest of Post-Soviet Press* 47, no. 2 (February 2, 1995): 2–4.

Doktorov, B. Z., A. A. Oslon, and E. S. Petrenko. *Epokha El'tsina: Mneniia rossiian. Sotsiologicheskie ocherki*. Moscow: Institut Fonda "Obshchestvennoe mnenie," 2002.

Duma i obshchestvennost': Informatsionnyi sbornik. Samara: Samarskaia Gubernskaia Duma, 2005.

Dunlop, John B. *Russia Confronts Chechnya: Roots of a Separatist Conflict*. Cambridge: Cambridge University Press, 1998.

———. "Do Ethnic Russians Support Putin's War in Chechnya?" Jamestown Foundation's *Chechnya Weekly* 6, no. 4, January 26, 2005, pp. 6–8. Available at www.jamestown.org (accessed August 10, 2008).

———. *The 2002 Dubrovka and 2004 Beslan Hostage Crises: A Critique of Russian Counter-Terrorism*. Stuttgart: Ibidem-Verlag, 2006.

Edele, Mark. *Soviet Veterans of the Second World War: A Popular Movement in an Authoritarian Society 1941–1991*. Oxford: Oxford University Press, 2008.

Egorov, Ivan. "Chechenskii sindrom." *Vremia Moskovskie novosti*, January 31, 2000.

Eichler, Maya. "Russia's Post-Communist Transformation: A Gendered Analysis of the Chechen Wars." *International Feminist Journal of Politics* 8, no. 4 (2006): 486–511.

———. "Gender and Nation in the Soviet/Russian Transformation." In Yasmeen Abu-Laban (ed.), *Gendering the Nation-State: Canadian and Comparative Perspectives*. Vancouver: University of British Columbia Press, 2008, pp. 46–59.

———. "Russian Veterans of the Chechen Wars: A Feminist Analysis of Militarized Masculinities." In J. Ann Tickner and Laura Sjoberg (eds.), *Feminist International Relations: Conversations about the Past, Present and Future*. London: Routledge, 2011.

Eifler, Christine. "The Armed Forces as a Place of Social Construction of Gender: Women in the Russian Military." In Gabriele Jähnert et al. (eds.), *Gender in Transition: Eastern and Central Europe Proceedings*. Berlin: Trafo Verlag, 2001, pp. 274–277.

———. "'Weil man nun mit ihnen rechnen muss...': Frauen in den Streitkräften Russlands." In Ruth Seifert and Christine Eifler (eds.), *Gender und Militär: Internationale Erfahrungen mit Männern und Frauen in den Streitkräften*. Königstein: Ulrike Helmer, 2004, pp. 103–137.

Elkner, Julie. "*Dedovshchina* and the Committee of Soldiers' Mothers under Gorbachev." *Journal of Power Institutions in Post-Soviet Societies* no. 1 (2004). Available at www.pipss.org/document243.html (accessed September 17, 2006).

Elshtain, Jean Bethke. *Women and War*. Chicago: University of Chicago Press, 1995.

———. "War." In Cheris Kramarae and Dale Spender (eds.), *Routledge International Encyclopedia of Women: Global Women's Issues and Knowledge*. New York: Routledge, 2000, pp. 2027–2032.

El'tsin, Boris. "Obrashchenie k grazhdanam Rossii." *Rossiiskaia gazeta*, December 14, 1994, p. 1.

———. "Obrashchenie Borisa El'tsina v sviazi s situatsiei v Chechne." *Rossiiskaia gazeta*, December 28, 1994, p. 1.

———. "O deistvennosti gosudarstvennoi vlasti v Rossii: Poslanie Presidenta RF Sobraniiu Rossiiskoi Federatsii," 1995. Available at http://public-service.narod.ru/appearance.html (accessed July 15, 2008).

———. "Rossiia, za kotoruiu my v otvete: Poslanie Presidenta RF Sobraniiu Rossiiskoi Federatsii," 1996. Available at http://public service.narod.ru/appearance.html (accessed July 15, 2008).

Engel, Christine. "Kulturelles Gedächtnis, Neue Diskurse: Zwei Russische Filme über die Kriege in Tschetschenien." *Osteuropa* 53, no. 5 (2003): 604–617.

Enloe, Cynthia. *Does Khaki Become You? The Militarization of Women's Lives*. London: Pandora: 1983.

———. *Bananas, Beaches and Bases: Making Feminist Sense of International Politics*. Berkeley: University of California Press, 1989.

———. *The Morning After: Sexual Politics at the End of the Cold War.* Berkeley: University of California Press, 1993.

———. *Maneuvers: The International Politics of Militarizing Women's Lives.* Berkeley: University of California Press, 2000.

———. "Masculinity as Foreign Policy Issue." *Foreign Policy in Focus* 5, no. 36 (October 1, 2000). Available at http://www.fpif.org/pdf/vol5/36ifmasculinity.pdf (accessed January 20, 2004).

———. "Military." In Cheris Kramarae and Dale Spender (eds.), *Routledge International Encyclopedia of Women: Global Women's Issues and Knowledge.* New York: Routledge, 2000, pp. 1370–1374.

———. *The Curious Feminist: Searching for Women in a New Age of Empire.* Berkeley: University of California, 2004.

Eremenko, I. N. *Rossiia i Chechnia (1990–1997 gody): Dokumenty svidetel'stvuiut.* Moscow: RAU-Universitet, 1997.

Eremitcheva, Galina, and Elena Zdravomyslova. "Die Bewegung der Soldatenmütter— Eine Zivilgesellschaftliche Initiative: Der Fall St. Petersburg." In Martina Ritter (ed.), *Zivilgesellschaft und Gender-Politik in Rußland.* Frankfurt: Campus Verlag, 2001, pp. 224–246.

Evangelista, Matthew. *The Chechen Wars: Will Russia Go the Way of the Soviet Union?* Washington, DC: Brookings Institution Press, 2002.

Fedyukhin, Igor. "No Alternatives: Experts Say the Law on Alternative Civilian Service Will Not Be Popular." *Vedemosti,* July 23, 2003. Reprinted in *CDI Russia Weekly* no. 266 (July 25, 2003). Available at www.cdi.org/Russia/266-9.cfm (accessed November 16, 2004).

Fel'gengauer, Pavel. "A sluzhit' vnov' pridetsia dva-tri goda: Prizyvnaia armiia pobedila kontraktnuiu." *Novaia gazeta,* March 1, 2010.

Felgenhauer, Pavel. "Call-up: No Professional Army Yet in Sight in Russia." *Segodnia,* May 4, 1995, p. 2. *Current Digest of Post-Soviet Press* 47, no. 18 (May 31, 1995): 16–17.

———. "The Russian Army in Chechnya Is Being Systematically Stripped of What Remains of Its Human Face." *Ekho Moskvy,* February 13, 2000. *Current Digest of Post-Soviet Press,* 52, no. 7 (March 15, 2000): 5.

———. "Russia's Forces Unreconstructed." Institute for the Study of Conflict, Ideology, and Policy's *Perspective* 10, no. 4 (March–April 2000). Available at www.bu.edu/iscip/vol10/Felgenhauer.html (accessed September 16, 2008).

———. "The Russian Army in Chechnya." *Crimes of War Project: The Magazine* (April 2003): 6–9. Available at http://www.crimesofwar.org/chechnya-mag/ChechnyaMagazine.pdf (accessed May 2, 2004).

———. "Medvedev Acknowledges Problems in the 'New Look' Armed Forces." *Eurasia Daily Monitor,* March 11, 2010. Available at http://www.jamestown.org/single/?no_cache=1&tx_ttnews[tt_news]=36145 (accessed June 1, 2010).

———. "Personnel Problems Impact on Russian Military Reform." *Eurasia Daily Monitor,* April 29, 2010. Available at http://www.jamestown.org/single/?no_cache=1&tx_ttnews[tt_news]=36329 (accessed June 1, 2010).

———. "Russian Military Personnel Crisis: Medvedev and the General Staff Join the Fray." *Eurasia Daily Monitor*, May 6, 2010. Available at http://www.jamestown.org/single/?no_cache=1&tx_ttnews[tt_news]=36350 (accessed June 1, 2010).

Felshtinsky, Yuri, Alexander Litvinenko, and Geoffrey Andrews. *Blowing up Russia: Terror from Within*. London: Gibson Square Books, 2007.

Ferretti, Maria. "'Neprimirimaia pamiat': Rossiia i voina." *Neprikosnovennyi zapas: Debaty o politike i kul'ture* no. 40–41 (2005): 78–82.

Fish, M. Steven. "Reform and Demilitarization in Soviet Society from Brezhnev to Gorbachev." *Peace and Change* 15, no. 2 (April 1990): 150–172.

Foley, Michael S. *Confronting the War Machine: Draft Resistance during the Vietnam War*. Chapel Hill: University of North Carolina Press, 2003.

Fond "Obshchestvennoe mnenie." "S ianvaria po oktiabr' dolia doveriaiushchikh prezidentu Rossii snizilis' na 12 punktov." December 11, 1994. Available at http://bd.fom.ru (accessed July 15, 2008).

———. "Bol'shinstvo rossiian odobriaiut soldatskikh materei, pytaiushchikhsia zabrat' svoikh detei iz chastei, voiuiushchikh v Chechne." February 3, 1995. Available at http://bd.fom.ru (accessed June 1, 2010).

———. "Bol'shinstvo rossiian polagaiut, shto sozdanie professional'noi armii—nailuchshii sposob usileniia ee boesposobnosti." February 24, 1995. Available at http://bd.fom.ru (accessed September 16, 2008).

———. "Esli god nazad na odnogo doveriaiushchego prezidentu prikhodilos' dva nedoveriaiushchikh, to seichas—desiat'." March 10, 1995. Available at http://bd.fom.ru (accessed July 15, 2008).

———. "Kak vy schitaete, prizyvniki dolzhny obiazatel'no prokhodit' sluzhbu v armii ili luchshe predostavit' im vozmozhnost' al'ternativnoi sluzhby v grazhdanskoi sfere (rabota na predpriiatiiakh, v bol'nitsakh i t.d.)?" May 6, 1998. Available at http://bd.fom.ru (accessed October 15, 2010).

———. "V. Putin samyi populiarnyi rossiiskii politik 1999 goda." January 13, 2000. Available at http://bd.fom.ru (accessed July 15, 2008).

———. "'Poteriannye gody' v 'shkole zhizni.'" November 23, 2000. Available at http://bd.fom.ru (accessed October 15, 2010).

———. "Glavnaia neudacha V. Putina—'ne utikhla Chechnia.'" March 21, 2002. Available at http://bd.fom.ru (accessed July 15, 2008).

———. "Srochnaia sluzhba v armii." October 3, 2002. Available at http://bd.fom.ru (accessed June 1, 2010).

———. "O sluzhbe v armii." July 8, 2004. Available at http://bd.fom.ru (accessed October 15, 2010).

———. "Politik goda—snova V. Putin." December 16, 2004. Available at http://bd.fom.ru (accessed July 15, 2008).

Fowkes, Ben (ed.). *Russia and Chechnia: The Permanent Crisis*. London: Macmillan Press, 1998.

Furman, Dmitrii E. (ed.). *Chechnia i Rossiia: Obshchestvo i gosudarstvo*. Moscow: Polinform, 1999.

Gagina, Marina. "Istoriia bolezni: Chechenskii sindrom." *Krasnyi sever*, February 25, 2003.

Gal, Susan, and Gail Kligman. *Reproducing Gender: Politics, Public, and Everyday Life after Socialism*. Princeton: Princeton University Press, 1997.

Galeotti, Mark. *Afghanistan: The Soviet Union's Last War*. London: Frank Cass, 1995.

Gall, Carlotta, and Tom de Waal. *Chechnya: A Small Victorious War*. London: Pan, 1997.

Gapova, Elena. "Conceptualizing Gender, Nation, and Class in Post-Soviet Belarus." In Kathleen Kuehnast and Carol Nechemias (eds.), *Post-Soviet Women Encountering Transition: Nation Building, Economic Survival, and Civic Activism*. Baltimore, MD: Johns Hopkins University Press, 2004, pp. 85–102.

"Gays Are Not Willingly Accepted in the Russian Army." *Pravda*, December 1, 2003. Available at http://english.pravda.ru/business/finance/01-12-2003/4207-gayarmy-0/ (accessed June 1, 2010).

"Genshtab podschital uklonistov." *Krasnyi voin*, April 5, 2008.

German, Tracey C. *Russia's Chechen War*. New York: RoutledgeCurzon, 2003.

Gerber, Theodore P., and Sarah E. Mendelson. "Strong Public Support for Military Reform in Russia." *PONARS Policy Memo* 288 (May 2003). Available at http://www.gwu.edu/~ieresgwu/assets/docs/ponars/pm_0288.pdf (accessed October 15, 2010).

———. "Casualty Sensitivity in a Post-Soviet Context: Russian Views of the Second Chechen War, 2001–2004." *Political Science Quarterly* 123, no. 1 (2008): 39–68.

Getmanenko, Oleg. "What War Can Do to a Man." *Novye izvestiia*, March 31, 2000, pp. 1–2. *Current Digest of the Post-Soviet Press* 52, no. 13 (April 26, 2000): 9.

Gill, Lesley. "Creating Citizens, Making Men: The Military and Masculinity in Bolivia." *Cultural Anthropology* 12, no. 4 (1997): 527–550.

Gillespie, David. "Confronting Imperialism: The Ambivalence of War in Post-Soviet Film." In Stephen L. Webber and Jennifer G. Mathers (eds.), *Military and Society in Post-Soviet Russia*. Manchester: Manchester University Press, 2006, pp. 80–93.

Gilligan, Emma. *Terror in Chechnya: Russia and the Tragedy of Civilians in War*. Princeton: Princeton University Press, 2010.

Glasser, Julie. "United People's Party of Soldiers' Mothers: An Analysis of a Grassroots Movement." *Же: Stanford's Student Journal of Russian, East European, and Eurasian Studies* 1 (Spring 2005). Available at http://zhe.stanford.edu/spring05/soldiers%20mothers2.pdf (accessed June 16, 2008).

Goldstein, Lyle J. "Russian Civil-Military Relations in the Chechen War, December 1994–February 1995." *Journal of Slavic Military Studies* 10, no. 1 (March 1997): 109–127.

Goldstein, Joshua S. *War and Gender: How Gender Shapes the War System and Vice Versa*. Cambridge: Cambridge University Press, 2001.

Golts, Alexander. "Putin and the Chechen War: Together Forever." *Moscow Times*, February 14, 2004. Available at http://www.countercurrents.org/golts140204.htm (accessed January 23, 2007).

Golts, Aleksandr. "The Social and Political Condition of the Russian Military." In Steven E. Miller and Dmitri Trenin (eds.), *The Russian Military: Power and Policy*. Cambridge, MA: MIT Press, 2004, pp. 73–94.

Golts, Alexander M., and Tonya L. Putnam. "State Militarism and Its Legacies: Why Military Reform Has Failed in Russia." *International Security* 29, no. 2 (Fall 2004): 121–158.

Gomart, Thomas. *Russian Civil-Military Relations: Putin's Legacy.* Washington, DC: Carnegie Endowment for International Peace, 2008.

"'Goriachaia Linia' Soldatskikh materei." *Izvestiia*, October 17, 1995.

Government of the Russian Federation. *Konstitutsiia Rossiiskoi Federatsii*, Moscow, December 12, 1993. Available at http://public-service.narod.ru/law.html (accessed July 15, 2008).

———. *Federal'nyi zakon "O Voinskoi obiazannosti i voennoi sluzhbe."* No. 53-F3, Moscow, March 28, 1998.

———. "Zaiavlenie Pravitel'stva RF o situatsii v Chechneskoi respublike i merakh po ee uregulirovaniiu." *Krasnaia zvezda*, October 23, 1999.

———. "Gossudarstvennaia Programma 'Patrioticheskoe Vospitanie Grazhdan Rossiiskoi Federatsii 2001–2005 Gody." February 16, 2001. Available at http://www.rg.ru/oficial/doc/postan_rf/122_1.shtm (accessed June 12, 2010).

———. *Federal'nyi zakon "Ob al'ternativnoi grazhdanskoi sluzhbe."* Moscow, 2003.

———. "Gossudarstvennaia Programma 'Patrioticheskoe Vospitanie Grazhdan Rossiiskoi Federatsii 2006–2010 Gody." July 11, 2005. Available at http://www.llr.ru/razdel3.php?id_r2=55 (accessed June 12, 2010).

Government of the USSR. *Women in the USSR.* Moscow: Progress Publishers, 1985.

Gross, Natalie. "Youth and the Army in the USSR in the 1980s." *Soviet Studies* 42, no. 3 (July 1990): 481–498.

Grossman, Lt. Col. Dave. *On Killing: The Psychological Cost of Learning to Kill in War and Society.* Boston: Little, Brown and Company 1995.

Gudkov, Lev. "Die Fesseln des Sieges: Rußlands Identität aus der Erinnerung an den Krieg." *Osteuropa* 55, no. 4–6 (April–June 2005): 56–73.

———. "The Army as an Institutional Model." In Stephen L. Webber and Jennifer G. Mathers (eds.), *Military and Society in Post-Soviet Russia.* Manchester: Manchester University Press, 2006, pp. 39–60.

Handelman, Stephen. *Comrade Criminal: Russia's New Mafiya.* New Haven: Yale University Press, 1995.

Hartmann, Kathrin. "Die Konstruktion von Männerbildern in Russland—Kontinuität und Wandel von Männerbildern in den 90er Jahren am Beispiel sowjetischer und postsowjetischer Filme." *Working Paper* no. 39. Berlin: Osteuropa-Institut der Freien Universität Berlin, 2002.

Herspring, Dale R. "Dedovshchina in the Russian Army: The Problem That Won't Go Away." *Journal of Slavic Military Studies* 18, no. 4 (2005): 607–629.

———. *The Kremlin and the High Command: Presidential Impact on the Russian Military from Gorbachev to Putin.* Lawrence: University Press of Kansas, 2006.

———. "Undermining Combat Readiness in the Russian Military, 1992–2005." *Armed Forces and Society* 32, no. 4 (2006): 513–531.

Higate, Paul R. (ed.). *Military Masculinities: Identity and the State.* Westport, CT: Praeger, 2003.

Hinterhuber, Eva Maria. *Die Soldatenmütter von Sankt Petersburg: Zwischen Neotraditionalismus und neuer Widerständigkeit.* Hamburg: LIT, 1999.

———. "Between Neotraditionalism and New Resistance—Soldiers' Mothers of St. Petersburg." *Anthropology of East Europe Review* 19, no. 1 (Spring 2001). Available at http://condor.depaul.edu/~rrotenbe/aeer/v19n1/Hinterhuber.pdf (accessed November 16, 2004).

Holloway, David. "War, Militarism, and the Soviet State." In Erik P. Hoffmann and Robbin F. Laird (eds.), *The Soviet Polity in the Modern Era.* New York: Aldine Publishing Company, 1984, pp. 359–391.

Hooper, Charlotte. "Masculinist Practices and Gender Politics: The Operation of Multiple Masculinities in International Relations." In Marysia Zalewski and Jane Parpart (eds.), *The "Man" Question in International Relations.* Boulder, CO: Westview Press, 1998, pp. 28–53.

———. *Manly States, International Relations, and Gender Politics.* New York: Columbia University Press, 2001.

Human Rights Watch. *"Welcome to Hell": Arbitrary Detention, Torture, and Extortion in Chechnya.* New York: Human Rights Watch, 2000.

———. "Conscription through Detention in Russia's Armed Forces." New York: Human Rights Watch, November 2002. Available at http://www.hrw.org/en/reports/2002/11/21/conscription-through-detention-russias-armed-forces (accessed October 15, 2008).

———. "To Serve without Health? Inadequate Nutrition and Health Care in the Russian Armed Forces." New York: Human Rights Watch, November 2003. Available at http://www.hrw.org/en/reports/2003/11/13/serve-without-health-0 (accessed October 15, 2008).

———. "The Wrongs of Passage: Inhuman and Degrading Treatment of New Recruits in the Russian Armed Forces." New York: Human Rights Watch, October 2004. Available at http://www.hrw.org/en/node/11940/section/1 (accessed October 15, 2008).

———. "Widespread Torture in the Chechen Republic: Human Rights Watch Briefing Paper for the 37th UN Committee against Torture." New York: Human Rights Watch, November 2006. Available at http://www.hrw.org/backgrounder/eca/chechnya1106/ (accessed July 15, 2008).

"Ia – Shamanov." Interview conducted by Anna Politkovskaia. *Novaia gazeta*, June 19–25, 2000.

Ilyina, Marina. "Critical Life Events and Downward Trajectories." In Sarah Ashwin (ed.), *Adapting to Russia's New Labour Market: Gender and Employment Behaviour.* New York: Routledge, 2006, pp. 193–212.

"I'm Afraid That I Won't Be Able to Forget the War: Psychological Rehabilitation of Chechen War Veterans." *Kommersant*, May 25, 2000, p. 9. *Current Digest of the Post-Soviet Press* 52, no. 21 (June 21, 2000): 18–19.

"In Brief: President's Rating Falls." *Nezavisimaia gazeta*, December 28, 1994, p. 1. *Current Digest of the Post-Soviet Press* 46, no. 52 (January 25, 1995): 16.

International Institute for Strategic Studies. *The Military Balance 1991–1992.* London: International Institute for Strategic Studies, 1991.

———. *The Military Balance 1996–1997*. London: International Institute for Strategic Studies, 1996.
———. *The Military Balance 1997–1998*. London: International Institute for Strategic Studies, 1997.
———. *The Military Balance 1998–1999*. London: International Institute for Strategic Studies, 1998.
———. *The Military Balance 1999–2000*. London: International Institute for Strategic Studies, 1999.
———. *The Military Balance 2000–2001*. London: International Institute for Strategic Studies, 2000.
———. *The Military Balance 2001–2002*. London: International Institute for Strategic Studies, 2001.
———. *The Military Balance 2002–2003*. London: International Institute for Strategic Studies, 2002.
———. *The Military Balance 2005–2006*. London: International Institute for Strategic Studies, 2005.
———. *The Military Balance 2008*. London: International Institute for Strategic Studies, 2008.
———. *The Military Balance 2009*. London: International Institute for Strategic Studies, 2009.
———. *The Military Balance 2010*. London: International Institute for Strategic Studies, 2010.
"Interview with Natal'ia Zhukova." Conducted by Anna Maria Tramonti. *Current*. CBC Radio, November 23, 2004.
"Interview of Tanya Lokshina, President of the Demos Center, Conducted by Olga Filippova, Moscow, 11 May 2007." *Journal of Power Institutions in Post-Soviet Societies* no. 6/7 (2007). Available at http://www.pipss.org/index772.html (accessed January 11, 2008).
Ipsa-Landa, Simone. "Russian Preferred Self-Image and the Two Chechen Wars." *Demokratizatsiya* 11, no. 1 (Winter 2003): 305–319.
Isachenkov, Vladimir. "State TV Runs Chechnya Ads." *Moscow Times*, January 26, 2005. Available at http://www.themoscowtimes.com/stories/2005/01/26/017.html (accessed January 30, 2005).
Isakova, Irina. "The Russian Defense Reform." *China and Eurasia Forum Quarterly* 5, no. 1 (2007): 75–82.
Issoupova, Olga. "From Duty to Pleasure? Motherhood in Soviet and Post-Soviet Russia." In Sarah Ashwin (ed.), *Gender, State and Society in Soviet and Post-Soviet Russia*. London: Routledge, 2000, pp. 30–54.
Jeffords, Susan. *The Remasculinization of America: Gender and the Vietnam War*. Bloomington: Indiana University Press, 1989.
Jones, Ellen. *Red Army and Society: A Sociology of the Soviet Military*. Boston: Allen and Unwin, 1985.
———. "Social Change and Civil-Military Relations." In Timothy J. Colton and Thane Gustafson (eds.), *Soldiers and the Soviet State: Civil-Military Relations from Brezhnev to Gorbachev*. Princeton: Princeton University Press, 1990, pp. 239–284.

Kagarlitsky, Boris. "Ethnic Problems and National Issues in Contemporary Russian Society." In Judyth L. Twigg and Kate Schecter (eds.), *Social Capital and Social Cohesion in Post-Soviet Russia*. Armonk, NY: M. E. Sharpe, 2003, pp. 55–73.

"Kak lechat 'chechenskii sindrom.'" *Svobodnyi kurs*, April 5, 2001.

Kalikh, Andrey, and Lev Levinson. "Implementation of the Right to Conscientious Objection in Russian Federation 2004 ¨C [sic] 2009." Available at http://www.ebcobeoc.eu/ (accessed June 15, 2010).

Karner, Tracy Xavia. "Engendering Violent Men: Oral Histories of Military Masculinity." In Lee H. Bowker (ed.), *Masculinities and Violence*. Thousand Oaks, CA: Sage Publications, 1998, pp. 197–232.

Kay, Rebecca. *Russian Women and Their Organizations: Gender, Discrimination, and Grassroots Women's Organizations, 1991–96*. New York: St. Martin's Press, 1999.

———. *Men in Contemporary Russia: The Fallen Heroes of Post-Soviet Change*. Aldershot: Ashgate, 2006.

Key, Joshua, and Lawrence Hill. *The Deserter's Tale: The Story of an Ordinary Soldier Who Walked away from the War in Iraq*. Toronto: House of Anasi, 2007.

Kirschenbaum, Lisa A. "'Our City, Our Hearths, Our Families': Local Loyalties and Private Life in Soviet World War II Propaganda." *Slavic Review* 59, no. 4 (Winter 2000): 825–847.

Klein, Uta. "The Military and Masculinities in Israeli Society." In Paul R. Higate (ed.), *Military Masculinities: Identity and the State*. London: Praeger, 2003, pp. 191–200.

Kliamkin, Igor', and Lev Timofeev. *Tenevaia Rossiia: Ekonomiko-sotsiologicheskoe issledovaniie*. Moscow: Rossiiskii gosudarstevennii gumanitarnii universitet, 2000.

Knight, W. Andy, and Tanya Narozhna. "Rape and Other War Crimes in Chechnya: Is There a Role for the International Criminal Court?" *spacesofidentity* 5, no. 1 (2005): 92–93. Available at http://pi.library.yorku.ca/ojs/index.php/soi/article/view/8002/7152 (accessed March 16, 2009).

Kon, I. S. "Dedovshchina v svete issledovanii zakrytykh muzhskikh soobshchestv." In *Muzhchina v ekstremal'noi situatsii*. St. Petersburg: Indrik, 2007, pp. 84–88.

Koval'skaia, Galina. "Shturm i glupost'." *Ezhenedel'nyi zhurnal*. April 1, 2003, pp. 16–17.

Krainova, Nataliia. "Vechnaia pamiat'." RIA "Samara," December 12, 2008. Available at http://www.riasamara.ru/rus/news/region/society/article36605.shtml (accessed April 15, 2009).

Kreisky, Eva. "Diskreter Maskulinismus: Über geschlechtsneutralen Schein politischer Idole, politischer Ideale und politischer Institutionen." In Eva Kreisky and Birgit Sauer (eds.), *Das geheime Glossar der Politikwissenschaft: Geschlechtskritische Inspektion der Kategorien einer Disziplin*. Frankfurt am Main: Campus, 1997, pp. 161–213.

Krylova, Ann. "Women Fighters in 1930s Stalinist Russia." *Gender and History* 16, no. 3 (November 2004): 626–653.

Kryshtanovskaya, Ol'ga, and Stephen White. "The Sovietization of Russian Politics." *Post-Soviet Affairs* 25, no. 4 (2009): 283–309.

Kucher, Aleksandr A. "Zhizn' posle voennoi sluzhby." *Nezavisimoe voennoe obozrenie* no. 43, November 21, 1997.

Kukhterin, Sergei. "Fathers and Patriarchs in Communist and Post-Communist Russia." In Sarah Ashwin (ed.), *Gender, State and Society in Soviet and Post-Soviet Russia*. London: Routledge, 2000, pp. 71–89.

Kuklina, Ida. "Acceptance Speech." Right Livelihood Award, December 9, 1996. Available at www.rightlivelihood.org/csmr_speech.html (accessed January 15, 2009).

Kwon, Insook. "A Feminist Exploration of Military Conscription: The Gendering of the Connections between Nationalism, Militarism and Citizenship in South Korea." *International Feminist Journal of Politics* 3, no. 1 (April 2000): 26–54.

Lambeth, Benjamin S. *The Warrior Who Would Rule Russia: A Profile of Aleksandr Lebed*. Santa Monica, CA: RAND, 1996.

Lapidus, Gail W. *Women in Soviet Society: Equality, Development, and Social Change*. Berkeley: University of California Press, 1978.

———. "Gender and Restructuring: The Impact of Perestroika and Its Aftermath on Soviet Women." In Valentine M. Moghadam (ed.), *Democratic Reform and the Position of Women in Transitional Economies*. Oxford: Clarendon Press, 1993, pp. 138–161.

———. "Contested Sovereignty: The Tragedy of Chechnya." *International Security* 23, no. 1 (1998): 5–49.

———. "Putin's War on Terrorism: Lessons from Chechnya." *Post-Soviet Affairs* 18, no. 1 (2002): 41–48.

Laruelle, Marlène. *In the Name of the Nation: Nationalism and Politics in Contemporary Russia*. New York: Palgrave Macmillan, 2009.

———. "Introduction." In Marlène Laruelle (ed.), *Russian Nationalism and the National Reassertion of Russia*. New York: Routledge, 2009, pp. 1–10.

Lebedev, Anna Colin. "The Test of Reality: Understanding Families' Tolerance regarding Mistreatment of Conscripts in the Russian Army." In Françoise Daucé and Elisabeth Sieca-Kozlowski (eds.), *Dedovshchina in the Post-Soviet Military: Hazing of Russian Army Conscripts in a Comparative Perspective*. Stuttgart: Ibidem-Verlag, 2007, pp. 47–74.

"Ledi v dospekhakh." *Interfaks Vremia*, August 23, 2006. Available at http://www.ifvremya.ru/cgi-bin/res.pl?FIL=work/arc/2006/0823/3_20060823.txt (accessed September 30, 2006).

Lentini, Peter. "Hegemonic Masculinities in Russia." In Vladimir Tikhomirov (ed.), *In Search of Identity: Five Years since the Fall of the Soviet Union*. Melbourne: University of Melbourne Centre for Russian and Euro-Asian Studies, 1996, pp. 157–169.

Levada-Tsentr. "Chechnia." Available at www.levada.ru/chechnya.html (accessed August 15, 2008).

———. "Delo polkovnika Budanova: Chechnia." July 31, 2002. Available at www.levada.ru/press/2002073100.html (accessed March 15, 2009).

———. "Armiia." Available at www.levada.ru/army (accessed October 15, 2010).

———. "Rossiiskaia armiia." February 17, 2010. Available at http://www.levada.ru/press/2010021701.html (accessed June 12, 2010).

Levinson, A. G. "The Role of Gender in Russians' Attitudes toward the Second Chechen Campaign." *Sociological Research* 43, no. 2 (2004): 79–95.

Levinson, Alexei. "Russia's People: What Is a Just War?" *openDemocracy Russia,* April 13, 2010. Available at http://www.opendemocracy.net/od-russia/alexei-levinson/russia%E2%80%99s-people-what-is-just-war (accessed June 15, 2010).
Liborakina, Marina. "Women Fight to Be Heard in Chechen Dialogue." Undated manuscript. Available at http://www.isar.org/pubs/ST/Chechwomen44.html (accessed October 23, 2003).
Lieven, Anatol. *Chechnya: Tombstone of Russian Power.* New Haven: Yale University Press, 1997.
Light, Margot. "Russia and the War on Terror." In Christopher Ankersen with Michael O'Leary (eds.), *Understanding Global Terror.* Cambridge: Polity Press, 2007, pp. 95–110.
Litovkin, Viktor. "Draftees Name the War in Chechnya, Hazing and Bad Food as Their Reasons for Refusing to Serve." *Izvestiia,* April 5, 1996, pp. 1–2. *Current Digest of Post-Soviet Press* 48, no. 15 (May 8, 1996): 5.
———. "The Army Is Shooting at Its Own Men: The Main Reason for Today's Tragedies Is Unbearable Living and Service Conditions." *Izvestiia,* June 6, 1997, pp. 1, 5. *Current Digest of the Post-Soviet Press* 49, no. 24 (July 16, 1997): 1–3.
———. "Opiat' prizyv, opiat' problemy." *Nezavisimoe voennoe obozrenie,* April 9, 2010.
Lokshin, Michael, and Ruslan Yemtsov. "Who Bears the Cost of Russia's Military Draft?" *Economics of Transition* 16, no. 3 (2008): 359–387.
Lokshina, Tanya. "Chechnya: Choked by Headscarves." *openDemocracy Russia,* September 27, 2010. Available http://www.opendemocracy.net/tanya-lokshina/chechnya-choked-by-headscarves (accessed October 15, 2010).
Lukanin, Mikhail. "Chechenskii sindrom." *Trud,* December 11, 2009.
Mangazeev, Igor'. "Chechenskii sindrom." *Veche Tveri,* September 6, 2007. Available at www.tverinfo.ru/analitika/chechenskii_sindrom.html (accessed December 1, 2010).
Mann, Michael. "The Roots and Contradictions of Modern Militarism." *New Left Review* no. I/162 (March–April 1987): 35–50.
Markwick, Roger D. "Stalinism at War." *Kritika: Explorations in Russian and Eurasian History* 3, no. 3 (Summer 2002): 509–520.
Marsh, Rosalind. "Women in Contemporary Russia and the Former Soviet Union." In Rick Wilford and Robert L. Miller, eds. *Women, Ethnicity and Nationalism: The Politics of Transition.* London: Routledge, 1998, pp. 75–103.
Mastykina, Irina. "When I Return: Psychiatrists Know a Very Terrible Truth about the 'Chechen Conflict.'" *Komsomolskaia pravda,* April 25, 1995, p. 3. *Current Digest of the Post-Soviet Press* 47, no. 17 (May 24, 1995): 9–10.
Mathers, Jennifer G. "Women in the Russian Armed Forces: A Marriage of Convenience?" *Minerva: Quarterly Report on Women and the Military* 18, no. 3–4 (2000): 129–143.
———. "Women, Society and the Military: Women Soldiers in Post-Soviet Russia." In Stephen L. Webber and Jennifer G. Mathers (eds.), *Military and Society in Post-Soviet Russia.* Manchester: Manchester University Press, 2006, pp. 207–227.
Matloff, Judith. "Russia's Army Faces Battle within Its Ranks." *Christian Science Monitor,* February 1, 1999.
———. "Russia's Powerhouses of Dissent: Mothers. The Soldiers' Mothers Committee

Takes on the Military in Ways Others Can't." *Christian Science Monitor*, February 24, 2000.
Matthews, Jill J. *Good and Mad Women: The Historical Construction of Femininity in Twentieth-Century Australia*. Sydney: George Allen and Unwin, 1984.
"Maybe Guilty, Maybe Sane: Supreme Court Reviews Yury Budanov Case." *Kommersant*, March 1, 2003, pp. 1, 3. *Current Digest of the Post-Soviet Press* 55, no. 9 (April 2, 2003): 9.
Mendelson, Sarah E. *Changing Course: Ideas, Politics, and the Soviet Withdrawal from Afghanistan*. Princeton: Princeton University Press, 1998.
Meshcherkina, Elena. "New Russian Men: Masculinity Regained?" In Sarah Ashwin (ed.), *Gender, State and Society in Soviet and Post-Soviet Russia*. London: Routledge, 2000, pp. 105–117.
Miaken'kii, Andrei. "Posle Boia: Vtoroi chechenskii sindrom?" *Moskovskaia pravda*, January 29, 2000.
Mickiewicz, Ellen. *Changing Channels: Television and the Struggle for Power in Russia*, 2nd ed. Durham, NC: Duke University Press, 1999.
Ministry of Defense of the Russian Federation. "Ob obrazovanii Obshchestvennogo Soveta pri Ministerstve Oborny Rossiiskoi Federatsii." Decree no. 490, November 16, 2006. Available at http://sovet.mil.ru/Documents.html (accessed June 15, 2010).
Moon, Seungsook. "Trouble with Conscription, Entertaining Soldiers: Popular Culture and the Politics of Militarized Masculinity in South Korea." *Men and Masculinities* 8, no. 1 (July 2005): 64–92.
Morgan, David H. J. "Theater of War: Combat, the Military, and Masculinities." In Harry Brod and Michael Kaufman (eds.), *Theorizing Masculinities*. London: Sage, 1994, pp. 165–182.
"Mothers' March to Grozny." *WRI Women* no. 19 (June 1995). Available at www.wri-irg.org/node/3778 (accessed January 15, 2009).
Nagel, Joane. "Masculinities and Nation." In Michael S. Kimmel, Jeff Hearn, and R. W. Connell (eds.), *Handbook of Studies on Men and Masculinities*. Thousand Oaks, CA: Sage Publications, 2004, pp. 397–413.
"Nesmotria na obeshchaniia Ivanova, soldat-srochnikov otpravliaiut Chechniu." *Novyi region*, February 28, 2006. Available at www.nr2.ru/society/57672.html (accessed September 16, 2008).
Nikonova, Ol'ga. "Zhenshchiny, voina i 'figury umolchaniia.'" *Neprikosnovennyi zapas: Debaty o politike i kul'ture* no. 40–41 (2005): 282–289.
Niva, Steve. "Tough and Tender: New World Order Masculinity and the Gulf War." In Marysia Zalewski and Jane Parpart (eds.), *The "Man" Question in International Relations*. Boulder, CO: Westview Press, 1998, pp. 109–125.
Nivat, Anne. "The Black Widows: Chechen Women Join the Fight for Independence—and Allah." *Studies in Conflict and Terrorism* 28, no. 5 (2005): 413–419.
Novikova, Asmik. "Reabilitatsiia veteranov Chechni." In *Militsiia mezhdu Rossiei i Chechnei: Veterany konflikta v rossiiskom obshchestve*. Moscow: Demos, 2007, pp. 76–99.
O'Brien, Mary, and Chris Jefferies. "Women and the Soviet Military." *Air University Review* 33, no. 2 (January–February 1982): 76–85.

Odnokolenko, Oleg. "Forgotten for Political Reasons: Chechen War Soldiers Denied Veteran Status." *Segodnia*, February 4, 2000, p. 4. *Current Digest of the Post-Soviet Press* 52, no. 5 (March 1, 2000): 5–6.

Oliinik, Aleksandr. "A uklonistov stanovitsia bol'she." *Krasnaia zvezda*, May 28, 1997.

Oliker, Olga, and Tanya Charlick-Paley. *Assessing Russia's Decline: Trends and Implications for the United States and the U.S. Air Force*. Santa Monica, CA: Rand, 2000.

Oushakine, Serguei Alex. *The Patriotism of Despair: Nation, War, and Loss in Russia*. Ithaca, NY: Cornell University Press, 2009.

Pain, Emil. "The Chechen War in the Context of Contemporary Russian Politics." In Richard Sakwa (ed.), *Chechnya: From Past to Future*. London: Anthem Press, 2005, pp. 67–78.

Parpart, Jane, and Marysia Zalewski (eds.). *Rethinking the Man Question: Sex, Gender and Violence in International Relations*. London: Zed Books, 2008.

Pennington, Reina. "'Do Not Speak of the Services You Rendered': Women Veterans of Aviation in the Soviet Union." *Journal of Slavic Military Studies* 9, no. 1 (March 1996): 120–151.

Peterson, V. Spike. "Security and Sovereign States: What Is at Stake in Taking Feminism Seriously?" In Spike V. Peterson (ed.), *Gendered States: Feminist (Re)Visions of International Relations Theory*. Boulder, CO: Lynne Rienner Publishers, 1992, pp. 31–64.

Petrone, Karen. "Masculinity and Heroism in Imperial and Soviet Military-Patriotic Cultures." In Barbara Evans Clements, Rebecca Friedman, and Dan Healey (eds.), *Russian Masculinities in History and Culture*. Houndsmills: Palgrave, 2002, pp. 172–193.

Pickel, Andreas, Frank Bönker, and Klaus Müller (eds.). *Postcommunist Transformation and the Social Sciences: Cross-Disciplinary Approaches*. Boulder, CO: Rowman and Littlefield, 2002.

Pinnick, Kathryn. "When the Fighting Is Over: The Soldiers' Mothers and the Afghan Madonnas." In Mary Buckley (ed.), *Post-Soviet Women: From the Baltic to Central Asia*. Cambridge: Cambridge University Press, 1997, pp. 143–156.

Pisarenko, Dmitrii. "Rany voiny: Chechenskii sindrom." *Argumenty i fakty*, August 21, 1996, p. 13.

Pleshakova, Svetlana. "Mamania-Kombat: Zhena-komandir—podarok dlia liubogo mushchiny." *Moskovskii komsomolets*, February 22, 2007, p. 4.

Pohl, Michaela. "Anna Politkovskaya and Ramzan Kadyrov: Exposing the Kadyrov Syndrome." *Problems of Post-Communism* 54, no. 5 (September/October 2007): 30–39.

Politkovskaia, Anna. "Peregovory o mire: Soldatskie materi uekhali dumat' nad predlozheniiami chechenskoi storony: Ostanovit li eto terakti?" *Novaia gazeta*, February 28, 2005, p. 2.

Politkovskaya, Anna. *A Dirty War: A Russian Reporter in Chechnya*. London: Harvill Press, 2001.

———. *Putin's Russia*. London: Harvill Press, 2004.

Popkova, Liudmila. "'Missiia nevypolnima': Zhenskie strategii politicheskogo uchastiia." In L. N. Popkova and I. N. Tartakovskii (eds.), *Gendernye otnosheniia v sovremennoi*

Rossii: issledovaniia 1990-kh godov. Samara: Isdatel'stvo "Samarskii universitet," 2003, pp. 221–241.

———. "Women's Political Activism in Russia: The Case of Samara." In Kathleen Kuehnast and Carol Nechemias (eds.), *Post-Soviet Women Encountering Transition: Nation Building, Economic Survival, and Civic Activism.* Washington, DC: Woodrow Wilson Center Press; Baltimore, MD: Johns Hopkins University Press, 2004, pp. 172–194.

Poroskov, Nikolai. "Call to Arms Barely Heard: Young Men in Russia Are Now Trying to Even Evade Alternative Service." *Vremia novostei*, October 1, 2004, p. 4. *Current Digest of the Post-Soviet Press* 56, no. 40 (November 3, 2004): 16.

Posadskaya, Anastasia (ed.). *Women in Russia: A New Era in Russian Feminism.* London: Verso, 1994.

Potts, Malcolm, and Thomas Hayden. *Sex and War: How Biology Explains Warfare and Terrorism and Offers a Path to a Safer World.* Dallas, TX: Benbella Books, 2008.

Pozhidaev, D. D. "Ot boevykh deistvii—k grazhdanskoi zhizni." *Sotsiologicheskie issledovaniia* no. 1 (1999): 70–74.

Putin, Vladimir. "Kakuiu Rossiiu my stroem: Poslanie Presidenta RF Sobraniiu Rossiiskoi Federatsii," 2000. Available at http://public-service.narod.ru/appearance.html (accessed July 15, 2008).

———. Interview with Mayak radio station, March 18, 2000. Available at www.kremlin.ru (accessed January 19, 2008).

———. "Ne budet ni revolutsii, ni kontrrevoliutsii: Poslanie Presidenta RF Sobraniiu Rossiiskoi Federatsii," 2001. Available at http://public-service.narod.ru/appearance.html (accessed July 15, 2008).

Putin, Vladimir, with Nataliya Gevorkyan, Natalya Timakova, and Andrei Kolesnikov. *First Person: An Astonishingly Frank Self-Portrait by Russia's President Vladimir Putin.* London: Hutchinson, 2000.

Racioppi, Linda, and Katherine O'Sullivan See. *Women's Activism in Contemporary Russia.* Philadelphia: Temple University Press, 1997.

Rakowska-Harmstone, Teresa. "Nationalities and the Soviet Military." In Lubomyr Hajda and Mark Beissinger (eds.), *The Nationalities Factor in Soviet Politics and Society.* Boulder, CO: Westview Press, 1990, pp. 72–94.

Rainsford, Sarah. "Putin Is Russia's New Pop Idol." BBC online, August 23, 2002. Available at http://news.bbc.co.uk/2/hi/europe/2212885.stm (accessed October 15, 2010).

Reese, Roger R. *The Soviet Military Experience: A History of the Soviet Army, 1917–1991.* London: Routledge, 2000.

Regamey, Amandine. "L'Opinion Public Russe et l'Affair Boudanov." *Journal of Power Institutions in Post-Soviet Societies* no. 8 (2008). Available at http://www.pipss.org/document1493.html (accessed April 1, 2009).

Renz, Bettina. "Putin's Militocracy? An Alternative Interpretation of *Siloviki* in Contemporary Russian Politics." *Europe-Asia Studies* 58, no. 6 (2006): 903–924.

Reuveny, Rafael, and Aseem Prakash. "The Afghanistan War and the Breakdown of the Soviet Union." *Review of International Studies* 25, no. 4 (1999): 693–708.

Riabova, Tat'iana, and Oleg Riabov. "'U nas seksa net': Gender, Identity and Anti-Communist Discourses in Russia." Undated manuscript. Available at nations.gender-ehu. org/text/Riabovy_u%20nas%20seksa%20net.doc (accessed July 29, 2008).

Rivkin-Fish, Michelle. "Anthropology, Demography, and the Search for a Critical Analysis of Fertility: Insights from Russia." *American Anthropologist* 105, no. 2 (2003): 289–301.

Roget, Olivier. "Eyewitness: Grozny under Siege. The Unheated City Is Short of Food and Medical Supplies." *Segodnia*, December 24, p. 3. *Current Digest of the Post-Soviet Press* 46, no. 51 (January 18, 1995): 8–9.

Roman, Meredith L. "Making Caucasians Black: Moscow since the Fall of Communism and the Racialization of Non-Russians." *Journal of Communist Studies and Transition Politics* 18, no. 2 (2002): 1–27.

"'Rossiiskaia Gazeta' otmenila alternativnuiu sluzhbu." *Regnum*, March 31, 2004. Available at http://www.regnum.ru/news/240003.html (accessed June 15, 2010).

"Rossiiskoi armii nuzhny zhenshchiny." *Nezavisimoe voennoe obozrenie* no. 22, June 23, 2000.

Rousseva, Valentina. "Rape and Sexual Assault in Chechnya." *Culture, Society and Praxis* 3, no. 1 (November 2004). Available at http://culturesocietypraxis.org/index.php/csp/article/viewFile/46/43 (accessed March 15, 2009).

Russell, John. "Mujahedeen, Mafia, Madmen: Russian Perceptions of Chechens during the War in Chechnya, 1994–96 and 1999–2001." *Journal of Communist Studies and Transition Politics* 18, no. 1 (2002): 73–96.

———. *Chechnya—Russia's "War on Terror."* London: Routledge, 2007.

"Russia Bans Gays, Alcohol and Drug Users from Army." *Agence France-Press*, March 13, 2003. Reprinted in *CDI Russia Weekly* no. 248 (March 14, 2003). Available at http://www.cdi.org/russia/248-11-pr.cfm (accessed April 1, 2009).

"Russia Launches Spring Military Draft Campaign." *Jamestown Foundation Monitor* 6, no. 68 (April 5, 2000). Reprinted in *CDI Russia Weekly* no. 96 (April 7, 2000). Available at http://www.cdi.org/russia/apr0700.html#10 (accessed September 16, 2008).

"Russians Believe Putin Will Restore Military and Economic Might." *Izvestiia*, February 19, 2000, p. 3. *Current Digest of the Post-Soviet Press* 52, no. 9 (March 29, 2000): 14.

"S otsrochkoi na god: L'goty voevavshim v Chechne." *Trud*, April 3, 2003, p. 30.

Sakaida, Henry, and Christa Hook. *Heroines of the Soviet Union, 1941–45*. Oxford: Osprey Publishing, 2003.

Sakwa, Richard. *Putin: Russia's Choice*. New York: Routledge, 2004.

———. *Russian Politics and Society*, 4th ed. London: Routledge, 2008.

———. (ed.). *Chechnya: From Past to Future*. London: Anthem Press, 2005.

Salmenniemi, Suvi. *Democratization and Gender in Contemporary Russia*. London: Routledge, 2008.

Sanborn, Joshua A. *Drafting the Russian Nation: Military Conscription, Total War, and Mass Politics, 1905–1925*. DeKalb: Northern Illinois University Press, 2003.

Sapper, Manfred. *Auswirkungen des Afghanistan-Krieges auf die Sowjetgesellschaft: Eine Studie zum Legitimitätsverlust des Militärischen in der Perestroijka*. Münster: LIT, 1994.

———. "Diffuse Militanz in Rußland: Ein Erbe des militarisierten Sozialismus?" *Berliner Debatte Initial* 8, no. 6 (1997): 93–107.
Sarin, Oleg L., and Lev Dvoretsky. *The Afghan Syndrome: The Soviet Union's Vietnam*. Novato, CA: Presidio, 1993.
Sarkisova, Ol'ga. "Skazhi mne, kto tvoi vrag . . . chechenskaia voina v rossiiskom kino." *Neprikosnovennyi zapas: Debaty o politike i kul'ture* no. 26 (2002): 94–101.
Sasson-Levy, Orna. "Military, Masculinity, and Citizenship: Tensions and Contradictions in the Experience of Blue-Collar Soldiers." *Identities: Global Studies in Culture and Power* 10 (2003): 319–345.
Scott, Joan W. "Gender: A Useful Category of Historical Analysis." *American Historical Review* 91, no. 5 (1986): 1053–1075.
Seager, Joni. *The Penguin Atlas of Women in the World*, 4th ed. New York: Penguin Books, 2009.
Seely, Robert. *Russo-Chechen Conflict, 1888–2000: A Deadly Embrace*. London: Frank Cass, 2001.
Service, Robert. *A History of Twentieth-Century Russia*. Cambridge: Harvard University Press, 1997.
Sharoni, Simona. "De-Militarizing Masculinities in the Age of Empire." *Austrian Political Science Journal* 37, no. 2 (2008): 147–164.
Shaw, Martin. *Post-Military Society: Militarism, Demilitarization and War at the End of the Twentieth Century*. Cambridge: Polity Press, 1991.
Shenfield, Stephen D. "Chechnya at a Turning Point." *Brown Journal of World Affairs* 8, no. 1 (Winter–Spring 2001): 63–69.
Shepeleva, Ol'ga. "Sem'i veteranov: Do i posle konflikta." In *Militsiia mezhdu Rossiei i Chechnei: Veterany konflikta v rossiiskom obshchestve*. Moscow: Demos, 2007, pp. 100–116.
Shevtsova, Lilia. *Yeltsin's Russia: Myths and Reality*. Washington, DC: Carnegie Endowment for International Peace, 1999.
———. *Putin's Russia*. Washington, DC: Carnegie Endowment for International Peace, 2003.
Shlapentokh, Vladimir. "Trust in Public Institutions in Russia: The Lowest in the World." *Johnson's Russia List* no. 9186 (June 27, 2005). Available at http://www.cdi.org/russia/johnson/9186-29.cfm (accessed May 15, 2009).
Shreeves, Rosamund. "Mothers against the Draft: Women's Activism in the USSR." *RFE/RL Report on the USSR* 2, no. 38 (1990): 3–8.
Shvedova, Nadezhda. "Gender Politics in Russia." In Linda Racioppi and Katherine O'Sullivan See (eds.), *Gender Politics in Post-Communist Eurasia*. East Lansing: Michigan State University Press, 2009, pp. 147–167.
Sieca-Kozlowski, Elisabeth. "Russian Military Patriotic Education: A Control Tool against the Arbitrariness of Veterans." *Nationalities Papers* 38, no. 1 (January 2010): 73–85.
Sil, Rudra, and Cheng Chen. "State Legitimacy and the (In)significance of Democracy in Post-Communist Russia." *Europe-Asia Studies* 56, no. 3 (2004): 347–368.

Simonsen, Sven Gunnar. "Putin's Leadership Style: Ethnocentric Patriotism." *Security Dialogue* 31, no. 3 (2000): 377–380.

Sivaeva, Tatiana. "Women NGOs and the War in Chechnya." Paper prepared for the Global Network for Women's Advocacy and Civil Society, 2000. Available at http://www.ciaonet.org/wps/sit03/sit03.pdf (accessed April 29, 2004).

Sjoberg, Laura, and Caron Gentry. *Mothers, Monsters, Whores: Women's Violence in Global Politics*. London: Zed Books, 2007.

Smirnov, A. I. "Zhenshchiny na sluzhbe v rossiiskoi armii." *Sotsiologicheskie issledovaniia* no. 11 (2000): 128–133.

Smirnov, Andrei. "From Military Butcher to Political Loser: A Portrait of General Shamanov." *North Caucasus Analysis* 8, no. 14 (April 5, 2007). Available at http://www.jamestown.org/single/?no_cache=1&tx_ttnews[tt_news]=4065 (accessed August 5, 2008).

Smirnov, Vasilii. "Iz pervykh ruk: Problemy osennogo prizyva." *Voenno-promyshlennyi kur'er*, December 1, 2004.

Sokirko, Viktor. "U rodiny—nastoichivyi prizyv." *Moskovskii komsomolets*, January 4, 2000.

Sokolov, Mikhail. "Predely primeneniia doktriny prav cheloveka v sovremennoi rossiiskoi kul'ture: Sud nad polkovnikom Budanovym i ego protivniki." Undated manuscript. Available at www.iie.ru/ifp/Alumni/Sokolov/Downloads/art2.doc (accessed April 10, 2009).

Soldiers' Mothers of St. Petersburg (SMSP). "The Facade Is Crumbling." 1996. Available at http://www.openweb.ru/smo/english/english.htm (accessed June 15, 2001).

———. "The Glorious Facade of the Russian Army." 1996. Available at http://www.openweb.ru/smo/english/english.htm (accessed June 15, 2001).

———. "Political Mentality in Russia." 1996. Available at http://www.openweb.ru/smo/english/english.htm (accessed June 15, 2001).

———. "Obshchestvennaia pravozashchitnaia organizatsiia 'Soldatskie Materi Sankt-Peterburga.'" 2002. Available at http://www.soldiersmothers.spb.org/rus/AboutUs/AboutUs_rus.htm (accessed November 16, 2004).

Soldner, Markus. *Rußlands Čečnja-Politik seit 1993: Der Weg in den Krieg vor dem Hintergrund innenpolitischer Machtverschiebungen*. Hamburg: LIT, 1999.

Sperling, Valerie. *Organizing Women in Contemporary Russia: Engendering Transition*. Cambridge: Cambridge University Press, 1999.

———. "The Gender Gap in Russian Politics and Elections." *PONARS Policy Memo* no. 259 (October 2002). Available at http://www.csis.org/files/media/csis/pubs/pm_0259.pdf (accessed July 30, 2008).

———. "The Last Refuge of a Scoundrel: Patriotism, Militarism and the National Idea." *Nations and Nationalism* 9, no. 2 (2003): 235–253.

———. "Making the Public Patriotic: Militarism and Anti-Militarism in Russia." In Marlène Laruelle (ed.), *Russian Nationalism and the National Reassertion of Russia*. New York: Routledge, 2009, pp. 218–271.

Spivak, Andrew, and William Alex Pridemore. "Conscription and Reform in the Russian Army." *Problems of Post-Communism* 51, no. 6 (2004): 33–43.

Stephen, Chris. "Chechen War Veteran Flexes Political Muscles, Sending Shiver Down the Spine of the Kremlin." *Irish Times*, January 14, 2003. *Johnson's Russia List* no. 7018 (January 15, 2003). Available at http://www.cdi.org/russia/johnson/7018-17.cfm (accessed August 15, 2008).

Stiehm, Judith. "The Protected, the Protector, the Defender." *Women's Studies International Forum* 5, no. 3–4 (1982): 367–376.

Strelets, Iurii. "Vechnaia pamiat' pavshim." *Samarskie izvestiia* 231, December 13, 2008.

Sturdee, Nick. "Chechen Syndrome." Aljazeera documentary, 2007. Available at http://english.aljazeera.net/programmes/witness/2007/04/200852518464052803.html (accessed March 16, 2009).

"'Sud dolzhen polnost'iu opravdat' polkovnika Budanova.'" *Na boevom postu*, March 7, 2001, p. 2.

Sundstrom, Lisa McIntosh. *Funding Civil Society: Foreign Assistance and NGO Development in Russia*. Stanford: Stanford University Press, 2006.

———. "Soldiers' Rights Groups in Russia: Civil Society through Russian and Western Eyes." In Alfred B. Evans, Jr., Laura A. Henry, and Lisa McIntosh Sundstrom (eds.), *Russian Civil Society: A Critical Assessment*, London: M. E. Sharpe, 2006, pp. 178–196.

Tëmkina, Anna D., and Elena Zdravomyslova. "Die Krise der Männlichkeit im Alltagsdiskurs: Wandel der Geschlechterordnung in Rußland." *Berliner Debatte Initial* 12, no. 4 (2001): 78–90.

"The Majority of Russia's People Are Against Putting Military Men Who Refuse to Serve [in Chechnya] on Trial." *Segodnia*, January 28, 1995, p. 3. *Current Digest of Post-Soviet Press* 47, no. 4 (February 22, 1995): 12.

"The State and the President Need Devoted Officers." *Rossiiskie vesti*, January 13, 1995, p. 2. *Current Digest of the Post-Soviet Press* 47, no. 2 (February 2, 1995): 5.

Thomas, Timothy L., and Charles P. O'Hara. "Combat Stress in Chechnya: 'The Equal Opportunity Disorder.'" *U.S. Army Medical Department Journal* (January–March 2000): 46–53.

Tickner, J. Ann. *Gender in International Relations: Feminist Perspectives on Achieving Global Security*. New York: Columbia University Press, 1992.

———. *Gendering World Politics: Issues and Approaches in the Post-Cold War Era*. New York: Columbia University Press, 2001.

Tishkov, Valery. *Chechnya: Life in a War-Torn Society*. Berkeley: University of California Press, 2004.

Tkachuk, Sergei. "Voiui ne spesha." *Novye izvestiia*, July 8, 2005, p. 2.

Trenin, Dmitri V., and Aleksei Malashenko with Anatol Lieven. *Russia's Restless Frontier: The Chechnya Factor in Post-Soviet Russia*. Washington, DC: Carnegie Endowment, 2004.

Troshev, Genadii. *Moia Voina: Chechenskii dnevnik okopnogo generala*. Moscow: Vagrius, 2001.

True, Jacqui. "Feminism." In Scott Burchill and Andrew Linklater (eds.), *Theories of International Relations*. New York: Macmillan, 1996, pp. 225–236.

———. *Gender, Globalization, and Postsocialism: The Czech Republic after Communism*. New York: Columbia University Press, 2003.

Tsygankov, Andrei P. "Double Standard, Lots of Blame: Russia, Chechnya and the West." *Los Angeles Times*, January 28, 2000, p. B13.

Tsymbal, Lt. Gen. Nikolai. "A Demoralized Army Cannot Be Combat-Ready." *Rossiiskie vesti*, January 10, 1995, p. 2. *Current Digest of Post-Soviet Press* 47, no. 2 (February 2, 1995): 4.

Tumarkin, Nina. *The Living and the Dead: The Rise and Fall of the Cult of World War II in Russia.* New York: Basic Books, 1994.

———. "The Great Patriotic War as Myth and Memory." *European Review* 11, no. 4 (2003): 595–611.

Udmantsev, Vadim. "'Reforma po Serdiukovu' glazami materi soldata." *Segodnia*, March 17, 2009.

Union of the Committees of Soldiers' Mothers of Russia (CSMR). "Annual Report 2002." 2002. Available at http://www.ucsmr.ru/english/ucsmr/report/report2002.htm (accessed January 7, 2005).

———. "Istoriia Soiusa Komitetov Soldatskikh Materei Rossii." 2003. Available at http://www.ucsmr.ru/ucsmr/history.htm (accessed January 7, 2005).

———. "Press-reliz 'Edinaia Narodnaia Partiia Soldatskikh Materei.'" 2003. Available at http://www.ucsmr.ru/party/pressrelease.htm (accessed January 7, 2005).

———. "To the History of the UCSMR." 2003. Available at http://www.ucsmr.ru/english/ucsmr/history.htm (accessed January 7, 2005).

United Nations Secretary-General. *Women, Peace and Security.* New York: United Nations: 2002. Available at http://www.un.org/womenwatch/daw/public/eWPS.pdf (accessed October 15, 2010).

Uzzell, Lawrence A. "Hero of Russia . . ." Jamestown Foundation's *Chechnya Weekly* 6, no. 1, January 5, 2005, p. 1. Available at www.jamestown.org (accessed August 10, 2008).

Vakhnina, Liudmila. "'Zashchitit' synovei: Ob organizatsii soldatskikh materei." *Informatsionnyi biulleten' pravleniia obshchestva "Memorial"* no. 25 (May 2002). Available at http://www.memo.ru/about/bull/b25/6.htm (accessed November 16, 2004).

Vallance, Brenda. "Russia's Mothers: Voices of Change." *Minerva: Quarterly Report on Women and the Military* 18, no. 3–4 (2000): 109–128.

Van Bladel, Joris. "Russian Soldiers in the Barracks: A Portrait of a Subculture." In Anne Aldis and Roger N. McDermott (eds.), *Russian Military Reform, 1992–2002.* Portland, OR: Frank Cass, 2003.

———. *The All-Volunteer Force in the Russian Mirror: Transformation without Change.* Ph.D. diss. (Proefschrift), Rijksuniversiteit Groningen, June 2004.

Vanderheeren, Hendrik. "Methods of 'The Soldiers' Mothers of St. Petersburg' in Conflict Resolution." August 2002–January 2003. Available at www.soldiersmothers.ru/pages/english/books.htm (accessed January 20, 2009).

Volkov, Vadim. *Violent Entrepreneurs: The Use of Force in the Making of Russian Capitalism.* Ithaca, NY: Cornell University Press, 2002.

"Vspominaia pogibshikh." Oblastnoi telekanal RIO, December 12, 2008. Available at http://www.rio-tv.ru/index.php?link=news&action=show&id=1232 (accessed March 15, 2009).

"Vy soglasny c prigovorom Budanovu?" *Kommersant Vlast'* no. 30, August 4, 2003, p. 7. Available at www.kommersant.ru/doc.aspx?DocsID=401110 (accessed March 15, 2009).

Wagensohn, Tanja. "Krieg in Tschetschenien." *Aktuelle Analysen* no. 18. München: Hans-Seidel-Stiftung, 2000.

Wagner, Claudia. *Rußlands Kriege in Tschetschenien: Politische Transformation und Militärische Gewalt*. Münster: LIT, 2000.

Ware, Robert Bruce. "Revisiting Russia's Apartment Block Blasts." *Journal of Slavic Military Studies* 18, no. 4 (2005): 599–606.

Webber, Stephen L., and Alina Zilberman. "The Citizenship Dimension of the Society-Military Interface." In Stephen L. Webber and Jennifer G. Mathers (eds.), *Military and Society in Post-Soviet Russia*. Manchester: Manchester University Press, 2006, pp. 159–206.

Wengle, Susanne, and Michael Rasell. "The Monetisation of L'goty: Changing Patterns of Welfare Politics and Provision in Russia." *Europe-Asia Studies* 60, no. 5 (2008): 739–756.

White, Anne. "New Mothers' Campaigning Organizations in Russia." In Anna Cento Bull, Hanna Diamond, and Rosalind J. Marsh (eds.), *Feminisms and Women's Movements in Contemporary Europe*. New York: St. Martin's Press, 2000, pp. 211–227.

Whitworth, Sandra. *Men, Militarism and UN Peacekeeping: A Gendered Analysis*. Boulder, CO: Lynne Rienner Publishers, 2004.

Women's Research and Education Institute. *Women in the Military: Where They Stand*, 7th ed. Arlington, Virginia: WREI, 2010.

Yeltsin, Boris N. *Midnight Diaries*. London: Phoenix, 2000.

Young, Iris Marion. "The Logic of Masculinist Protection: Reflections on the Current Security State." *Signs: Journal of Women in Culture and Society* 29, no. 1 (2003): 1–25.

Yurchak, Alexei. "Muzhskaia ekonomia: Ne do glupostei kogda kar'eru kuësh.'" In Sergei Ushakin (ed.), *O Muzhe(n)stvennosti*. Moscow: Novoe literaturnoe obozrenie, 2001, pp. 245–267.

Yuval-Davis, Nira. *Gender and Nation*. London: Sage Publications, 1997.

Yuzhny, Arkady. "Trial of Col. Budanov Postponed: Atmosphere Surrounding Trial Is Becoming More and More Tense." *Segodnia*, March 6, 2001, p. 2. *Current Digest of the Post-Soviet Press* 53, no. 10 (April 4, 2001): 13.

Zalewski Marysia, and Jane Parpart (eds.). *The "Man" Question in International Relations*. Boulder, CO: Westview Press, 1998.

Zarakhovich, Yuri. "Chechnya's Walking Wounded." *Time Europe*, September 28, 2003. Available at http://www.time.com/time/europe/html/031006/syndrome.html (accessed June 10, 2009).

Zawilski, Valerie. "Saving Russia's Sons: The Soldiers' Mothers and the Russian-Chechen War." In Stephen L. Webber and Jennifer G. Mathers (eds.), *Military and Society in Post-Soviet Russia*. Manchester: Manchester University Press, 2006, pp. 228–240.

Zdravomyslova, Elena. "Ot sotsial'noi problemy k kollektivnomu deistviiu: Pravozashchitnaia organizatsiia 'Soldatskie materi.'" In Vladimir V. Kostiushev (ed.),

Obshchestvennye dvizheniia v sovremennoi Rossii: Ot sotsial'noi problemy k kollektivnomu deistviiu. Moscow: Rossiiskaia akademiia nauk, 1999, pp. 51–64.

———. "Peaceful Initiatives: Soldiers' Mothers Movement in Russia." In Ingeborg Breines, Dorota Gierycz, and Betty Reardon (eds.), *Towards a Women's Agenda for a Culture of Peace.* Geneva: UNESCO Publishing, 1999, pp. 165–180.

———. "Soldiers' Mothers Fighting the Military Patriarchy: Re-invention of Responsible Activist Motherhood for Human Rights' [sic] Struggle." In Ilse Lenz, Charlotte Ullrich, and Barbara Fersch (eds.), *Gender Orders Unbound: Globalisation, Restructuring and Reciprocity.* Opladen: Barbara Budrich, 2007, pp. 207–227.

Zhurzhenko, Tatiana. *Sotsial'noe vosproizvodstvo i gendernaia politika v Ukraine.* Kharkov: Folio, 2001.

Zuckerman, Fredric S. "To Justify a Nation: Inter-War Soviet Nationalism." *History of European Ideas* 15, no. 1–3 (1992): 383–390.

Zürcher, Christoph. *The Post-Soviet Wars: Rebellion, Ethnic Conflict, and Nationhood in the Caucasus.* New York: New York University Press, 2007.

Zvereva, Galina. "'Rabota dlia muzhchin?' Chechenskaia voina v massovom kino Rossii." *Neprikosnovennyi zapas: Debaty o politike i kul'ture* no. 26 (2002): 102–109.

Index

40th Army (Soviet Union), 28
81st Motor-Rifle Regiment (Russia), 133

Aachener-Friedenspreis (2004), 181n53
accountability, in Soviet Union, 33
activism, 87–88, 133, 142; CSMR and SMSP, 89–91, 93–94; motherhood and, 94; soldiers' mothers groups (Soviet Union), 31–33; women's, 147–148n29. *See also* antiwar protests; soldiers' mothers groups
afganky (female Afghan war veterans), 155n102
afgantsy (male Afghan war veterans), 30
Afghan veterans movement, fragmentation of, 191n137
Afghan war. *See* Soviet-Afghan war
aggressiveness, 123, 124
alcohol abuse, 122–123, 124, 170n63, 172n86
Alexander II, 19
Alexseev, Mikhail A., 45, 160–161n44
Alkhan-Iurt, massacre in, 53, 118
Alkhanov, Alu, 54
All-Union/All-Russian Center for the Study of Public Opinion (VTsIOM), 30, 62, 119, 160–161n44, 168n23
all-volunteer force, 2, 3; adoption of, 137; resistance to, 72; soldiers' mothers groups and, 97, 98, 99; support for, 46, 76–77, 79, 82, 139, 141, 175n129. *See also* military volunteers
Amandine Regime, 118
ambiguity: of enemy, 114, 134; of militarized masculinity 36, 43, 58, 141; of war heroes, 52; of war outcome, 126–127
Analytical Center of Iurii Levada. *See* Levada Center
Andropov, Iurii, 28
antidraft activism. *See* Antimilitarist Radical Association; soldiers' mothers groups
Antifascist Committee of Soviet Women, 20, 21
Antimilitarist Radical Association (ARA), 95
antimilitarism, 30, 81, 95, 141–142
antiterrorist campaign, of Putin, 39, 91. *See also* counterterrorism; terrorism
antiwar protests: CSMR and SMSP, 89,

91, 92; Mothers' March for Life and Compassion, 91; women and, 87–88. *See also* soldiers' mothers groups
Argentina, 137
Article 63 of the 1977 Soviet Constitution, 21
Ashwin, Sarah, 152n46
attitudes, generational differences and, 68–69, 175n128
Attwood, Lynn, 153n68
Australia, 137
Austria, 137
Azerbaijan, 153n60

Babchenko, Arkady, 76, 114, 126, 174–175n126
Babichev, Ivan, 44, 161n61
Baev, Pavel, 52
"bandits," 42, 45, 48, 50, 53
Bannikov, Konstantin, 70
Barany, Zoltan, 162n74
Barylski, Robert, 44, 45
Basaev, Shamil, 38, 47, 165n144
Baskaev, Arkadii, 118
Baysayev, Usam, 118
benefits, 190–191n128; in-kind, 191n129; military officers, 192–193n8; Russian-Chechen war veterans, 103, 128–134, 141, 191n132; Soviet Union, 18, 22, 25, 140, 155n102
Beslan hostage taking, 39, 55
betrayal, 30, 47, 50, 116–117, 120–121
Betz, David J., 37
Bickford, Andrew, 152nn41, 44
biological reproduction, 22–24, 94, 100, 101
Boevoe Bratstvo, 161n53, 191n137
Bolshevik Revolution, 18
Bolsheviks, 17, 19
Border Guard Service, 167n7
Borenstein, Eliot, 55–56
Brazil, 137
Breslauer, George, 40
Brezhnev, Leonid, 15, 18, 19, 23, 27
Brown, Sarah, 67

Budanov, Iurii, 117–121, 134, 142, 190n125
Budennovsk hostage taking, 38, 55
Buinaksk, bombings in, 47
Burawoy, Michael, 8

Caiazza, Amy, 77, 94, 95
Canada, 137
capitalism: identities and values, 171n72; masculinity/masculinities and, 4, 67–72; militarized masculinity and, 72, 141; patriotism and, 80–81; post-Soviet Russia, 59–60; PTSD and, 125–126; Russian postcommunist transformation and, 9
careers: conscription and, 67, 83; female soldiers and, 73
casualties: CSMR and SMSP, 88, 90–92; draft evasion and, 75; Great Patriotic War 18; peacetime deaths 28, 31, 85; Russian-Chechen wars, 39, 76, 112, 159n23, 165n144, 187n65; Samara *Oblast'* 132; Soviet-Afghan war, 28
cease-fire agreement (1996), 38, 46
Central Asian republics, 24
Chechen fighters, 38, 42, 47, 104, 115–116, 119, 159n23; as "beasts" 48, 104. *Also see* "bandits"
Chechen-Ingush Republic, 37
Chechenization, 53–55, 58
Chechen National Congress, 37
Chechens: deportation of, 10; femininity and, 48; mothers, 90, 93, 104; as "others," 41–42, 48, 93, 116; Putin's rhetoric and masculinity, 48; scapegoating of, 90, 160n39; stereotypes of, 119, 160n42; suicide bombings, 48, 93, 104, 163n96; terrorist characterization of, 163n92; Yeltsin's rhetoric and masculinity, 42
chechenskii "kvadrat," 103
"Chechenskii sindrom," 188–189n89
Chechen syndrome, 121–127, 131–132, 188–189n89
chechentsy. *See* Russian-Chechen war veterans

Chechnya (Samara Committee), 130, 132–133, 148n30
Chechnya: independence (1996–1999), 47; Putin on, 52; sovereignty and political struggles, 37–38; Yeltsin on, 41
Chernenko, Konstantin, 28
Chernomyrdin, Viktor, 41, 160n36, 165n144
chernye, 42
children: daughters, 101; education for, 130; military service and, 97; patriotic education for, 131–133; protection of, 6; responsible motherhood and, 86, 94, 100; sons, 7, 21, 28, 32, 54, 75, 93, 95, 98, 99, 100, 102, 128, 130, 148n30, 174–175n110, 189n102; Soviet Union, 23, 24, 25; supportive motherhood, 100–101; in war 53, 102, 104
Christian women, 24
citizens, 13–14, 50, 53, 112, 114, 134, 135; gendered protection of, 41–42, 48, 55, 133; Putin and, 50; Soviet 140; Yeltsin and, 45
citizenship: CSMR and SMSP 89; Great Patriotic War and, 15, 109; militarized masculinity and, 7, 8, 78–79, 140; masculinized military service and, 60, 62, 67–68, 72, 80, 82–84, 106, 109, 131, 136–137; military wages and, 78; patriotism and, 79–82, 131; Samara soldiers' mothers groups and, 98–99; social and militarized, 140; Soviet-Afghan war and, 28; Soviet Union and military service, 2, 19, 21, 25–26, 28–31, 109; spectator militarism and, 80; veterans and, 131
citizen-soldier, 59, 72, 74, 80, 139–141
civilian deaths, 53, 75, 113, 117–121
civilian-military sphere, in Soviet Union, 17
civilians: Russian generals and, 53; violence against, 115, 117–121
civil society groups. *See* soldiers' mothers groups
Civil War (1918–1921), 17, 19

class: masculinity and, 6, 13, 67–72, 139, 171n73, 175; military service and, 19, 30, 60, 70–72, 138, 174–175n126; women and, 171n73; Soviet Union and, 18, 149n9
Coca-Cola, 64
Cold War, 19, 21, 32, 33
Colton, Timothy J., 151n34
combat: conscripts and, 1, 76–77; *dedovshchina* and, 76, 155n99; fear and, 112–113, 121–123, 186n33; male bonding and, 111; masculinity and, 3–4, 8, 110, 111, 138–139; morale and, 112; nostalgia for, 126; pay, 176n144; police officers and, 111; public distaste for, 3; return from, 1, 13, 17, 89, 103, 109, 121, 123–125, 127, 131–132, 155n102; veterans of, 128–129, 135; women in Great Patriotic War, 16, 20, 22, 151n27; women's recruitment and, 73
combatants, 115, 119
combat readiness, 65, 73, 75, 112–114
combat-related stress. *See* post-traumatic stress disorder
Committee of Soldiers' Mothers (Soviet Union), 31, 32
Committee of Soldiers' Mothers of Briansk, 118
Committee of Soldiers' Mothers of Russia (CSMR), 77, 102; antiwar movement and, 89, 91–92, 180–181n45; financial support for, 179n18; international peace prize for, 181n53; letters sent to, 184n124; masculinity and, 182n78; militarized masculinity and, 89, 90; militarized patriotism and war, 88–95; patriotic motherhood and, 89, 90, 93; responsible motherhood, 94, 95; Samara mothers' groups and, 97, 105–106. *See also* soldiers' mothers groups
communism: Soviet gender order and, 25; Yeltsin and, 45. *See also* Soviet Union
Communist Party, 15, 17
community, sense of, 126

compulsory military service. *See* conscription
comradeship, military brotherhood and, 126
Connell, R. W., 6, 145–146n8
conscientious objectors, 61
conscription, 2: abolition of, 13, 46, 51, 84, 89, 97, 99, 106, 137, 162n74; Border Guard Service and, 167n7; capitalism and, 59–60, 67–72, 83, 141; class and, 70–71; continuation (2010), 3; contract soldiers and, 72, 74; controversy over, 2–3; costs of, 171n78, 172n90; CSMR and SMSP, 88, 89; emigration and, 173–174n110; gendered power relations and, 8; global politics and, 137; homosexuality and, 172n86; market economy and, 67–72; masculinity and, 3; militarized identities and, 7; militarized masculinity and, 138, 140; motherhood and, 138; patriotism and, 82–83; Peter the Great and, 19; Putin and, 51, 139; Russia (post-Soviet), 59, 60–62, 74–79; Samara soldiers' mothers groups and, 97–98, 101, 106; Serdiukov and, 84; Soviet-Afghan war, 30, 31; Soviet Union, 16, 21, 26, 59; students (Soviet Union), 85; tenuousness of, 139; women in Great Patriotic War, 20; Yeltsin and, 44–45, 46, 51. *See also* citizen-soldier; *dedovshchina*; military service
Constitution (Russian, 1993), 40, 41, 60, 61
Constitution (Soviet, 1977), Article 63 of, 21
constitutional referendum (Chechen Republic, 2003), 54
contract soldiers, 3, 72–74, 77–79, 83–84, 128, 176n144; attraction of, 60, 78. *See also* military volunteers
corruption, 40, 41, 62, 65, 78, 81
Council of Mothers and Widows, 86
Council of Servicemen's Parents, 86, 105, 106, 184n125

counterterrorism 39, 52, 128. *See also* antiterrorist campaign; terrorism
crime: Chechens and, 41–42, 57, 116, 160n42; masculinity and, 171n72; Russian army and, 81; Russian-Chechen War (1994–1996) and, 41–42, 160n40; Russian-Chechen war veterans and, 125, 127, 132. *See also* war crimes
CSMR. *See* Committee of Soldiers' Mothers of Russia

Dagestan, 38–39, 47
deaths: as a result of *dedovshchina*, 64, 66; civilian, 53, 75, 113, 117–121; CSMR and SMSP, 31, 39, 90; Elza Kungaeva, 117; Grozny, 112; noncombat-related, 63, 169n31; peace-time, 28, 31, 85; Russian-Chechen wars, 39, 51, 62, 114, 159n23; Samara soldiers' mothers, 105; soldiers' mothers groups and, 31, 85; Soviet-Afghan war, 28. *See also* casualties
decrees, of Yeltsin, 45–46, 77, 158n15
dedovshchina: combat zone (Russian-Chechen wars), 76; conscription and, 82, 83; details of, 63–67; gendered hierarchy, 66; masculinity and, 63–67; soldiers' mothers groups and, 85, 88, 98; Soviet-Afghan war and, 30, 31, 34, 155n99; special forces and, 169n38. *See also* hazing
dedy, 63, 64, 65, 66, 76
defender, masculine role of, 24–27, 86, 96, 97, 99, 101–103, 106, 110, 132
"Defend the Defender of the Fatherland," 96, 97
defense industry: Soviet Union, 19; Stalinist period, 17
defense-mindedness, of Soviet Union, 16
deferment, 59, 60–61, 78, 89
demilitarization, 4, 14, 16, 17, 33, 83, 87, 105–106, 109, 138–139
democracy: CSMR and SMSP, 89; disillusionment with, 49; transition

to, 8, 140; women's recruitment and, 173n103; Yeltsin and, 45
democratization, 9
demographics: conscription, 27, 62; "demographic crisis," 23–24; post-Soviet Russia, 153n56; Soviet gender order and, 23, 24, 27; women's recruitment and, 21
Demos Center, 111, 124
deportation, of Chechens and Ingushes, 10
Deriglazova, Larisa, 92, 168n29
derzhava, 29
desertion, 4, 7, 16, 17, 19, 59, 60, 63, 66, 77, 83, 89, 114; CSMR and SMSP, 88, 90, 97
development strategy, in Stalinist period, 17
dignity, of servicemen, 96, 129–130; masculinity and, 169–170
Dinamo stadium (Grozny), 54
displacement, from Russian-Chechen wars, 75, 174nn111, 114
divorce, 124, 170n63
domesticity, 7, 100–101
draft. *See* conscription
"draft dodging," 61, 62, 66, 69, 78, 114, 139. *See also* draft evasion
draft evasion, ix, 2, 3, 16; acceptance of, 69; attitudes and, 69, 71; casualty rate and, 75; class and masculinity, 174–175n126; CSMR and SMSP, 88; market economy and, 68; masculinity and, 108–109; militarization and, 4; patriotism and, 79–80, 81, 82, 83, 84; post-Soviet Russia, 60, 61–62, 63; public opinion of, 114; Russian-Chechen wars, 74, 76, 77, 84, 135, 141; social status and, 70; soldiers' mothers groups and, 101; Soviet Union, 19, 30, 59; sympathy for, 69, 171n71, 175n129
draft exemptions, 19, 59, 62, 88, 89, 168n20
draft resistance, 77
drug abuse. *See* substance abuse

Dubrovka Theater hostage-taking, 39
Dudaev, Dzhokhar, 37–38, 41, 43, 44
dukhy, 63
Duma, 38; conscription and, 61; CSMR and, 90, 92; opposition in, 40; Samara soldiers' mothers groups and, 103; women in, 57
duty, of male citizens (military service), ix, 2, 3, 8, 11, 15, 34, 45, 60, 66–68, 70, 71–72, 83, 84, 100, 140–141; mothers and, 32, 90, 93, 97–101, 103; "patriotic," 11, 32, 44, 45, 81–82, 103; masculinity and, 36; veterans and, 118, 133;
Dvoretsky, Lev, 154n89

economic conditions: Soviet gender order and, 23; post-Soviet Russia, 9, 49, 138, 140
economic cost, of military draft, 171n78
economic development, Soviet gender order and, 24
economic policy, in Russian postcommunist transformation, 9, 40, 55
economic transformation: masculinity and, 67–72; militarized masculinity and, 72, 140, 141; patriotism and, 80–81; post-Soviet Russia, 9, 59–60; Putin and, 55; women and, 73; Yeltsin and, 40. *See also* capitalism
education: draft evasion and, 67, 171n71; military service and, 71; Soviet conscription and, 21. *See also* patriotic education
Egorichev, N. G., 15
Egorov, Ivan, 188–189n89
Eifler, Christine, 73, 192n6
election. *See* presidential elections
Elkner, Julie, 31, 33, 156n112
emigration, conscription and, 173–174n110
empathy, 77, 114, 186n46
employment: Soviet men, 24–27; Soviet women, 22–25; post-Soviet women, 73; post-Soviet men, 68, 170n63; veterans, 125, 141, 189–190n105

224   Index

enemies, construction of, 41–42, 48–49, 115–121
Enloe, Cynthia, 1; foreign policy, 157n8; gender roles and militarization, 87; masculinity, 36, 157n8, 164n113; masculinized humiliation, 50; nationalism, 164n113; patriotism and motherhood, 32; rape, 188n83; women's recruitment, 73–74
entrepreneurship, 70
equality, in Soviet Union. *See* gender equality
Eritrea, 137
essentialist ideas: femininity and motherhood, 21, 86, 93–94, 104; masculinity, 21, 98
estrangement, 123–124
ethnic cleansing, rape and, 188n83
ethnicity, 24; cross-ethnic motherhood 104, 180n40; CSMR and SMSP and, 90, 91–92; ethnoterritorial federalism, 10; marginalized masculinity and, 6; Russian postcommunist transformation and, 10; Samara soldiers' mothers groups and, 104; Soviet-Afghan war and, 30–31; Soviet gender order and, 24, 26–27
excessive warriors, 13, 109, 115–121, 133, 134, 135
exemptions, from military service, 19, 59, 62, 88, 89, 168n20
extremism, 48

family, 100–101; Chechen syndrome and, 124; military service and, 110–111; Soviet gender order and, 24–25; women's recruitment and, 73–74. *See also* children; husbands; mothers; wives
fear: militarized masculinity and, 112–113, 121–123, 186n33; mothers', 101; parents', 2, 3, 46, 60; of terrorism, 36, 48–49, 58
federalism, ethnoterritorial, 10
Federal Security Service (FSB), 3, 35, 36, 53, 73, 166n151

Felgenhauer, Pavel, 39, 113, 159n23
Femininity/femininities, 5–7, 12, 85, 87–88; Chechen femininity, 48; CSMR and SMSP, 94; *dedovshchina* and, 66; Great Patriotic War and, 20, 151n27; militarized masculinity and, 112, 121, 123; military training and, 112; military women, 73–74; Muslim, 152n46; PTSD and, 121, 123; post-Soviet period, 94; Samara soldiers' mothers groups, 102; Soviet gender order and, 16, 22–23, 27–28, 33; state legitimation and, 7; states and, 6; suicide bombing and, 48
feminism: analysis, 37, 146n13, 146n14; consciousness, 20; in post-Soviet Russia, 95; Russian, 160n36; scholarship, 22, 86–67, 93, 115, 120, 136, 146n11, 147–148n29
feminist International Relations (IR), ix, 4–8, 85–86
feminization, of conscripts, 65–66; *dedovshchina* and, 32, 65–66; disarmament, 156n114; Soviet men, 25–26; of Soviet society, 32, 98, 132
fieldwork (Samara), x, 11–12, 13, 63, 74, 96, 132, 147–148n29, 178n15
financial incentives, for volunteers, 78–79
First Person (Putin), 48
food provisions, military service and, 2
"For Life and Freedom" (CSMR congress), 90, 91
"For Russia We Stand and Will Always Stand" (Chernomyrdin speech), 41
fragile warriors, 121–127, 131, 133
Friedrich Ebert Foundation Award (2000), 181n53
FSB-ization, 166n151

Galeotti, Mark, 30, 154n81
Gapova, Elena, 153n68
gay men: conscription and, 172n86; subordinate masculinity and, 6
gender, ix, 2, 5, 8, 9, 11, 12, 13, 14; Chechen men and, 42; class privilege and, 171n73; conscription and, 3;

dedovshchina and, 65–66; draft evasion and, 171n71; foreign research and, 185n20; Great Patriotic War and, 15–16; ideology and sociopolitical processes, 13–14; Kadyrov's Chechen rule and, 54; militarization and, 4, 13, 80, 138–139; military service and, 111; military volunteers, 173n103; motherhood and, 94–95; PTSD and, 121, 124; Russian government positions (1993–2008), 57; Soviet Union and, 15–16, 33–34; Soviet Union armed forces, 192n6; Soviet Union militarized socialism and, 16–21; Soviet Union military service and, 19–21; Soviet-Afghan war and, 27–33; suicide bombings and, 163n96; women's recruitment, 72–74; Yeltsin and, 41–42, 49. *See also* feminism; feminist International Relations; femininity/femininities; masculinity/masculinities; men; women

gendered militarization, global politics of, 136–138

gendered power relations, 5, 8

gender equality: German Democratic Republic and, 152n44; Great Patriotic War and, 20, 22; Russian armed forces and, 74, 137; Soviet Union, 20, 22, 94, 151n27

gender order, 5–7, 87, 88, 138, 145–146n8, 152n41; military's, 20, 74; post-Soviet Russia, 94, 138, 157n125; Soviet Union, 12–13, 20, 22–28, 94, 153n68; women's recruitment, 73, 74

gender relations, 5–7; Soviet Union, 16, 23. *See also* gender order; gender equality

gender roles: CSMR and SMSP, 88–95; militarized, 2, 7, 13, 30, 85–87, 138, 152n44; motherhood and militarization, 86–88; mothers, 93–95, 100–102; Samara soldiers' mothers groups, 100, 101, 102; Samara, 96–105. *See also* femininity/femininities; gender order; masculinity/masculinities; militarized masculinity; motherhood

Gender Studies Center at Samara State University, 147–148n29, 148n30

generals: "generals' crisis," 43; militarized masculinity and, 35–36, 43–44, 47, 52–53, 57–58; Russian-Chechen war (1994–1996), 43–44, 47; Russian-Chechen war (1999–2009), 52–53; soldiers' morale and, 113; soldiers' mothers groups and, 97

generational differences, in attitudes toward military service, 68–69, 175n128

Geneva Conventions, 115, 119

German, Tracy C., 147n26

German Democratic Republic, militarization in, 152n44

glasnost', 2, 13, 29, 31, 33, 175

global politics, of gendered militarization, 136–138

Goffman, Erving, 65

Goldstein, Joshua, 112

Golts, Alexander M., 54, 149n3

Gomart, Thomas, 51, 166n151

Gorbachev and Yeltsin as Leaders (Breslauer), 40

Gorbachev, Mikhail, 2, 13, 49; *glasnost'*, 2; military status and conscription, 16; reform policies of, 27; soldiers' mothers groups and, 33, 85; Soviet-Afghan war and, 28–29

Grachev, Pavel, 43, 44, 51

Great Patriotic War (World War II), 81, 82; cult of, 26; commemoration of, 33; military service policy, 20; motherhood and, 15–16, 20; On Veterans (law), 128; patriotism and, 81; society's attitude toward, 109, 111, 131, 141, 150n14; social mobilization, 17–18; Soviet gender order and, 22, 23; Soviet state formation and, 17; Tomb of the Unknown Soldier, 15; welfare system and, 18, 190–191n128; women and, 15–16, 20–21, 23

Grebennikov, Andrei, 126

Gromov, Boris, 43, 191n137
Grozny: military casualties at, 75, 112, 185n25; Kadyrov's death, 54; Russian-Chechen war veterans, 112; Russian conscripts and, 60, 75; storming of, 38, 44, 60, 75, 112, 161n61; Troshev on, 53
gruppovshchina, 31
Gudkov, Lev, 18
guilt syndrome, 50

Haiti, U.S. intervention in, 159n32
hazing: masculinity and, 3, 63–67, 110, 139; military service and, 2, 3, 30, 62, 63–67, 110, 139, 170n47, 185n14; Russian-Chechen wars, 76; soldiers' mothers groups, 16, 85, 97–98, 110. See also *dedovshchina*
hegemonic masculinity, 6, 7, 16, 71–72, 109, 138, 170n50
"Hero of Russia," 44, 53, 58
"Heroes of the Soviet Union," 20
heroic warrior, 13, 108, 109, 126, 131, 134, 135
heroism, 52–53, 117, 131; Budanov and, 117, 120; militarized masculinity and, 15, 44–45, 51–53, 57, 58, 120, 131, 140; Russian-Chechen War (1994–1996), 44–45, 57; Russian-Chechen War (1999–2009), 51–53, 58, 77; Russian generals and, 58; Soviet Union, 15, 20, 30, 140, 150n14; veterans and, 109, 127, 131–133; women and, 20. See also heroic warrior
Herspring, Dale R., 71
Hinterhuber, Eva M., 89–90, 94
homosexuality: conscription and, 172n86; subordinate masculinity and, 6
hostage takings, 38, 39, 55, 165n144
humanitarian aid, 90–91, 97, 103
human rights: *dedovshchina* and, 65; soldiers' mothers groups and, 88
human rights groups, 61, 63, 65, 66, 78, 83, 88–93, 105, 118, 120; sexual violence and, 120
human rights violations: Chechnya, 39, 54, 58, 159n25; CSMR and SMSP, 88, 89, 91–92; public reactions to, 187n65
Human Rights Watch, 63, 65, 66, 78
humiliation: *dedovshchina*, 65–66; Soviet Union collapse, 49–50, 53
Hungary, 137
husbands: PTSD and, 124; wages (Soviet Union), 25; women soldiers and, 74; veterans as, 134

Iaroslavets, Aleksandr, 133
Iastrzhembskii, Sergei, 118
identity: capitalism and, 4; conscription and, 3; economic transition and, 67; feminist International Relations and, 5; militarism and, 7; militarized masculinity and, 8; military service and, 109–111; Soviet gender order and, 25; urbanization and modernization, 171n72. See also femininity/femininities; masculinity/masculinities; militarized masculinity; motherhood
ideology: gender(ed), 5–6, 14, 20, 35, 57, 66, 94, 97, 101, 114, 140; militarism as, 4; post-communist crisis in, 5, 9, 11, 14, 101, 114, 130, 135, 139, 140
Ilyina, Marina, 68
imperialism: Russian, 10
Imperial Russia, 17
income: of military officers, 192–193n8; military volunteers, 79; Soviet gender order, 23, 25
individualism, 70, 80, 82, 83
industrialization, 17, 19
Ingushes, deportation of, 10
in-kind benefits, 128, 191n129
internationalist duty, 28
International Relations (IR). See feminist International Relations
Ipsa-Landa, Simone, 160n40
Iraq War veterans (U.S.), 142
Islam, 153n60. See also Muslims
Islamic fundamentalists, 48, 163n92
Islamic State of Dagestan, 47

Israel, 137
Italy, 137
Iushenkov, Sergei, 40
Ivanov, Sergei, 92–93, 97

Jones, Ellen, 26, 151n34

Kadyrov, Akhmed, 54
Kadyrov, Ramzan, 54, 58
Kadyrovites, 54
Kadyrov syndrome, 54
kadyrovtsy, 54
Karner, Xavia, 122
Kay, Rebecca, 67
Kazakhstan, 153n60
Kazantsev, Viktor, 53
KGB, 36
Khasaviurt cease-fire agreement (1996), 38, 46
Khrushchev, Nikita, 18, 19
killing, soldiers' reluctance toward, 113–114
Kirghizia, 153n60
Kisliar (Dagestan), 38
Klein, Uta, 137
Knight, Andy, 120–121
Kondrat'ev, Georgii, 43
kontraktnaia sluzhba, 72
kontraktniki, 72. *See also* contract soldiers; military volunteers
Kotliarova, V., 128
Kremlin, 44, 54, 55
Krylova, Anna, 20, 151n27
Kucher, Aleksandr, 127, 190n125
Kuibishev. *See* Samara
Kukhterin, Sergei, 25
Kuklina, Ida, 91, 182n78
Kungaeva, Elza, 117, 119, 120, 134
Kvashnin, Anatolii, 52–53, 118

labor: conscription and, 63–64; *dedovshchina* and, 63–64; gendered division of, 5; Soviet conscription and, 21; Soviet men's, 24–27; Soviet women's, 22–24, 34

labor force: PTSD and, 125; Soviet conscription and, 21
labor market, 67–68, 73, 141
Lapidus, Gail, 23
Latvia, 137
lawlessness, Yeltsin and, 41, 42, 160n40
Law on Military Obligation and Service, 60, 72
leadership. *See* state leadership
Lebed, Aleksandr, 44, 46, 53, 162n77
Lebedev, Anna Colin, 184n124
legal aid, by soldiers' mothers groups, 88, 96, 97
legal reform, for veterans' benefits, 130
legitimacy effects, 29
Lenin, Vladimir, 17, 19
Lentini, Peter, 40
Levada, Iurii, 168n23
Levada Center, 62, 168n23, 176n150
Levinson, A. G., 165n138
l'goty, 191n129
Liborakina, Marina, 160n36
Libya, 137
Lieven, Anatol, 27, 69–70, 171n73
living conditions: *dedovshchina* and, 66–67; military service, 62, 63, 65
Lobov, Oleg, 40, 159n32
Lokshin, Michael, 70
Lokshina, Tanya, 12, 111

Mal'tseva, Ol'ga, 74
Malaysia, 137
male collective, *dedovshchina* and, 66
male identity, military service and, 109–111
Malofeev, Mikhail, 113
mandatory military service. *See* conscription
manhood, military service and, 1. *See also* masculinity/masculinities; militarized masculinity
Manifesto: Russia at the Turn of the Millennium (Putin), 50
Mann, Michael, 150n19, 151n34
marginalized masculinity, 6, 71–72

Markelov, Sergei, 120
market economy: masculinity and, 67–72; militarized masculinity and, 72; patriotism and, 80–81; PTSD and, 125–126. *See also* capitalism
Markov, Nikolai, 62
Markwick, Roger D., 18, 149n9
Masculinity/masculinities: alternative notions of, 171n72; antimilitarism and remilitarization, 141–142; capitalism and, 4, 60; characteristics of, 7; Chechen, 48; Chechen syndrome and, 121–127; class and, 71–72; conscription and, 3; CSMR and, 94, 182n78; in elections 45–48; essentialist ideas of, 98; femininity and, 6; feminist International Relations and, 5; gender and, 5; gender roles and, 85–87; global politics of gendered militarization, 136–138; leadership and, 36, 55–57; market economy and, 69–70; militarism/militarization and, 7, 8, 138–139; military service and, 3–4, 97–99, 174–175n126; military training and, 112; morale, 3, 97; nationalism and, 164n113; patriotism and, 131–133; power and, 6; PTSD and, 126; Putin and, 48, 55–56; rape and, 120; Russian-Chechen wars and, 55–57; Russian-Chechen war veterans and, 109–111; Russian conscripts in Russian-Chechen war (1994–1996), 44–45; Russian government positions (1993–2008), 57; Soviet Union and, 16, 25, 26, 29–31, 69; state legitimation and, 3; states and, 6; toxic, 122; types of, 6–7; war and, 36, 108–109; Yeltsin and, 40, 41–42, 48–49. *See also* gay men; gender order; militarized masculinity
Masculinization: of Soviet women, 25; of Russia's bureaucratic and political elite, 56
masculinized: adulthood, 32; humiliation, 50, 58, 164n113; protection 49; states 49, 50; task of soldiering, 112, 128

Maskhadov, Aslan, 39, 46, 53
Matthews, Jill J., 145–146n8
media: conscription, 51, 63, 66–67; *dedovshchina* and, 64, 66–67; PTSD and, 122; Putin and, 51; Russian-Chechen wars, 51, 75–76; soldiers' excessive violence and, 116, 117; soldiers' mothers groups and, 89, 92; Soviet-Afghan war and, 28, 29; women soldiers, 74
medical care, military service and, 2, 63, 83
Mel'nikova, Valentina, 93, 95
Memorial (human rights group), 61
memorials, 104, 132–133
men: Great Patriotic War and, 15; identity and conscription, 3–4; identity and military service, 109–111; militarization and respect/benefits, 128–131; Soviet citizenship and conscription, 21; Soviet Union gender order and, 24–27. *See also* citizenship; conscription; gender; gender order; masculinity/masculinities; militarized masculinity; military service
Meshcherkina, Elena, 70
mesta boevoi slavy, 103
mesta boevykh deistvii, 103
militaries: CSMR and SMSP, 89; femininity and, 6; gendered power relations and, 8; gender roles and, 86; masculinity and, 6, 7; militarism and, 7; Putin and, 37; social makeup (post-Soviet Russia), 70–71; Soviet Union, 16–21, 29–31; Yeltsin and, 37. *See also* military service; Russian military
militarism: definition of, 4; excessive warrior representations and, 121; gender and, 7, 14, 85–86, 108, 131; masculinity, 36, 135, 138; militarization and, 4–5; motherhood and, 87; Putin and, 4; rhetoric of, 80; Russian postcommunist transformation and, 4, 9–10, 14, 80, 138–139, 142; Russian state legitimation, 11; Russia's political

leadership and, 139; Soviet Union, 16–18, 21, 28, 79–80, 150n19; state legitimation and, 4; veterans and, 131; Yeltsin and, 36

militarization: challenges and reinforcements, 4, 139; citizenship and military service, 137; definition of, 4; FSB-ization and, 166n151; gender and, 4, 7, 11, 13, 138; gender order and, 6–7; German Democratic Republic, 152n44; global politics of, 136–138; masculinity/masculinities/men and, 56–67, 136, 138–139, 142; militarism and, 4–5; motherhood and, 7, 86–88; patriotism and, 82; as process, 4; Russia, 35, 80, 138–139; Russian postcommunist transformation and, 9–10, 140; soldiers' mothers groups and, 4, 90, 105–107; Soviet-Afghan war and, 27–33; Soviet gender order, 22–27; Soviet socialism, 16–21; Soviet Union, 16, 140; state legitimation and, 6; veterans' groups and, 4. *See also* demilitarization; remilitarization

militarized citizenship, 80, 131, 140

militarized femininity, 151n27. *See also* women soldiers

militarized gender roles, 2, 7, 13, 30, 85–87, 138, 152n44; CSMR and SMSP, 88–95; motherhood and militarization, 86–88; mothers, 100–102; Samara, 96–105. *See also* militarized masculinity; military service

militarized masculinity, 4–8, 12–14; challenges to, 16, 27, 30, 36, 43–45, 112; conscription (Russian-Chechen wars), 60–62, 74–79; contract soldiers, 72–74; crisis of, 55, 59–84, 89, 114, 128, 131, 141; CSMR, SMSP, and, 89–90; *dedovshchina*, 63–67; excessive violence and, 115; feminist analysis of, 4–8, 146n14; global politics of, 136–138; market economy and class, 67–72; nationhood and state leadership,

55–57; patriotic motherhood and, 87, 100; patriotism and, 79–83; PTSD and, 121, 123; Putin's restoration of, 50–53; Russian-Chechen wars, 35–39, 57–58, 59–60, 83–84; Russian postcommunist transformation and, 11, 135, 139–141; Samara soldiers' mothers groups and, 97–99, 100–101; sexual violence and, 120; soldiers' mothers groups and, 32, 106–107; Soviet Union and, 25, 27–28, 32; veterans and, 131–135; veterans' benefits and, 128, 131; war and, 87–88, 108–109; Yeltsin's leadership and, 40–45. *See also* citizen-soldier; military service; warriors

militarized men: privileging of, 56–58, 130; respect and benefits for, 128–131; supportive mothers of, 106; wives of, 130. *See also* militarized masculinity; military veterans; warriors

militarized patriotism, 4, 36, 84, 136, 139, 142; conscripts and, 77, 80; CSMR and SMSP, 88–95; Putin and Russian-Chechen war (1999–2009), 48–49, 51–52, 55, 77; Samara soldiers' mothers groups, 96–105; soldiers' mothers groups and, 105–107; veterans and, 131–133; Yeltsin and Russian-Chechen war (1994–1996), 43. *See also* patriotism

militarized socialism, 16–21, 150n19

Military Balance, 61

military draft. *See* conscription

military education. *See* education

military effects, 29

"military glory," 103

military leadership: militarized masculinity and, 43–45, 50–53; soldiers' morale and, 113. *See also* Russian generals

military logic, of Soviet Union, 16

military officers: compensation of, 130, 140, 192–193n8; *dedovshchina* and, 64–65. *See also* Russian generals

military performance, morale and, 44, 76, 112–113
military personnel: in Soviet Union (1991), 61; in post-Soviet Russia, 61
military professionalism, 45, 51–52, 58, 89, 99, 139. *See also* all-volunteer force; contract soldiers; military volunteers
military recruitment, 3, 72–74, 78–79, 138
military service: class and masculinity, 174–175n126; compulsory (*see* conscription); conditions (post-Soviet) during, 62; conscription and, 2–3; Council of Servicemen's Parents and, 184n125; CSMR and SMSP, 89, 90, 105–106; hazing and, 2, 185n14; length of, 19, 60, 65, 78, 84, 167n5; living conditions and violence (post-Soviet Russia), 60; male citizenship and, 68, 83, 89, 98, 137; male identity and, 109–111; mandatory (*see* conscription); manhood and, 1, 2, 7, 83, 97, 99, 111, 140; market economy and, 67; masculinity and, 1, 3–4, 59, 69, 79, 83, 97–99; militarization and, 7–8; militarized masculinity and, 7–8, 139–140; money-making through, 78; motherhood and, 87, 94, 100; patriotic education and, 131–132; patriotism and, 80, 82, 139; Putin on, 82; Russia (eighteenth century), 19; Russia (post-Soviet), 60–62; Russian-Chechen war (1994–1996), 44–45; Samara soldiers' mothers groups and, 97–100, 106; socialization and, 2, 7, 8, 21, 25, 26, 31, 98, 99, 109–111, 132; socioeconomic backgrounds and, 70–71; soldiers' mothers groups and, 31, 85, 139; Soviet-Afghan war and, 28; Soviet Union, 15, 19–21; Soviet Union gender order and, 25, 26; Soviet Union law (1967), 21; Soviet men and, 24–27; Soviet Union public opinion on, 30; Soviet students, 85; suicide and, 33, 83, 169n31; women's recruitment and, 72–74, 137. *See also* conscription; contract soldiers; *dedovshchina*; military volunteers
military-society relations, 9, 59, 81, 105
military spending, 168n29
military training, 112, 115
military veterans: Great Patriotic war veterans, 18, 109, 150n17, 190–191n128; Soviet-Afghan war veterans, 30, 127, 131, 155n102, 189–190n105, 191n137. *See also Boevoe Bratstvo*; Russian-Chechen war veterans
military volunteers: attraction of, 60, 73, 78–79, 84, 139; conscription and, 3; Russian-Chechen wars, 3, 78; women, 21, 73–74, 137, 173n103. *See also* all-volunteer force; contract soldiers
Miliutin, Dmitrii, 19
Ministry of Defense (Russia): Chechenization and, 53; conscription and, 3, 60, 61, 77, 78; CSMR and, 93; Grozny and, 38
Ministry of Defense (Soviet Union), 86
Ministry of Interior Affairs (Russia), 38, 53, 60, 111, 157n3, 113
Mironov, Valerii, 43
missing soldiers: CSMR and SMSP, 88; in Soviet-Afghan war, 28
mobilization: anti-war, 92; for Great Patriotic War, 17–18, 20; men's, 60, 77–78, 81–82; militarism as a source for, 139; for Russian-Chechen wars, 60, 77–78
modernization (Soviet), 10, 26, 171n72
moral authority, of motherhood, 32, 94–95
morale: of mothers, 102, 106; militarized masculinity and, 3, 97; of soldiers, 44, 76, 97, 106, 112–114, 133, 134–135, 185n28
morality, of war, 112–114
Moscow, bombings in, 47
Moscow Committee of the Communist Party, 15
Moscow hostage-taking, 39

Moscow Military District, 73
Moscow soldiers' mothers group. *See* Committee of Soldiers' Mothers of Russia
motherhood: conscription and war, 138; essentialist ideas of, 93–94, 104; gender roles and, 85–86; Great Patriotic War and, 15–16, 20; Madonna image, 87; *mater dolorosa* (archetype), 87; militarization and, 86–88; politics of, 93–95; responsible, 94–95, 100–102, 104, 106; Soviet Union gender order and, 22–24; Spartan mother (archetype), 87; supportive, 100–102. *See also* mothers; soldiers' mothers groups
"motherland," 100–101
"Mother of the Defender of the Fatherland," 102
mothers: demilitarization, 87; militarization, 7, 87; post–Great Patriotic War, 21; role of, 100–102. *See also* motherhood; soldiers' mothers groups
Mothers' March for Life and Compassion, 91
Muslims: femininity, 152n46; as nationality term, 153n60; Russian-Chechen war (1994–1996), 41; Russian-Chechen war (1999–2009), 48, 163n92; Soviet conscription and, 27; women, 24

Nagel, Joane, 36
Narozhna, Tanya, 120–121
nationalism: domesticity and family, 101; masculinity and, 36, 164n113; masculinized humiliation and, 50, 164n113; nationalist forces (Russia), 40, 42, 46; Russian postcommunist transformation and, 9; Soviet conscription and, 31; Soviet gender order, 24; war, militarism, and, 36
nationalities: Putin and, 48; soldiers' mothers groups and, 90, 104;

Soviet Union, 10, 16, 25, 29, 30–31, 153n60; Yeltsin and, 41. *See also* ethnicity
nationality policy (Soviet), 10
"national security" rape, 188n83
nation-building: masculinity and, 36; militarized masculinity and, 6, 10; Yeltsin and, 40
nationhood: masculinity and, 55–57; Russian-Chechen wars and, 49–50
NATO, 49
Nazi Germany, 10, 17–18, 20. *See also* Great Patriotic War
negotiations: Chernomyrdin and, 165n144; Russian-Chechen war (1994–1996), 39, 53; support for, 54, 165n138
New Russians, 70
New Thinking (Gorbachev), 28
New Zealand, 137
North Caucusus Military District Court, 117
North Caucusus Military Institute, 126
North Korea, 137
Novye Aldy, massacre in, 118
NTV, 76, 116, 186–187n50

October Revolution, 17
Orden Muzhestva, 1
officers. *See* military officers
O'Hara, Charles P., 122
oil, 10, 55, 161n45
OMON, 124
On Veterans (law), 128
Order of Courage, 1
organized crime, 41, 69–70
"others," killing of, 115–121
otsrochka, 60–61
Oushakine, Serguei, 39, 104, 147n28, 147–148n29

pacifism: CSMR and SMSP, 89, 91; gender roles and, 86–87; Soviet youth and, 26. *See also* antimilitarism
Pain, Emil, 49

Pamiat' (committee), 132, 148n30
parliamentary elections: Chechen-Ingush Republic (1990), 37; Chechen Republic (2005), 54
patriarchal: authority, 25; gender roles, 100
patriotic education: draft compliance and, 82, 131, 139; patriotic education programs (2001–2005, 2006–2010), 82, 131–133, 139; Samara soldiers' mothers and, 106; Soviet Union, 21, 26; veterans and, 131–133
patriotic heroes, 109, 131–133, 134–135
patriotism: capitalism and, 4; conscription and, 60, 77, 79–83; CSMR and, 89, 91; Great Patriotic War and, 15, 18; masculinity and, 36, 131–133; militarism and, 139, 142; militarization and, 3–4, 36; militarized masculinity and, 139–140; motherhood and, 87; Putin and, 9, 49–50, 51–52, 55–56, 77; Russian-Chechen wars and, 43, 48–52, 57–58, 79–83; Russian postcommunist transformation and, 9, 11; SMSP and, 89; soldiers' mothers groups (Moscow and St. Petersburg), 88–95; soldiers' mothers groups (Samara), 96–105, 106; Stalin and, 17; Soviet Union, 15, 17, 18, 20, 25–26, 28; state legitimation and, 3; veterans and, 131–133; war and, 36; women and, 7, 20. *See also* militarized patriotism
peacemaking, Yeltsin and, 45, 46–47
peace march, 91
Pennington, Reina, 20
pensions. *See* benefits
"people as power" discourse, 24
perception effects, 29
perestroika, 27, 31, 34
Persian Gulf War, 138
Peru, 137
Peter the Great, 19
Petrone, Karen, 22
physical disabilities, 188–189n89
Pinnick, Kathryn, 155n102

Pisarenko, Dmitrii, 114
Plekhanov, Sergei, 37
Poliakova, Ella, 87
police, 12, 52, 65, 78, 83, 111, 121, 124
policies. *See* state policies
Politburo, 33
political activism, 142; by soldiers' mothers groups, 87–88, 89–90, 91. *See also* activism
political ideology, Soviet conscription and, 21
political party formation, by CSMR, 92–93
political power, in Russian postcommunist transformation, 10
political power relations, gendered, 8
political processes, gender and, 13–14
politics: CSMR and, 92–93; masculinity and, 5, 56–57; motherhood, 93–95; patriotism, militarized masculinity and, 140; Samara soldiers' mothers groups and, 103, 105; Soviet gender order and, 23; women and militarization, 87
Politkovskaya, Anna, 54, 108, 118
Popkova, Liudmila, x, 147–148n29
popularity. *See* public opinion
population, Soviet gender order and, 23, 24, 27
Poroskov, Nikolai, 78–79
postcommunist transformation, 8–11
post-military society, 79–83
post-traumatic stress disorder (PTSD), 121–127, 188–189n89
power, militarized masculinity and, 6, 8
power ministries, 55, 58, 60
Prakash, Aseem, 29, 155n90
Presidential Committee on Human Rights, 93
presidential elections: Chechen-Ingush Republic (1990), 37; Russia (1996), 36, 38, 45–47; Russia (2000), 47–50
prisoners of war, 90, 115
private security firms, 72, 125–126, 137–138, 141

production, Soviet gender order and, 23
propaganda: Cold War and motherhood, 32; Great Patriotic War, 20
protests. *See* activism; antiwar protests
psychological problems, 121–127
public debate: *dedovshchina*, 30; Soviet-Afghan war and, 28, 29, 30
public image management, for Yeltsin, 40
public opinion: all-volunteer force, 175nn128, 129; Budanov, 117, 119; Chechnya (1999), 47; conscription, 62, 82–83; desertion, 114; draft evasion, 69, 77, 114, 175n129; Putin, 47, 48–49, 50, 54, 56, 166n148, 176n150; Rokhlin, 44; Russian-Chechen war (1994–1996), 42–43; Russian-Chechen war (1999–2009), 54, 92, 165n138; soldiers' mothers groups, 91; Soviet military service, 30; use of military force, 160–161n44; Yeltsin, 40, 42–43, 45, 46
Public Opinion Foundation, 47
public services, *l'goty* and, 191n129
Pulikovskii, Konstantin, 53
Putin, Vladimir: Budanov and, 118–119; Chechenization, 54–55, 58; conscription and, 75, 77; contract soldiers, 77; CSMR and SMSP, 92, 93; *Manifesto: Russia at the Turn of the Millennium*, 50; masculinity and, 55–56, 57; militarism and, 4; military service and, 3, 83; military spending, 168n29; nationalism and patriotism, 9; patriotism, 134, 135, 139; popularity of, 47–49, 54, 56, 162n79; post-military society and, 80; public opinion, 47, 48–49, 50, 54, 56, 166n148, 176n150; public trust in, 176n150; Russian-Chechen war (1999–2009), 38, 39, 47–55; secret service career, 157n4; as sex symbol, 166n148; soldiers' mothers groups and, 93; terrorists and, 58; welfare state reform (2005), 191n129; Yeltsin and, 35–37, 157n2, 157n4
Putnam, Tonya L., 149n3

race: marginalized masculinity and, 6–7; military training and, 115; Yeltsin's messages and, 41–42
racialization, of Chechen men, 41–42
Raduev, Salman, 38, 48
Rakowska-Harmstone, Teresa, 25
rape: 117, 120–121; same-sex, 169–170n46; types of, 188n83
recreational rape, 188n83
recruitment, 3, 72–74, 78–79, 138
Red Army, 15, 18–20, 29, 73
reenlistment, 126
Reese, Roger R., 154n81
reform, Yeltsin and, 40
refugees, from Russian-Chechen wars, 75, 174nn111, 114
regional location, military service and, 71
Regional *Oblast'* Organization of Participants of Combat Operations in Chechnya and Dagestan, 129, 148n30
Regional Voluntary Organization of Parents of Servicemen. *See Synov'ia*
rehabilitation, 124, 127
religion, 24. *See also* Muslims
remilitarization, 4, 14, 106–107, 109, 133, 139, 141–142
reproduction, 22–24, 94, 100, 101
respect, 128–131
responsibility, motherhood and, 94–95, 100–102, 104, 106
Reuveny, Rafael, 29, 155n90
Riabov, Oleg, 56
Riabova, Tat'iana, 56
rights: soldiers', 96–105; soldiers' mothers groups and, 88. *See also* human rights
Rokhlin, Lev, 44
Roman, Meredith L., 42
Rostov-Baku highway and railway, 10
rural regions, military service of men from, 71
Russia (post-Soviet): militarized masculinity of, 3–4, 13, 138–139; military service in, 1–2, 59–84; motherhood in, 94–95;

postcommunist transformation, 8–11. *See also* Imperial Russia; Russian-Chechen wars; Soviet Union

Russian-Chechen war (1994–1996), 1, 2–3; conscription and, 2–3, 77; draft evasion, 76–77; extension of military service length, 78; overview, 57–58; postcommunist transformation and, 10–11; refugees, 75, 174n111; public opinion on, 42–43; soldiers' mothers groups and, 89–91, 102–103; Yeltsin and, 36, 40–47, 55

Russian-Chechen war (1999–2009): as antiterrorism operation, 47; civilian deaths, 75; conscription and, 77–78; contract soldiers and volunteers, 3, 78; *dedovshchina*, 76; draft evasion, 76–77; media and, 75–76; overview, 58; postcommunist transformation and, 10–11; public opinion on, 54, 92, 165n138; Putin and, 36, 47–55; refugees, 75, 174n114; Russian humiliation and, 49; soldiers' mothers groups and, 91–93

Russian-Chechen wars, 35–37; antimilitarism and remilitarization, 141–142; conscription, 60–62, 74–79; contract soldiers and women's recruitment, 72–74; CSMR and SMSP, 89–93; *dedovshchina*, 63–67; market economy and class, 67–72; masculinity, nationhood, and state leadership, 55–57; militarized masculinity and, 59–60, 83–84, 138–141; overview, 37–39, 57–58; patriotism, 79–83; Samara soldiers' mothers groups, 102–105; unpopularity of, 4

Russian-Chechen war veterans, 108–109; Chechen syndrome and masculinity, 121–127; citizenship and, 140–141; marginalization of, 140; military service and male identity, 109–111; new relationships, 124–125; patriotism and masculinity, 131–133; respect and benefits for, 128–131; soldiers' morale and morality of war, 112–114; violence, excessive, 115–121

Russian Constitution (1993), 40, 41, 60, 61

Russian generals: "generals' crisis," 43; militarized masculinity and, 35–36, 43–44, 47, 52–53, 57–58; Russian-Chechen war (1994–1996), 43–44, 47; Russian-Chechen war (1999–2009), 52–53; soldiers' morale and, 113; soldiers' mothers groups and, 97

Russian imperialism, Russian-Chechen wars and, 10

Russian military: personnel, 61; reform, 72, 89, 149n3, 192–193n8; social makeup, 70–72; women's recruitment, 72–74. *See also* conscription; draft evasion; military service

Russian soldiers: heroism and, 51–52; morale, 112–114; visits by Samara soldiers' mothers groups to, 97

sacrifice: citizens', 15, 103, 142; mothers', 7, 16, 28; soldiers', 45, 52, 116, 132

St. Petersburg soldiers' mothers group. *See* Soldiers' Mothers of St. Petersburg

salaries, for military officers, 192–193n8. *See also* income

Salmenniemi, Suvi, 23

Samara (Russia), x, 1, 11, 64, 69, 70, 86, 96, 109, 125, 129, 130, 132, 133

Samara fieldwork, 11–12, 13, 63, 74, 96, 132, 147–148n29, 148n30. *See also* soldiers' mothers groups

Samara *Oblast'* Committee of Parents of Servicemen. *See Sodeistvie*

Samara Regional Chechen National-Cultural Organization, 148n30

Samara Regional Parliament, 148n30

Samara Regional Public Fund Offering Social Support to Retired Military Personnel, Invalids, Veterans of Local Wars, and Liquidators of the Chernobyl' Accident, 148n30

Samara soldiers' mothers groups, 1,

96–105, 106, 109, 125, 132, 147–148n29, 148n30; *See also Sodeistvie; Synov'ia*
Samara State University, x, 147–148n29, 148n30
Samara veterans' organizations, 109, 129–130, 132–133
same-sex rape, 169–170n46
Sanborn, Joshua A., 149n5, 150n21
Sapper, Manfred, 17, 154n78, 155n96
Sarin, Oleg L., 154n89
scapegoating, 90, 160n39
scarcity, 63–67
School Number 1 hostage-taking (Beslan), 39
Scott, Joan, 5
Security Council, 40, 46
security, Yeltsin's discourse of, 49
security firms, 72, 125–126, 137–138, 141
security services, 3, 35, 36, 53, 57, 73, 166n151
Serbia, NATO's 1999 war against, 49
Serdiukov, Anatolii, 84
Sergeev, Igor, 52
sexual violence, 117, 120–121
Shaldikova, Galina, 105, 106
Shamanov, Vladimir, 53, 117–118
Shaw, Martin, 80
Shenfield, Stephen, 78
Shevtsova, Lilia, 49, 50, 157n3
Shlapentokh, Vladimir, 176n150
"shock therapy" (economic policy), 9
Sieca-Kozlowski, Elisabeth, 131
siloviki, 57
Simonsen, Sven Gunnar, 163n92
Sivaeva, Tatiana, 49, 92
Slavic republics (Soviet Union), 24
slogans, of Samara soldiers' mothers groups, 96
Slovenia, 137
Smirnov, A. I., 192n6
SMSP. *See* Soldiers' Mothers of St. Petersburg
SOBR, 124
Social Chamber of the Ministry of Defense, 93

social citizenship, 140
social contract, 80, 130, 132–133, 140
social cost, of military draft, 171n78
socialism, militarized, 16–21
socialization, 2, 7, 8, 21, 25, 26, 31, 98, 99, 109–111, 132. *See also* femininity/femininities; gender; masculinity/masculinities; militarized masculinity; military service
social mobilization, for Great Patriotic War, 17–18, 20
social order, in Russian postcommunist transformation, 9, 11
social processes, gender and, 13–14
social rejection, 124
social relations, in Russian postcommunist transformation and, 10, 14, 138
social stratification, Russian military and, 70
social welfare benefits. *See* benefits
society: Budanov and, 118; Chechen syndrome and, 127; conscription (post-Soviet) and, 62; economic transformation (post-Soviet), 59–60; generational differences in attitudes, 68–69; Great Patriotic War and, 17–18; militarized masculinity and, 8; post-military, 79–83; soldiers' mothers groups and, 92, 103; Soviet-Afghan war and, 28, 30; Soviet Union, 16–21, 23; states and, 6; violence against civilians, 115
society-military relations. *See* military-society relations
society-state relations. *See* state-society relations
socioeconomic inequality, conscription and, 60, 70–71
Sodeistvie (Samara soldiers' mothers group), 96, 97–99, 100, 101, 103–105, 106, 125, 148n30
Sokolov, Mikhail, 119
soldiering (post-Soviet Russia): antimilitarism and remilitarization,

141–142; global politics of gendered militarization, 136–138; militarized masculinity and, 112, 128, 138–141

soldiers: heroism and, 51–52; morale, 112–114; visits by Samara soldiers' mothers groups to, 97. *See also* Russian soldiers

soldiers' mothers groups, 1, 11, 85–86, 105–107, 178n6; activism of, 2, 4, 27, 28, 31–33, 34, 142, 155n90; antiwar movement and, 180–181n45; benefit claims, 103, 191n132; citizenship and, 140–141; conscription and, 139; co-opted and independent, 86; CSMR and SMSP, 88–95; *dedovshchina* and, 30; draft evasion and desertion, 77, 89, 90, 92–93, 97; militarization and, 4; motherhood and militarization, 86–88; political attacks against, 91, 92–93, 181n47; PTSD and, 125; Samara, 96–105; Soviet Union and, 31–33, 85. *See also* Committee of Soldiers' Mothers of Russia; *Sodeistvie*; Soldiers' Mothers of St. Petersburg; *Synov'ia*; Union of Committees of Soldiers' Mothers of Russia

Soldiers' Mothers of St. Petersburg (SMSP), 86, 181n53; antiwar position, 102; *dedovshchina*, 64, 65; militarized patriotism and war, 88–95; military service, 105–106. *See also* soldiers' mothers groups

soldiers' rights, 95, 96–98, 105, 121, 178n14

Soldner, Markus, 40, 147n26

"Someone Like Putin" (pop song), 56

sotsial'nyi lift, 71

South Africa, 137

sovereignty, militarized masculinity and, 6

Soviet-Afghan war, 126–127, 154n78; challenges to militarization during, 27–33; combat readiness in, 113–114; soldiers' mothers groups and, 28, 30, 31–33, 34, 85, 86

Soviet-Afghan war veterans, 30, 127, 131, 155n102, 189–190n105, 191n137

Soviet armed forces, women in, 137, 192n6

Soviet Union, 15–16, 33–34; collapse of, 49, 50; conscription (1970s), 59; Constitution (1977), Article 63 of, 21; Defense Ministry, 86; gender order in, 22–27; mandatory military service, 2; militarized socialism, 16–21; policies of, 10, 16, 140; soldiers' mothers groups, 28, 30, 31–33, 34, 85, 86. *See also* Great Patriotic War; Russia; Soviet-Afghan war

Soviet Women's Committee, 21

special forces, 124, 138, 169n38

spectator militarism, 80

Sperling, Valerie, 57

spouses, PTSD and, 124

Stalin, Joseph, 10, 15–16, 17, 18

Staropromyslovskii district, massacre in, 118

state agencies, militarized, 3

state-building: militarized masculinity and, 6, 13; Yeltsin and, 40

state leadership: masculinity and, 55–57; military professionalism and, 139; motherhood and, 86; Putin, 47–55; Russian-Chechen wars and, 35–39, 57–58; soldiers' morale and, 113; Yeltsin, 40–47. *See also specific leaders*

state legitimation: femininity and, 7; gender order and, 5–7; masculinity and, 3; militarism and, 4, 11; Russian postcommunist transformation, 9; war and militarized gender roles, 7

state policies: militarism and, 4; militarized masculinity and, 8; Putin, 56–57; Soviet Union, 10, 16, 140

states: loyalty to soldiers, 120; masculinity and, 7, 136–137; military violence and, 136–137; political leadership and militarism, 139; Soviet Union and military, 16–21, 29–31; veterans' benefits and, 131; violence against civilians, 115

state security sector, 126

state security services. *See* security services

state-society relations, in post-Soviet Russia, 4, 14, 80, 81, 84, 136, 138, 140
statist ideology, of Putin, 51
Statute 59 (Russian Constitution, 1993), 60
Stepashin, Sergei, 157n3
stereotypes, 119, 160n42
stress. *See* post-traumatic stress disorder
students, draft and, 60–61, 70, 85
subordinate masculinity, 6, 7, 170n50
substance abuse: combat and, 122–123; conscription and, 172n86; toxic masculinity and, 122; veterans and, 124
suffering mothers, 87, 95
suicide bombings, 48, 93, 104, 163n96
suicide, conscripts and, 33, 83, 169n31
Sundstrom, Lisa, 95, 147n28
superpresidentialism, 40
supportive motherhood, 100–102
Sychev, Andrei, 2
Synov'ia (Samara soldiers' mothers group), 96–97, 99, 100–103, 104, 105, 106, 148n30

Taiwan, 137
Tajikistan, 153n60
Tangi-Chu (city), 117
territorial integrity, Russian-Chechen wars and, 41, 48, 50
terrorism: CSMR statement on, 91; excessive violence and, 115, 119, 135; global war against, 39, 108; Putin and, 39, 48, 50, 52; rhetoric on, 93; Russian-Chechen war (1999–2009), 47, 48, 50, 52, 54
Thomas, Timothy L., 122
Tomb of the Unknown Soldier, 15
toxic masculinity, 122
Transcaucasian republics (Soviet Union), 24
transportation routes, 10
Troshev, Gennadii, 53
Tsymbal, Nikolai, 113
Tumarkin, Nina, 26
Turkmenistan, 153n60

ukas (decree) 2166 and 1360, 158n15
Union of Committees of Soldiers' Mothers of Russia, 39, 86, 88, 105, 106. *See also* Committee of Soldiers' Mothers of Russia
United Nations Decade for Women: Government of the USSR, 156n114
United People's Party of Soldiers' Mothers, 92, 105
United Russia, 55, 118
United States, 19, 137, 138, 142, 173n103, 173–174n110
United States Vietnam War, 29–30
unrecognized warriors, 128–131, 133
unwilling warriors, 112–114, 133, 135
urbanization, 171n72
"us versus them": Russian-Chechen war (1994–1996), 41; war on terror, 93
Uzbekistan, 153n60

Vainakh, 148n30
Vakhnina, Liudmila, 61
values, urbanization and modernization, 171n72
Van Bladel, Joris, 65, 169–170n46
Verdery, Katherine, 8
veterans. *See* military veterans; Russian-Chechen war veterans; Soviet-Afghan war veterans
veterans' organizations, militarization and, 4, 131–133
Victory Day (May 9), 18
Vietnam War (U.S.), 29–30
Vietnam War veterans (U.S.), 142
violence: desensitization to, 186n35; domestic, 124; excessive, 115–121; sexual, 120–121
voennosluzhaiushchie, 183n86
Volga-Ural Military District, 73
Volgodonsk, bombings in, 47
Volkov, Vadim, 72
volunteers. *See* all-volunteer force; contract soldiers; military volunteers
Vorob'ev, Eduard, 43

VTsIOM, 30, 62, 119, 160–161n44, 168n23
VTsIOM-A, 168n23

wages. *See* income
war: masculinity and, 36, 108–109; militarized gender roles and, 7; militarized masculinity and, 138; morality of, 112–114; motherhood and, 87, 138; Russian-Chechen war veterans and, 128; soldiers' mothers groups and, 88–95. *See also* Great Patriotic War; Soviet-Afghan war; Russian-Chechen wars
war crimes, 53, 108, 117–121, 133–135, 190n125
war on terror. *See* counterterrorism; terrorism
war protests. *See* antiwar protests
war resisters, 186n46
warriors: excessive, 13, 109, 115–121, 133, 134, 135; fragile, 121–127, 131, 133; masculinity of, 108–109; patriotic, 40, 43; unrecognized, 128–131, 133; unwilling, 112–114, 133, 135. *See also* militarized masculinity
Webber, Stephen L., 80
welfare benefits. *See* benefits
welfare state reform (2005), 191n129
welfare system, 190–191n128
Whitworth, Sandra, 115, 121, 126
wives: PTSD and, 124; veterans' benefits and, 130
women: conscription and, 137; draft evasion and, 171n71; global politics and conscription, 137; Great Patriotic War and, 15–16, 20; men's class privilege and access to, 171n73; men's military service and, 60, 111; in the military (post-Soviet Russia), 73–74; as military volunteers, 21, 73, 136–137, 173n103; military wives, 124, 130; patriotism and, 7; politics and militarization, 87–88; post–Great Patriotic War, 20–21; PTSD and, 124–125; Putin and, 56; recruitment, 72–74; Russian government positions (1993–2008), 57; Soviet armed forces, 192n6; Soviet gender order and, 22–24; as veterans, 155n102; veterans' benefits and, 130. *See also* femininity/femininities; gender; motherhood; mothers; soldiers' mothers groups
"Women and Development, Law, Reality, and Perspectives" (conference), 160n36
Women in the USSR (UN Decade for Women: Government of the USSR), 156n114
women's equality, in Soviet Union, 16. *See also* gender equality
women's movement: in Russia, 74; in Soviet Union, 21
women's rights, Chechen republic, 54
women's rights groups, sexual violence and, 120
women soldiers, 20–21, 73–74
work. *See* labor
Workers-Peasants Red Army, 19
workforce. *See* labor force
working-class men: marginalized masculinity and, 6; military service and, 71
World War I, 17
World War II, U.S. soldiers firing during, 186n35. *See also* Great Patriotic War
wounded: Grozny, 112; Russian-Chechen wars, 39; Soviet-Afghan war, 28

Yeltsin, Boris, 40, 41–43, 44, 45; conscription, 51, 77, 162n74; distrust of, 159n31; health of, 55; management of image, 40; masculinity crisis, 55, 56, 57; militarized masculinity and, 51–52; negotiations and, 165n144; patriotism and, 135; personnel reductions by, 61; popularity of, 42; presidential election (1996), 36, 45–47, 58; public opinion, 40, 42–43, 45, 46; Putin and, 35–37, 48–49, 50, 52, 157n2, 157n4; Russian-

Chechen war (1994–1996), 38, 40–47, 159n32; Russian-Chechen war (1999–2009), 38; "shock therapy," 9
Yemtsov, Ruslan, 70
Young, Iris Marion, 55
Yuval-Davis, Nira, 23–24

Zdravomyslova, Elena, 89, 91, 93, 94, 180–181n45
zemliachestvo, 31
Zilberman, Alina, 80
Ziuganov, Gennadii, 46
Zürcher, Christoph, 159n23

The authorized representative in the EU for product safety and compliance is:
Mare Nostrum Group
B.V Doelen 72
4831 GR Breda
The Netherlands

www.ingramcontent.com/pod-product-compliance
Lightning Source LLC
Chambersburg PA
CBHW021807220426
43662CB00006B/217